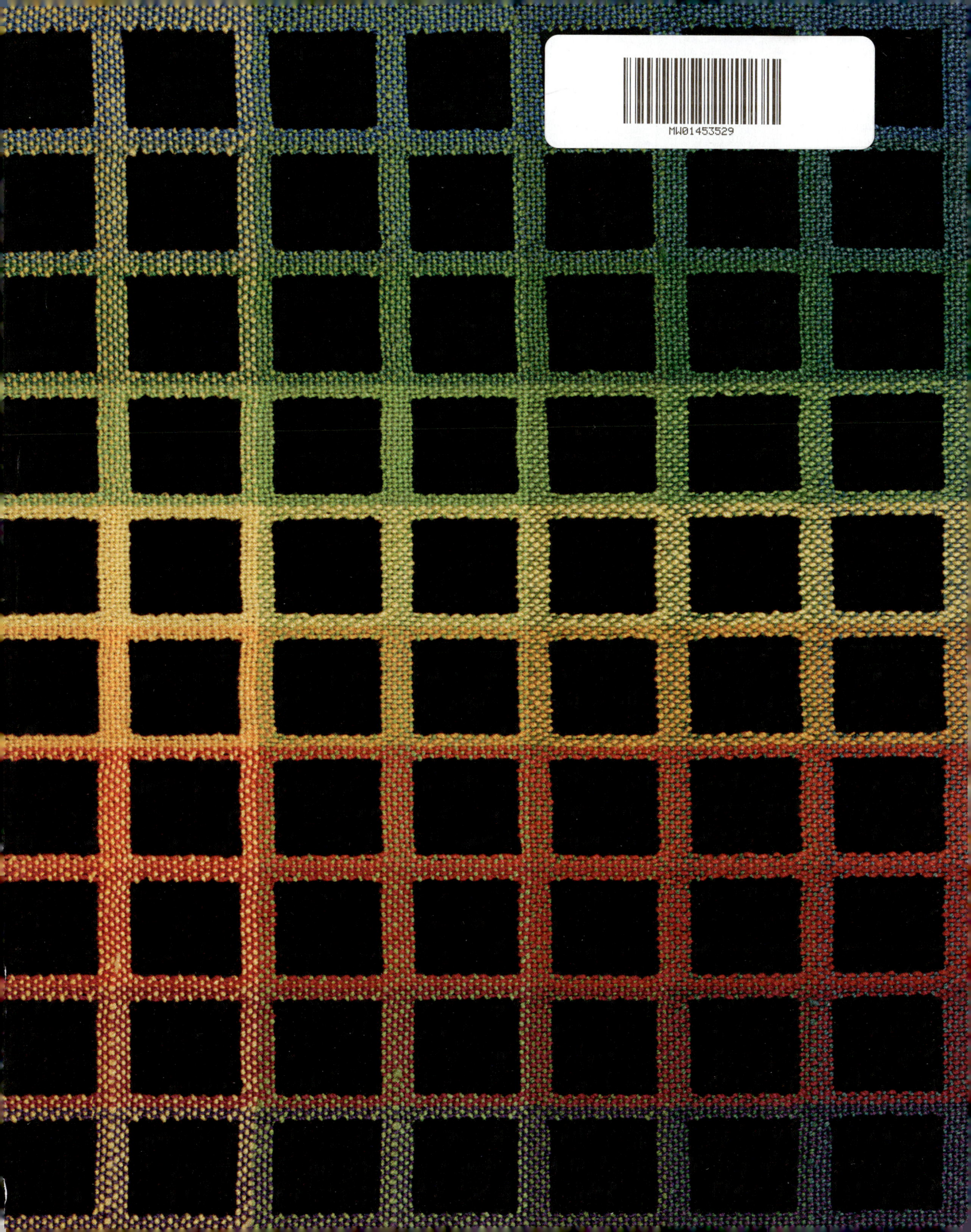

The best of Weaver's

20 innovative designers

28 unique and beautiful projects

11 in-depth articles on double-weave theory

from

twenty years of

Weaver's and *Prairie Wool Companion*

THE MAGIC OF DOUBLE WEAVE

DOUBLE WEAVE

PUBLISHER
Alexis Yiorgos Xenakis

PUBLISHING DIRECTOR
David Xenakis

EDITOR
Madelyn van der Hoogt

COPY EDITOR
Wendy Siera

GRAPHIC DESIGNER
Bob Natz

PHOTOGRAPHER
Alexis Yiorgos Xenakis

PRODUCTION DIRECTOR
Denny Pearson

BOOK PRODUCTION MANAGER
Carol Skallerud

PRODUCTION ARTISTS
Ev Baker
Nancy Holzer
Jay Reeve

MIS
Jason Bittner

FIRST PUBLISHED IN USA IN 2006 BY XRX, INC.
PO BOX 1525, SIOUX FALLS, SD 57101-1525

COPYRIGHT © 2006 XRX, INC.

All rights reserved.
No part of this publication may be reproduced, stored in a retrieval system, or transmitted, in any form or by any means, electronic, mechanical, photocopying, recording or otherwise, without the prior permission of the copyright holder.

We give permission to readers to photocopy the instructions and graphics for personal use only.

ISBN 1-933064-04-8

Produced in Sioux Falls, South Dakota, by XRX, Inc., 605.338.2450

Printed in USA

XRX BOOKS

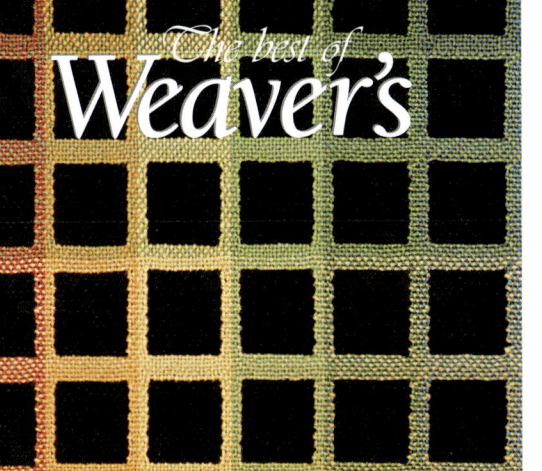

double weave double weave double weave double weave double weave double weave double weave double weave double weave double weave double weave double weave
weave double weave double weave double weave double weave double weave double weave double weave double weave double weave double weave double weave double
double weave double weave double weave double weave double weave double weave double weave double weave double weave double weave double weave double weave we
ble weave double weave double weave double weave double weave double weave double weave double weave double weave double weave double weave double weave dou

XRX BOOKS

The best of Weaver's

THE MAGIC OF
DOUBLE WEAVE

Edited by Madelyn van der Hoogt
Photography by Alexis Xenakis

designers & authors &

double weave, double width — 5

twice as wide: a herringbone blanket
by Doramay Keasbey

double wide, double warm throw
by Tracy Kaestner

double-width overshot tablecloth
by Doramay Keasbey

a double-width coverlet
by Charles Billings

it's an 'L' of a shawl!
by David Xenakis and Ruth Morrison

stitched double cloth — 21

ruana in stitched double cloth
by Doramay Keasbey

she fancies plush: two self-lined jackets
by Nish Raymond

double tartan with extra-weft stitching
by David Xenakis

designing stitched double cloth
by Doramay Keasbey

double-weave blocks and color — 35

double-weave jacket in interlocking crosses
by Gretchen Romey-Tanzer

color windows
by Judie Yamamoto

windows coat
by Bonnie Luckey

reversible panel vest with color windows
by Priscilla Lynch

mixed color effects in double weave
by Doramay Keasbey

summer sherbet runner
by Doramay Keasbey

color in loom-controlled double weave
by Paul O'Connor

patchwork jacket in double-woven twill
by Doramay Keasbey

contents

overshot-patterned double weave   57

4-block, 4-shaft double weave
by Madelyn van der Hoogt

shamrock table runners
by Bobbie Irwin

mug rugs
by Judie Eatough

'colonial' double-weave table runner
by Madelyn van der Hoogt

symmetrical turning blocks
by Madelyn van der Hoogt

overshot-patterned double-weave coverlet
by Helen Jarvis

network solutions: overshot to double weave
by Doramay Keasbey

playing with texture and design   77

grandma's game bags
by Diane Ferguson

sequins and silk: camisole and skirt
by Sigrid Piroch

baffle weave: mixing layers on the loom
by Alice Schlein

'double, double toil and trouble' runner
by Barbara Walker

network drafting: double weave
by Alice Schlein

double weave a la carte
by Alice Schlein

raising eyelashes
by Alice Schlein

eyelash vest
by Alice Schlein

unconventional double-weave shawl
by Miriam Taylor

playing with double weave
by Nish Raymond

introduction

Weaver's Editor Madelyn van der Hoogt presents in this volume thirty-four articles and projects from Weaver's magazine and Prairie Wool Companion that focus on loom-controlled double weave. Gathered in one place, these articles become a unique and comprehensive text on all aspects of double weave in addition to a collection of beautiful fabrics to weave. All techniques are clearly explained and illustrated by the bright and creative designers who made PWC and Weaver's so beloved by their readers.

Madelyn succeeded David Xenakis as Editor of Prairie Wool Companion in 1986, and was Editor of Weaver's from 1988 to 1999.

"Magic" is a word that weavers are sometimes accused of overusing. But so many aspects of weaving truly *are* magical! Placing your first pattern pick in overshot, taking a piece of huck lace out of the dryer, unwinding a shawl from the cloth beam, fulling a wool fabric to soft fuzziness—some form of magic happens with nearly every handwoven cloth. With double weave, you'll find your sense of magic is more than doubled.

The several structures we call double weave all derive from our ability to weave two layers of cloth on the loom at the same time. Although we could use this technique to produce two independent cloths, doing so provides no real advantage over weaving them singly. Instead, when we weave two layers, we connect them together in some way. The magic of double-weave comes from the ways the layers are connected.

• If a single weft travels across the top layer, across the bottom layer, back across the bottom layer, and then back across the top layer, the selvedges will be separate on the starting side but connected on the other side. The two layers can then be unfolded to become a single cloth twice their original width when they are removed from the loom. Double-wide cloths can be designed in any weave structure—twill, overshot, summer and winter, laces, and more.

• If threads from the top layer (warp or weft or both) weave with threads from the bottom layer (warp or weft or both) the two layers are connected by "stitching." Stitching can be designed to show decoratively or it can be invisible. With invisible stitching, a cloth can have two very different faces—either in texture, structure, color, or any combination of these.

• If two differently-colored layers exchange faces in some parts of the cloth but not in others, block designs can be produced (one layer weaves pattern, the other weaves background). As few as eight shafts can produce multicolored framed windows, four-block designs that look like overshot, and much more. Layers can also be exchanged to create pockets to stuff and eyelashes to cut.

Try them all and make your own double-weave magic!

Madelyn

double weave, double width

twice as wide: a herringbone blanket	6
double width, double warm throw	10
double-width overshot tablecloth	12
a double-width coverlet	16
it's an 'L' of a shawl	18

twice as wide: a herringbone blanket

Doramay Keasbey

Weaving wide blankets in one or more panels and sewing them together can certainly be done successfully, but what a joy it has been to explore the possibilities of weaving a single twill blanket double the width of my new loom! Because it has eight shafts instead of four, this loom offers many intriguing possibilities for double-width weaving.

My very first blanket was woven in Finland on a borrowed loom larger than my own but only wide enough to produce a 'matka huopa,' literally a trip blanket or carriage throw. I wove the next one for a double bed in two panels, each the full width of my 4-shaft loom, joined them together, and had them brushed commercially to produce a lush, fuzzy surface that helped to conceal the seam. For a later blanket I joined three panels to span the width of a queen-sized bed. All were woven in a balanced 2/2 straight twill that allows the yarns to be fairly close yet provides enough flexibility to drape softly.

With eight shafts, an enormous variety of additional patterns and interlacements can be woven as single-layer fabrics. Another less common use for eight shafts is to weave two 4-shaft fabrics simultaneously, one above the other. For blankets, two perfectly matching panels can be woven at the same time and joined at one side so that when the fabric is removed from the loom it can be opened to double width. Since twice the number of shafts is needed for weaving double width as for a single layer, double-width plain weave can be produced on as few as four shafts. For most double-width pattern weaves, at least eight are required.

In theory, any single-layer fabric can be woven double width if enough shafts are available. Since warp ends are usually sett at almost twice their usual density to produce two layers, a limitation might be the relative stickiness of the yarn chosen for warp. I've had good results with smoothly spun wool yarn for blankets and with smooth cotton for other projects. Balanced straight twills, herringbone, various broken twills, and unbalanced twills emphasizing warp colors on one side and weft colors on the other are especially suitable for blankets. For lightweight textiles such as tablecloths, there is an even wider range of suitable weaves including twills, satins, lace weaves, and supplementary-weft pattern weaves such as overshot or summer and winter. These structures are described in most general weaving books, usually for a single layer of fabric. Do you wonder how they can be woven double width?

1. Write the threading for each layer

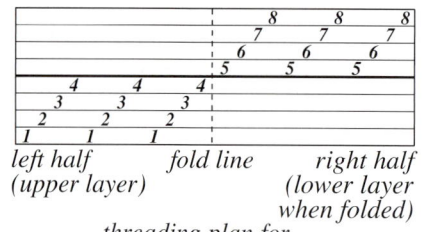

left half (upper layer)   fold line   right half (lower layer when folded)

threading plan for two layers imagined as if unfolded

2. Fold the threading in half

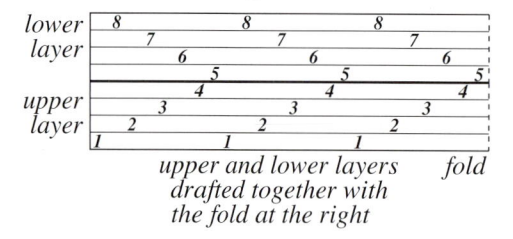

lower layer / upper layer

upper and lower layers drafted together with the fold at the right

3. Plan the path of the shuttle

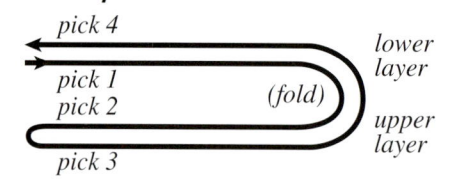

pick 4
pick 1
pick 2   (fold)
pick 3

lower layer
upper layer

THREADING

In order to be entirely free to choose any structure and not be restricted to a 'recipe' for double-width fabrics, it is necessary to understand how the threading and treadling affect the woven product. Let's start with a simple example: 2/2 straight twill. It is usually threaded in straight order on four shafts: 1, 2, 3, 4. For a double-width fabric, this threading will form the upper layer. The lower layer must be threaded on a different set of shafts but with the same threading order: 5, 6, 7, 8, The lower-layer threading can be placed at either side of the upper-layer threading—on the right if the fold is to be on the right, on the left if the fold is to be on the left. In *1*, the fold is designed to be on the right so the lower-layer threading is placed on the right.

After our hypothetical fabric is woven, removed from the loom, and opened to its full width, the portion threaded on shafts 1–4 will be on the left and the half threaded on shafts 5–8 on the right just as they appear in *1*. The fold, where the two layers join, is indicated in *1* by a dashed vertical line. If you folded this threading draft along the vertical line so the fold is at the right and the numbers 5–8 are underneath and if you could read these numbers through the paper, the result would look like the threading draft in *2*: one layer is above the other and the individual warp ends of the two layers alternate with each other.

The threading draft for double width can be written directly without the step shown in *1*. First mark the fold line in the single-layer draft. If the fold is to be on the right side in the double-width fabric, write the draft on the first set of shafts from left to right as far as the fold leaving a space after each number; then continue writing the draft from right to left on the second set of shafts in the empty spaces. For a fold on the left side, first write the draft from right to left as far as the fold leaving a space after each number; then continue writing left to right on the second set of shafts in the empty spaces.

This is the essence of drafting double width for any weave. The fold should not seem a barrier to stop the continuity of a pattern that develops in a single direction such as straight twill, and yet it can also be a logical place for a change of direction or a change from one texture to another, as in the case of block weaves, for example. In our threading draft of double-width straight twill, the direction of the threading for the lower layer only appears to reverse at the fold. This is an illusion because we are looking at the draft for both layers plotted on a single plane. When the fabric is opened full width the twill line will continue in the same direction from edge to edge. If reversal of the twill line had been intended at the center of the opened fabric, the threading of the lower layer could have been written in the opposite direction from the draft in *2*. Similar control is possible for the placement of designs such as herringbone or diamond twill. The repeat can be centered on the fold line or the repeat can be completed there.

TREADLING AND TIE-UP

After the threading is determined, the next step is to consider how to form the sheds in their proper sequence. The general method of weaving double width is illustrated in *3*: the weft travels from the open edge through the upper layer as far as the fold in the first shed, passes around the fold and through the

Careful weaving (avoiding draw-in or unsightly weft loops) produces a nearly invisible 'fold' in a double-width blanket. Another aid to disguising the fold is to plan a dark warp stripe where the fold occurs.

lower layer to its open edge, returns to the fold through the lower layer, passes around the fold, and travels through the upper layer back to its starting position at the open edge. This means that for a single-shuttle weave, four sheds return the shuttle to its starting position. However, except for double-width plain weave, which completes its full treadling sequence for both layers in four sheds, more sheds are required to complete a full treadling repeat in other weave structures—twice the usual quantity of sheds for any given weave are required when weaving two layers.

The first two sheds of a 2/2 twill sequence are shown in *4*, one in the upper and the second in the lower layer. Together they equal a single pick across the opened double-width textile. The next two picks are added in *5*, bringing the shuttle back to its starting point although only half of the full twill sequence has been completed. In our straight-twill example, four more sheds, making eight altogether, constitute a full treadling repeat—four for the upper layer and four for the lower layer.

It is easy to recognize which shafts should be raised for the upper layer because they are the same as those raised when you are weaving the structure as a single layer. If you isolate just the upper-layer sheds and write them in order in their allotted positions according to the sequence in *3*, you have half of the treadling as shown in *6*.

Now all that remains is to figure out which shafts to raise for the lower-layer sheds in the sequence. Since we know that all of the upper-layer warp threads must be raised for each lower-layer pick (so that the lower-layer weft weaves *under* the upper layer), we can fill in those numbers automatically as shown in *7a*. Added to each shed must be the appropriate lower-layer shafts that allow the weft to continue the same interlacement it is making in the upper layer. In *7b*, the sheds are separated into four pairs (representing the four picks across the entire double-width fabric) and the raised shafts are indicated. To trace the way these shafts are chosen, refer to *4* and note the under-two/over-two progress of the weft to see how it maintains this relationship as it curves around the fold, imagining the result when the fabric is spread out double-width. Note that after shafts 1, 2 are raised in the upper layer, shafts 7, 8 plus all of the upper-layer shafts are raised to allow the 2/2 interlacement to continue uninterrupted through the lower layer. In the next lower-layer shed, shafts 1-2-3-4 are raised automatically with shafts 5, 8 so the weft flows smoothly into the following upper-layer shed. The rest of the treadling is derived by continuing this procedure.

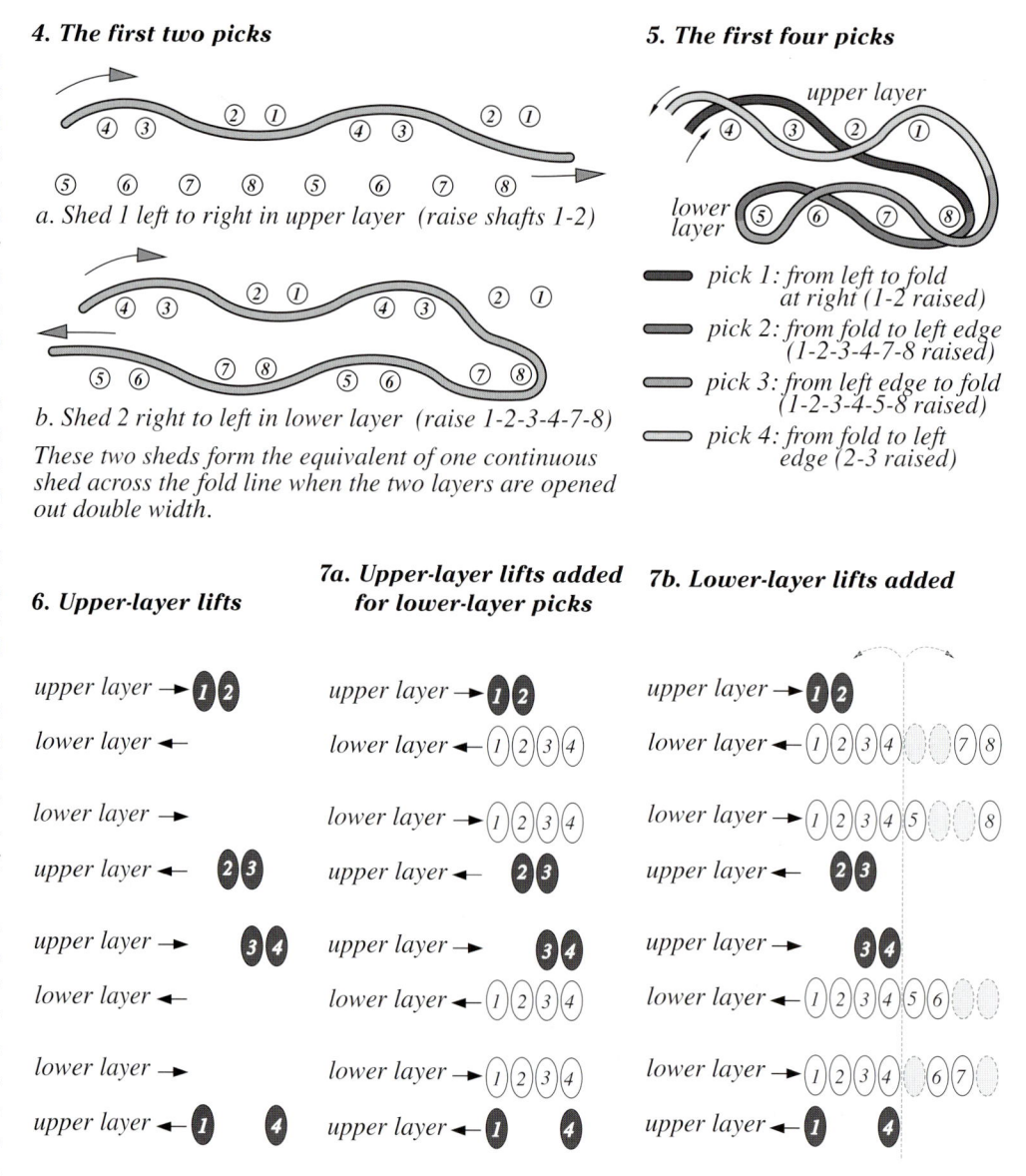

In each pair of sheds in *7b*, the shafts raised for one layer are exactly opposite to the shafts selected for the other. For example, shafts 1, 2 (closest shafts in the first set) are opposite to shafts 7, 8 (farthest shafts in the second set); shafts 2, 3 (middle shafts in the first set) are opposite to shafts 5, 8 (outer shafts in the second set), etc.

Another way to think about this is to remember that the second set of shafts mimics the first set but causes the corresponding shafts to move in opposite directions since the surface that faces the floor during weaving will be turned to face up when unfolded. Thus, the threads on shafts 1, 2 are counterparts of threads on shafts 5, 6; threads on shafts 2, 3 counterparts of threads on shafts 6, 7; and so on. So when shafts 1, 2 are raised in one shed, shafts 5, 6 sink in the other shed of the pair; when shafts 2, 3 rise, shafts 6, 7 sink in the paired shed; etc. This relationship should become clear by studying *7b*. And now, you are ready to design double-wide pieces! ✂

4. The first two picks

a. Shed 1 left to right in upper layer (raise shafts 1-2)

b. Shed 2 right to left in lower layer (raise 1-2-3-4-7-8)

These two sheds form the equivalent of one continuous shed across the fold line when the two layers are opened out double width.

5. The first four picks

— pick 1: from left to fold at right (1-2 raised)
— pick 2: from fold to left edge (1-2-3-4-7-8 raised)
— pick 3: from left edge to fold (1-2-3-4-5-8 raised)
— pick 4: from fold to left edge (2-3 raised)

6. Upper-layer lifts

upper layer → ❶❷
lower layer ←
lower layer →
upper layer ← ❷❸
upper layer → ❸❹
lower layer ←
lower layer →
upper layer ← ❶   ❹

7a. Upper-layer lifts added for lower-layer picks

upper layer → ❶❷
lower layer ← ①②③④
lower layer → ①②③④
upper layer ← ❷❸
upper layer → ❸❹
lower layer ← ①②③④
lower layer → ①②③④
upper layer ← ❶   ❹

7b. Lower-layer lifts added

upper layer → ❶❷
lower layer ← ①②③④   ⑦⑧
lower layer → ①②③④⑤   ⑧
upper layer ← ❷❸
upper layer → ❸❹
lower layer ← ①②③④⑤⑥
lower layer → ①②③④   ⑥⑦
upper layer ← ❶   ❹

8a. Herringbone twill draft for single-layer cloth

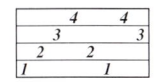

8b. Draft for herringbone blanket double width

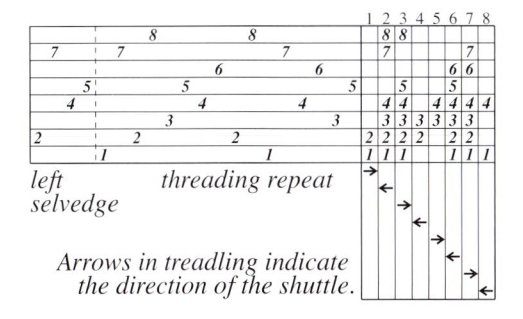

left selvedge — threading repeat

Arrows in treadling indicate the direction of the shuttle.

HERRINGBONE BLANKET

Practice your drafting skills by deriving the double-width draft for this blanket, starting with the basic herringbone threading shown in 8a. Plan to have the fold on the right side. Don't look at the complete draft until you've finished, and then compare your draft with 8b (ignore the threading for the left selvedge). Have fun!

- Equipment. 8-shaft loom, 33" weaving width; 10-dent reed; 3 shuttles.
- Materials. Warp and weft: 2-ply wool (1620 yds/lb, Munkagarn, Nordic Studio) in assorted colors. For the warp and weft color orders used in this blanket: 1 lb, 2 oz medium green; 7 oz white; 5 oz light green; 3 oz light blue; small amounts of dark blue and blue-green. Total yarn amounts are about 3400 yds (2 lb, 1 oz).
- Wind a warp of 660 ends 3 yds long (includes 24" loom waste and allows 13% shrinkage) in the following color order: 120 light green, 80 white, 88 light green, 32 light blue, 100 white, 20 light blue, 40 white, 8 dark blue, 32 light blue, 16 blue-green, 84 light green, 40 light blue.
- Sley 2/dent in a 10-dent reed, 20 epi (10 epi/layer), centered for 33".
- Thread 41 repeats of the draft in **8b** and end with the 4 ends at the left selvedge.
- Weave 20 ppi following the treadling in **8b** and the weft color order as follows (or use your own!). For the border at the beginning: 4¼" white, 2" light green, 1¼" white; for the body: 70" medium green; for the border at the end: 1¼" white, 2" light green, 4¼" white.
- Note: Any harmonious colors can be chosen and arranged in stripes or other proportions in both warp and weft as desired. For other wool yarns, choose a sett that is double that of a single-layer fabric if woven in 2/2 twill. Remember that washing and finishing a blanket will full the yarns, so choose setts that are slightly loose to allow fulling and create a soft drape.
- Finish by making a twisted fringe: twist two adjacent groups of four threads each separately in one direction; then twist them together in the opposite direction and secure the ends with an overhand knot. Wash the blanket by hand in cool water with mild suds; spin by machine to extract excess water; tumble 10 minutes at low setting in dryer; brush gently with a stiff brush. After shrinkage of 13% or less, the final dimensions should be about 57" x 76", a generous size for a soft, fluffy throw.

WEAVING TIPS

- Whenever the shuttle passes through the upper layer, the treadling is the same as if a single layer were being woven. When the shuttle passes through the lower layer, all of the upper layer must be raised to keep it above the lower layer while the appropriate shed of the lower layer is formed. Treadling for the top layer is fairly light, therefore, while treadling for the lower layer requires raising a large number of shafts. Observing the relationship between the relative weight of the lifts and the corresponding treadling order (upper/lower/lower/upper) can help in keeping track of one's place in the sequence.
- Another useful practice is to make it a rule to complete a full treadling sequence (eight picks for double-width 2/2 twill) without interruption and taking breaks only after the sequence is completed.
- It is helpful to note the position of the shuttle or shuttles at the beginning of a full treadling sequence and to be consistent about always starting the sequence from that position. If you are about to start a sequence and your shuttles are in the wrong place, you will know that you have made a mistake.

DOUBLE-WIDTH NOTES
from Bonnie Inouye

- Use warp yarns that are not fuzzy. Wool yarns stick together when they are sleyed double. To cut static electricity, spritz warp threads just above the fell with a garden-variety mister.
- If the warp is at all sticky, put a mirror on one side of your loom and use it to check the shed in each row. It is very hard to see a skipped warp on the bottom half of the work and very tedious to correct many mistakes off the loom for a large piece.
- Use extra threads at the fold edge. I like to thread a smooth, strong cotton warp end with each of the last three to five ends at the fold edge in both layers without changing the spacing in the reed of the regular warp threads. The cotton ends prevent the threads from drawing in at the fold and can be easily pulled out after the piece is off the loom and before it is washed.
- Watch the tension on the cloth beam. One layer might slide against the other in the center. It is better not to advance the warp quite as far as usual or a slight gap may form between the weft threads in the center of the bottom layer.
- Join new weft threads at the selvedge side and not at the fold side.
- Calculate the percent of shrinkage accurately by sampling in order to judge the width and length of the finished piece.
- Arrange the treadles so that they make logical sense to you. You may want to arrange a walking order, or a sequential order, or place all top-layer treadles together and all bottom-layer treadles together so that one foot operates one layer and the other foot the other layer.

Double-width pros and cons

- Pros: Double-width weaving eliminates the difficulty of matching patterns or subtle changes in weft colors across two or more panels. Warp color orders can be placed symmetrically for both layers on the warping board. A well-woven fold is less visible than a seam.
- Cons: Twice as many shafts are required to weave any structure double width, one set for each layer. The weaving process is harder and slower. The denser warp threads can cling together, making sheds difficult to separate. Mistakes in the bottom layer are hard to prevent since they are not visible. Special effort must be made to ensure that the fold does not show in the final piece.

double wide, double warm throw

Tracy Kaestner

An extra warp thread in the gold stripe at the fold compensates for draw-in.

This article was originally published as a Microweave Cookbook recipe. Microweave 'recipes' are projects that can be budgeted into busy lives. Usually they require from a weekend to a week of weaving—or they can be spread over a longer period without overwhelming an active schedule. However you plan your weaving time, Microweave recipes give quick results!

Double the maximum weaving width of your loom and warm up this winter with a woolly throw. A large-scale plaid is a great way to try a first double-width project. Stripes in the warp can help disguise any irregularities at the fold. With a bit of practice you'll learn the techniques for successfully treating the 'fold' so only your loom really knows for sure!

Why weave double width? If your loom is not very wide, say 32", a throw is not usually considered even a possibility. A 32"-wide loom can produce a 64"-wide throw, however, if it is woven 'double-width.' (Even if you *have* a 64"-wide loom, you may not be able to manage the reach—someone really ought to tell us *before* we buy our looms at what width we can comfortably weave!)

TIPS FOR DOUBLE-WIDTH WEAVING

- Keep it simple, at least at first. Double-width plain weave can be achieved on just four shafts. With eight shafts, try a double-width 2/2 twill.
- Make sure the sheds are clear, especially when you are weaving in the bottom layer, to prevent the two layers from being stitched together in spots. Also, if threads in the bottom layer stick together, you'll have floats to repair. Use a weaving sword or pick-up stick to clear sheds if necessary.
- To minimize draw-in for this throw, an extra warp thread of 3/2 pearl cotton is added to the fold edge and removed after weaving (its smoothness allows it to be pulled out easily).
- To make any irregularities at the fold less apparent to the eye, design the fold to coincide with a vertical stripe, as in this throw. (In addition, in the throw, the fold stripe uses seven gold threads instead of the six used in the other stripes. The extra thread ensures that all stripe widths match in spite of slight drawing-in at the fold.)
- As the shuttle turns at the fold, before beating, tuck your index finger inside the fold and gently position the weft to make sure there is sufficient yarn (but no loops!) going around the turn.
- After carefully removing the 3/2 pearl cotton warp thread when the throw is off the loom, lay the throw out and pull diagonally in both directions to align the threads and straighten the fold.
- Use a tapestry needle to repair any skips on the bottom layer.

THE THROW

- Preparation time. One week and one day.
- Equipment. 4-shaft loom, 32" weaving width; 8-dent reed; 2 rag or ski shuttles.
- Ingredients. 2-ply wool (1000 yds lb, Savoy, Webs; or substitute a similar wool yarn such as Harrisville Highland, 900 yds/lb), navy 1½ lbs, deep green 1 lb, gold 2 oz, rust 2 oz. To plan other colors or stripe designs, draw stripes for the full throw to scale on graph paper. Then fold the paper in half to plan the warp color order (review double-wide drafting principles in "Twice as Wide," pp. 6–9).

Saturday AM

- Wind a warp of 511 ends 4 yds long in color order: 96 navy, 12 gold, 96 navy, 96 green, 12 rust, 96 green, 96 navy, 7 gold.
- Sley 2/dent in an 8-dent reed, 8 epi/layer, 16 total epi; center for 32".

Saturday PM

- Thread the heddles following the draft. The first thread on shaft 1 should be on the right side of the loom as you are sitting in front of it. Thread, sley, and weight one end of 3/2 pearl cotton on shaft 4 at the left edge.

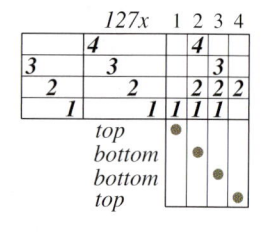

	127x	1	2	3	4
	4		4		
3	3			3	
2	2			2	2	2
	1	1	1	1	
	top	•			
	bottom		•		
	bottom			•	
	top				•

Sunday-Friday

- For a finished length of about 90" (not including fringe), weave the throw following the treadling in *1*: [6" navy, 1" gold, 6" navy, 6" green, 1" rust, 6" green] x3; 6" navy, 1" gold, 6" navy; allow 8" at each end for fringe. (Shafts 1-2 weave the top layer, shafts 3-4 the bottom layer.) It takes four double-layer picks to equal two picks across the cloth when it's opened into a single layer. The shuttle order (for a fold at the left and open edges at the right) is top, right to left; bottom, left to right; bottom, right to left; top, left to right.

Saturday AM

- Cut the throw from the loom. Unfold, check for errors, and repair as needed. Carefully pull out the single end of 3/2 pearl cotton. Tie fringe in 1" bouts (8 ends each). Machine wash, delicate cycle; air dry. Trim fringe. Now rent a movie and curl up in your new throw!

Wish you had a wide loom? Wish no more! Weave your first double-width project with this simple quick throw—twice as wide as the width of your loom—and add warmth to an early winter.

double-width overshot tablecloth

Doramay Keasbey

So you decided not to give up the dining room and get a really wide loom? Luckily, this doesn't mean you can't weave a really wide cloth. Weave two layers on a narrow loom 'double-wide,' and look—no seams!

Before reading this article, review 'Twice as Wide,' pages 6–9, to learn the basic principles for drafting and weaving double-wide fabrics. Study this article, weave this tablecloth, and you'll be ready to design your own—twice as wide as the width of your loom.

Two layers—woven one above the other with a fold at one side and free edges at the other side—can be opened out to produce a fabric twice as wide as the original woven width. This feat is easily accomplished in plain weave or twill (see the blanket, pp. 8–9, and the throw, pp. 10–11). With a little more preparation and concentration while you are weaving, the same method can be applied to textiles patterned by a supplementary weft, such as overshot.

THE THREADING

The threading draft for double-width weaving must include both the top and bottom layers—on separate sets of shafts. One way to do this is to draft the top layer on the first set and the bottom layer on the following set. Since 4-block overshot requires four shafts for a single layer, the top layer can be drafted on shafts 1–4 and the bottom layer on shafts 5–8. For both layers to be woven simultaneously (one above the other), an end from the top layer must alternate with an end from the bottom layer.

To understand the process, first imagine that we want to use the overshot draft in *1* for a double-wide fabric. (Note that the treadling draft in *1* shows only the pattern picks; tabby is used alternately throughout using treadles 1 and 2).

The draft in *1* is rewritten in *2* so that the right half, which is to become the top layer, remains on shafts 1–4, and the left half, which is to become the bottom layer, continues the threading but on shafts 5–8. (The draft in *2* still represents a single-layer cloth. The center thread on shaft 1, in the position where the fold will occur when the draft is rewritten in two layers, is marked with an *.)

To become a draft for two layers as in *3*, the draft in *2* is then rewritten as if it had been folded at the center thread (compare the * in *2* and *3*) and

Create double-width overshot drafts in three easy steps. Write the complete draft (right to left), but at the center point change to shafts 5–8. Rewrite the draft (right to left), skipping a space after each thread to the midpoint. Then place threads on 5–8 (left to right) in the spaces.

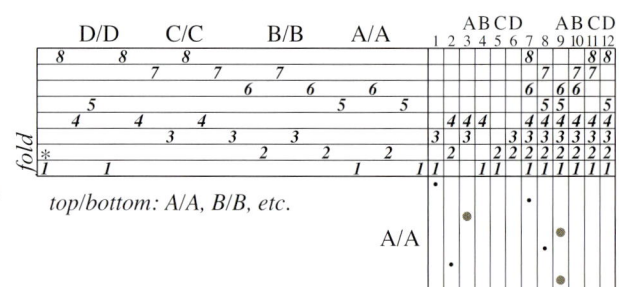

1. Step 1: write an overshot draft.

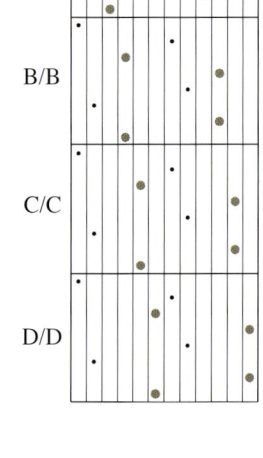

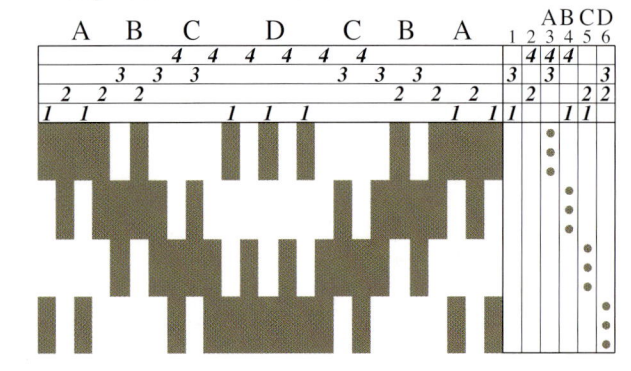

2. Step 2: divide the draft in half.

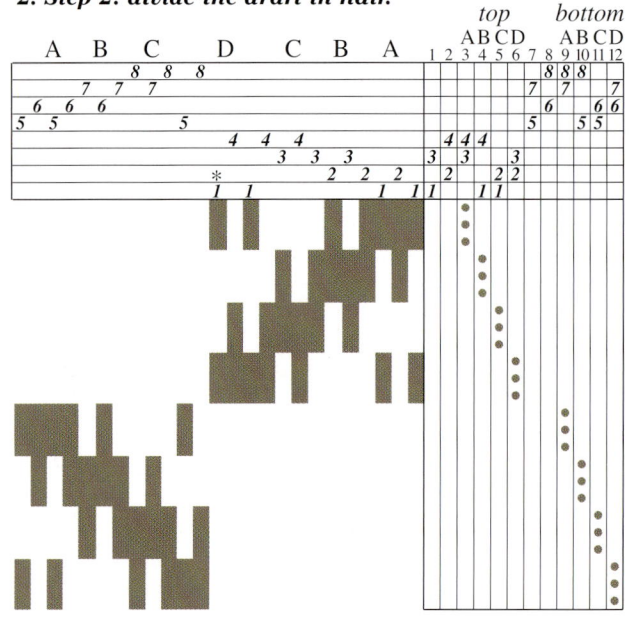

3. Step 3: 'fold' the divided draft.

top/bottom: A/A, B/B, etc.

4. Skeleton tie-up

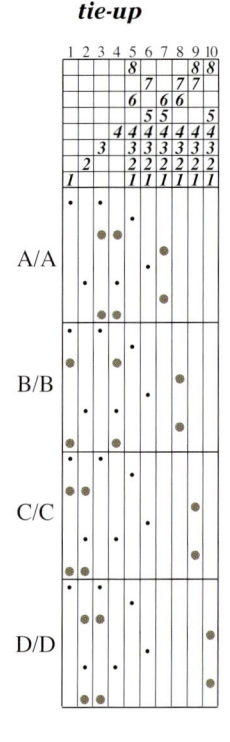

the lower layer continued around this fold back to the starting edge at the right. To do this, first enter the warp threads on shafts 1–4 (top layer) leaving a space after each thread for the bottom layer. Then enter the threads for the bottom layer in these spaces (5–8), but write from the left (center) to the right edge (therefore, in *3*, the bottom-layer ends from left to right are threaded 8-5-8-7-8-7-6-7-6-5-6-5, in the opposite order from their order in *2*).

THE TIE-UP
The shafts that weave the top layer are tied up just as they would be for a single cloth. Two adjustments must be made to the tie-up for the shafts that weave the bottom layer, however.

First: the supplementary-weft pattern floats must weave the pattern on the outer side, which is now facing down in the lower layer. This means that to produce floats in the correct position when the cloth is unfolded, the tie-up that weaves shafts 5–8 as a single-layer cloth in *2* must be reversed; i.e., all shafts that are raised for the single-layer cloth remain down in the double-layer cloth; all shafts that are down in the single-layer cloth are raised in the double-layer cloth. (Note that the tie-up for tabby must also be reversed in the bottom layer).

Second: when a weft is inserted in the bottom layer, all of the shafts in the top layer must be raised. The four top-layer shafts are therefore added to the tie-up for treadles 7–12. Compare the tie-ups for shafts 5–8 in *2* and *3* to see how these two adjustments are applied.

Since many looms are not equipped with 12 treadles, a skeleton tie-up is suggested in *4* in which two feet are used together to depress treadles for the top layer (indicated by two marks in a treadling row).

THE TREADLING
The treadling order in *3* includes tabby picks and pattern picks in both layers (in *3* the tabby treadles for the top layer are 1 and 2, for the bottom layer, 7 and 8; the pattern treadles are 3–6 for the top layer, 9–12 for the bottom layer). The treadling sequences in *3*, *4*, and *5* (p. 14) assume a fold at the left side and open edges at the right side with the shuttle sequence beginning from the right in the top layer. A full sequence to return each shuttle (tabby and pattern) back to its starting place is: top, right (R) to left (L); bottom L to R; bottom R to L, top L to R.

The combined treadling sequence for both shuttles in *3* and *4* is: tabby top, tabby bottom, pattern top, pattern bottom, tabby bottom, tabby top, pattern bottom, pattern top. This means that tabby goes all the way from the right edge to what will later become the left edge of the tablecloth (while on the loom, this edge is at the right in the lower layer) before the pattern weft follows in both layers. The handling of each shuttle for two consecutive picks this way is actually more efficient than if they alternate one and one.

SLEYING THE REED
Since each layer must be sleyed at its usual density for a single layer, the overall sett for two woven layers is twice what it would be for a single layer. For the tablecloth, p. 15, the appropriate sett for a single layer is 20 epi; therefore the sett for the double-width fabric is 40 epi.

CONTROLLING THE FOLD
Slight drawing in by the weft at the selvedges is a natural occurrence in weaving. The fold edge of a double-width cloth therefore requires special care. Depending on whether the weft interlaces regularly or produces pattern floats inside the fold, drawing in can produce irregularities down the center of a double-width fabric when it is unfolded (warp threads may appear condensed there; weft-float blocks can show narrowed widths). One way to compensate for the compression of threads at the fold edge is to sley the fold-edge threads more openly than the rest; see directions for the project tablecloth, p. 14.

CONTROLLING THE SELVEDGES
In theory it should be possible to twist pattern and tabby wefts around each other at the selvedges (which are both on the same side in double-width weaving) to ensure that the pattern weft reaches each selvedge and is not withdrawn in a subsequent pick in the same pattern shed. In double-width weaving, it is difficult to accomplish this.

Floating selvedges are a useful alternative in single-layer weaving and can also be used with double-width weaving. Since both floating selvedges occur at the same side, however, it is necessary to devise a way to keep track of which floating selvedge belongs to which layer. The following system works well: add doubled floating selvedges for both of the edges at the right side by placing each doubled thread alone in its own reed dent. The outer one belongs to the lower layer, the inner one, the upper.
❏ When the shuttle enters the upper layer first (on its path from selvedge to selvedge), pass it over both floating selvedges and exit from the lower layer under both.
❏ When the shuttle enters the lower layer first, pass it over the outside floating selvedge and under the inner floating selvedge; exit from the top layer under the inner and over the outer floating selvedge (on entering and exiting, the shuttle passes between the floating selvedges the same way: outer is down, inner is up for both entrance and exit).

Special care must be taken that wefts do not lock the layers together even once. To avoid such a catastrophe, place the shuttles methodically as they exit at the right. When a shuttle exits from the top layer, place it on top of the woven cloth. When a shuttle exits from the lower layer, place it on a shelf, chair, bench, or table beside the loom. Develop the following rhythm: pick up the shuttle on top of the cloth, enter it over both floating selvedges, and in the next shed exit under both; pick up the shuttle from the table, enter between the floating selvedges (over the outer, under the inner) and exit the next shed from the other layer between the floating selvedges the same way. If you are consistent, you will have no trouble keeping track of where each shuttle should go by looking at its position at the right edge. Slide your finger between the layers at the open edge frequently to be sure it is always open.

TIPS FOR EASY THREADING
For symmetrical overshot threading drafts, make a chained warp with a 2/2 cross; select a reed that produces the right sett at 4/dent (4/dent in a 10-dent reed for the tablecloth); sley. Turn one lease stick on edge to separate the warp into two levels of alternating pairs. Since for the tablecloth, the threading for 5–8 is the same as the threading for 1–4, thread the first warp end of a pair on the first set of shafts (1–4) and the other warp end of that pair on 5–8 in the corresponding heddle (see *5*, p. 14). Keep track of your place by blocking off a group of eight threads (four for each set of shafts); check heddle positions to verify that the two sets look identical. (This is easiest to do if you are using string heddles without frames around the heddle bars—in this case, the heddles can be seen clearly on their respective shafts.)

5. Draft for double-width overshot tablecloth

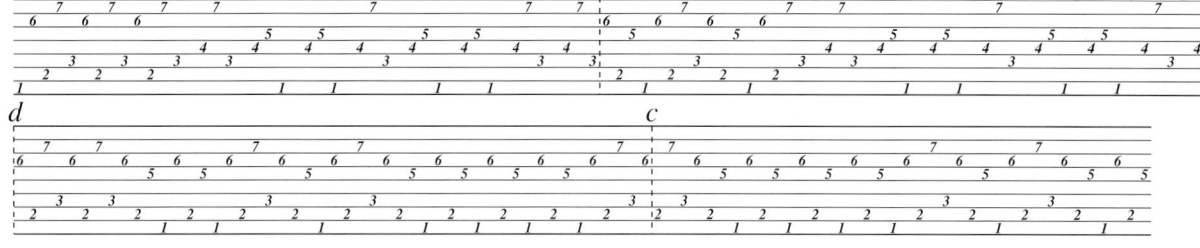

Dream no longer about that wide loom you thought you had to have. You, too, can weave tablecloths and coverlets! Here is a great first project in double-width overshot. Both the threading and treadling sequences are straightforward and easy to follow.

This tablecloth is 46" x 78". To increase tablecloth size, add to repeats *a–d* (at 180 ends or picks per repeat). Warp and tabby weft for the tablecloth are white, and there are four pattern-weft colors (dark and light tan for the major table motif; medium and light blue for the minor star motif). Consider using one or more hues in the ground cloth with other pattern-weft colors.

- Equipment. 8-shaft loom, 26" weaving width; 10-dent reed; 2 shuttles.
- Materials. Warp and tabby weft: 10/2 pearl cotton (4200 yds/lb), white or natural, 1½ lbs. Pattern weft: 8/2 cotton (3360 yds/lb, Homestead, Halcyon); light blue (L) 2½ oz; medium blue (B) 2½ oz; light tan (T) 4 oz; dark tan (D) 5 oz.
- Wind a warp of 1043 ends 10/2 white or natural cotton, 3½ yds long.
- Sley 4/dent in a 10-dent reed, 40 epi; center for 26". Sley the 5 threads at left side (the fold): 1 in last dent and 2/dent in next 2 dents. Add 2 doubled ends at the right side for floating selvedges, each pair in a single dent.
- Thread as in *5* in the following order: *a* to *b* 4x; *a* to *d* 4x; *a* to *c* 1x.
- Weave following the treadling draft in *5*. See p. 13 for efficient shuttle order and floating selvedge treatment. For looms with 10 treadles, substitute corresponding treadles from the skeleton tie-up in *4*, p. 12.

Start with the tabby weft at the right edge; weave 1" plain weave for hem: treadle 1 (top), treadle 7 (bottom), treadle 8 (bottom), treadle 2 (top). Then weave the tablecloth following tabby with pattern (tabby is shown only in the first eight picks of *5*): *a* to *b* 4x; *a* to *d* 14x (or number desired); *a* to *b* 5x; *b* to *c* 1x. End with 1" plain weave.

(Motif order is *a–b* [star, join] 4x; *a–d* [star, join, star, table] 14x; *a–b* [star, join] 5x; *b–c* [star to balance] 1x.)

For pattern-weft color order in the star, use 6B, 8L, 4B, 8L, 6B. For the join, use 2T, 4D, 4T, 4D, 2T. For the table, use 10T, 8D, 4T, 4D, 4T, 4D, 12D, 8T, 16T, 4T, 4D, 4T, 8D, 10T.

Change pattern-weft colors by turning weft tails around the floating selvedge and into the shed at the beginning or end of each two-color section only. Save time and avoid weft buildup by carrying the inactive color of each pair along the edge within these sections, enclosing the inactive weft with the active weft occasionally to avoid selvedge loops.

- Finish by machine zigzagging raw ends. Turn under a narrow hem at both ends; stitch by hand. Leave any weft tails at color changes. Machine wash, warm, gentle cycle; tumble dry. After fulling fabric by laundering, trim off tails at weft color changes. Spread on your table and enjoy!

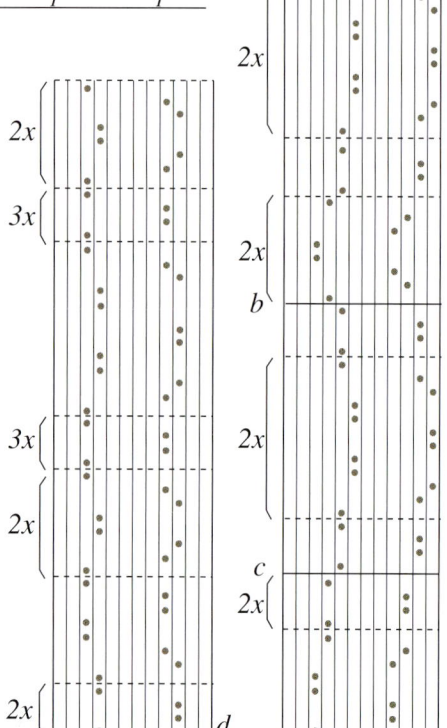

6. 4-shaft unpatterned alternative

Weave double-width plain weave on four shafts by threading the top layer on shafts 1 and 2, the bottom layer on shafts 3 and 4. Arrange warp and weft color stripes for interest. Use 10/2 or 8/2 cotton, 40 epi.

Looser spacing of ends at the fold prevents unsightly draw-in.

Weave this soft, drapable tablecloth—it needs no ironing!—on a loom with a weaving width as narrow as twenty-six inches. Change warp and weft colors or overall size to fit your loom, your table, and your taste!

a double-width coverlet

Charles Billings

1. Threading for shafts 1–8; see instructions

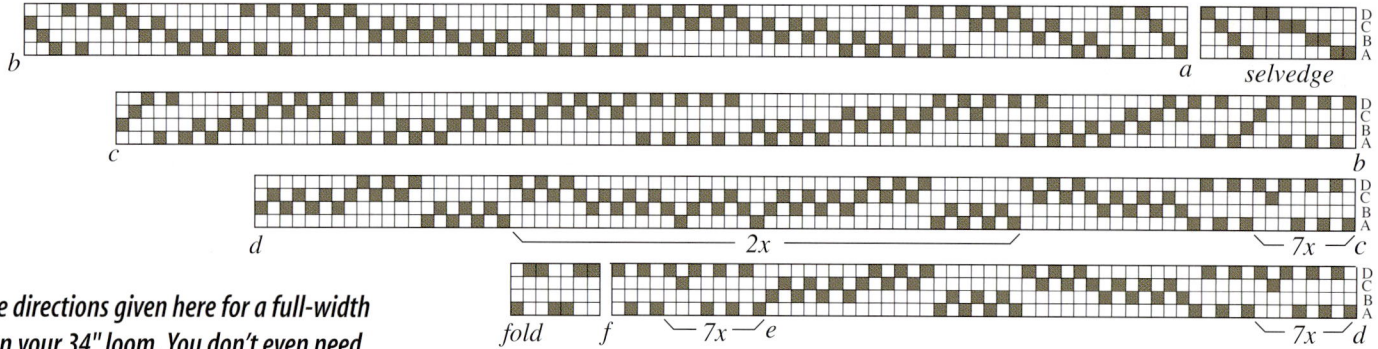

Follow the directions given here for a full-width coverlet on your 34" loom. You don't even need a loom with a lot of treadles! Instead, you can use an ingenious and convenient skeleton tie-up for this double-wide overshot fabric.

Each square in the threading in **1** (above) represents 2 ends: A = 1 & 5, B = 2 & 6, C = 3 & 7, D = 4 & 8.
Shafts 1–4 weave the top layer, 5–8 the bottom layer.
Thread: selvedge, a–b, b–c, c–d, d–e, c–d, e–f, a–b, fold.
For each square in **3** (A–H) substitute a 4-pick sequence from **2**.
Shuttles travel from top to bottom in A–D, bottom to top in E–H.
Weave a–b, [b–c, c–d, d–e, c–d, e–f] 3x, b–c, f–g.

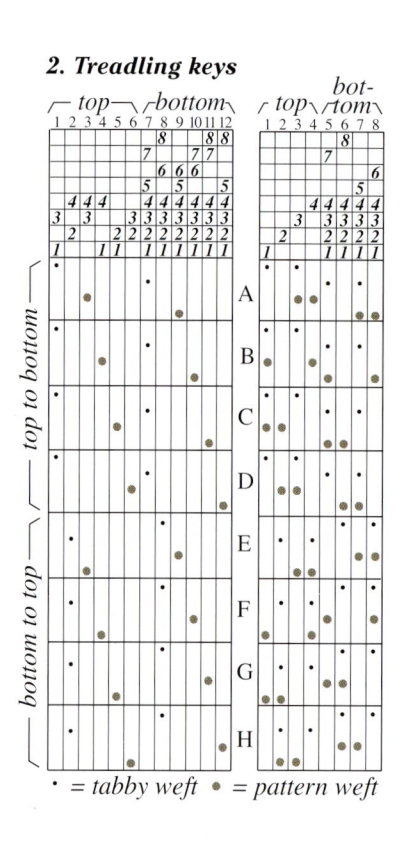

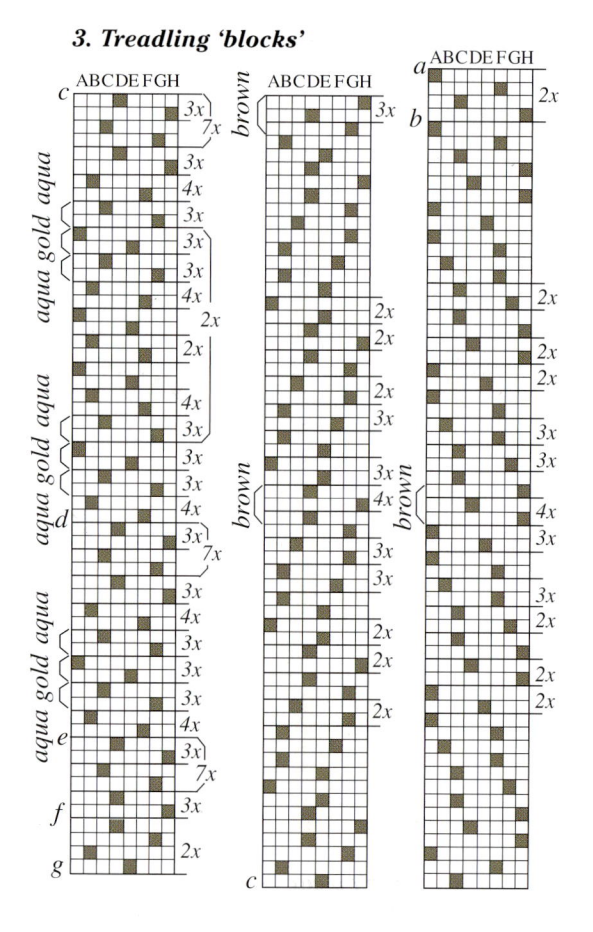

The design for this coverlet combines two common overshot coverlet patterns, 'Virginia Snowball' and 'Blooming Leaf.'

- Equipment. 8-shaft loom, 34" weaving width; 12-dent reed; 2 or more shuttles.
- Materials. Warp and tabby weft: 20/2 unmercerized cotton (8400 yds/lb), natural, 2 lbs. Pattern weft: 10/2 wool (2800 yds/lb), 2 lbs total, navy and optional accent colors (i.e., aqua, brown, gold).
- Wind a warp of 1600 ends 5 yds long, enough for one coverlet 96" x 62".
- Thread following the draft in **1**; note that ends are doubled at selvedge and fold (AA = 1, 1, 5, 5, etc.).
- Sley 4/dent in a 12-dent reed, 48 total epi; 24 epi per layer; sley 2/dent in the last 3 dents on both sides; center for 33 1/3"; add 2 doubled floating selvedges 1/dent on the right side.
- Review Doramay Keasbey, 'Double-width Overshot Tablecloth,' pp. 13–14, for an explanation of adding and using floating selvedges, proper weft order, shuttle placement, and weft color changes.
- Weave 2½" with scrap yarn for fringe area and then weave ½" with tabby weft only (alternate sequences A and E omitting pattern picks). Weave the body of the coverlet following the block order in **3** substituting treadling keys in **2**; end with ½" tabby and then 2½" waste yarn as at the beginning. For a longer coverlet, repeat the section in brackets. To minimize stress at fold, use a temple and/or adjust to ensure sufficient weft slack.
- Finish by removing from loom; hemstitch between tabby headers and scrap yarn; trim fringe and remove scrap yarn. Hand wash in bathtub or laundry sink, warm water; line dry. ✄

2. Treadling keys

• = tabby weft   • = pattern weft

3. Treadling 'blocks'

double weave *double* **weave** *double* weave *double* **weave** *double* weave *double* **weave** *double* weave *double* **weave** *double* **weave** *double* weave *double* **weave** *double* weave *double* **weave** *double* **weave** *double*

Billings Charles Billings Charles Billings Charles Billings Charles Billings Charles Billings Charles Billings

Doubled threads at the fold prevent draw-in.

"I can't weave a coverlet," you say. "My loom (and my reach) aren't wide enough to weave it in one piece, and I'd never be able to weave two panels that match." But you can weave a full coverlet 'double-width.'

DOUBLE WEAVE

it's an 'L' of a shawl!

David Xenakis and Ruth Morrison

The oddest things snare my attention: "...a woven tube, if cut along the bias from end to end, makes a long piece of bias-cut fabric without any waste."

People who sew probably know all about interesting things like that, but the information, delivered with the casual brilliance that distinguishes most of Nish Raymond's conversation, brought me to full attention. It's like catnip is to a cat: Why does it work that way? What would happen if...?

In this case, I wondered what would happen if, at some point, the cut reversed direction to move along the opposite bias. The unexpected answer? The long bias strip bends around a right angle into an L shape. That discovery and a superb weaver, Ruth Morrison, are responsible for bringing you this 'L' of a shawl! Not only that, but the shawl is an unpieced 25" wide from a weaving width of only 18"!

Note: Nish Raymond allows a generous warp length for her garment fabrics. After weaving, she threads her thrums on a small 4-shaft table loom to make the bias bindings which give her garments a superbly finished look; see pp. 24–27.

- Equipment. 4-shaft loom, 18" weaving width; 12-dent reed; 1 boat shuttle; 7 bobbins.
- Materials. Warp and weft: 2-ply Shetland wool (1800 yds/lb, Harrisville Designs), White, 1700 yds; Midnight Blue, 120 yds; Rose, 175 yds; Mist Blue, 235 yds; Garnet, 235 yds; Aster, 235 yds; Cobalt, 350 yds.
- Wind two warp chains 4 yds long each: one chain of 215 ends following the upper-layer color order in *1* and one chain of 216 ends White.
- Sley each chain (one above the other) 1/dent in a 12-dent reed (2 total ends/dent, 24 epi), centered for 18".
- Thread following the draft in *3*. Take special care with the threading to ensure that the all-white chain is threaded on only shafts 2 and 4 and the multicolored chain on only shafts 1 and 3.
- Weave a short heading in scrap yarn following the treadling in *3*. Then weave the body of the shawl following the treadling in *3*, the weaving order in *2*, and the color order in *1*. *This is very important:* when you read the color order in *1* for the weft, *every color and number listed equals 2 picks of weft*. For example, 4 Midnight Blue in *1* will mean to weave 8 picks of Midnight Blue.
- Begin the shawl by weaving half of the lower cloth

1. Warp and weft color orders

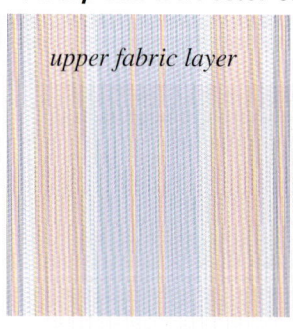

upper fabric layer

lower fabric layer

2. Weaving order

- half of back layer color order
- front layer color order
- back layer color order
- front layer color order
- back layer color order
- front layer color order
- half of back layer color order

a. Color order for upper fabric layer (left to right):

8 White
4 Midnight Blue
4 Rose
4 Midnight Blue
8 Mist Blue
4 Garnet
2 Rose
4 Garnet
16 Aster
4 Garnet

2 Rose
4 Garnet
8 Mist Blue
24 Cobalt
4 Rose
16 Cobalt
4 Rose
24 Cobalt
8 Mist Blue
4 Garnet
2 Rose
4 Garnet
16 Aster
4 Garnet

2 Rose
4 Garnet
8 Mist Blue
4 Midnight Blue
4 Rose
4 Midnight Blue
7 White

(Total: 215 ends)

b. Color order for lower fabric layer (left to right)

216 White

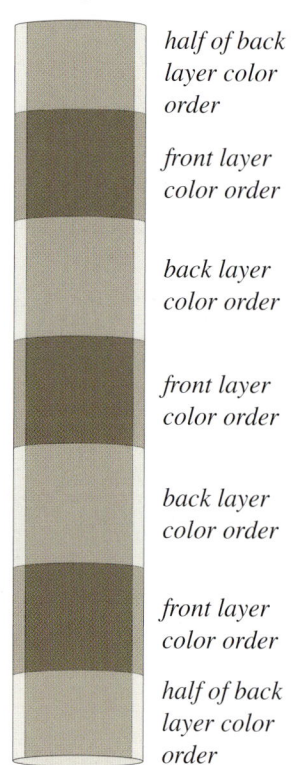

3. Draft

Upper cloth layer (shafts 1 and 3) is colored. Lower cloth layer (shafts 2 and 4) is all white.

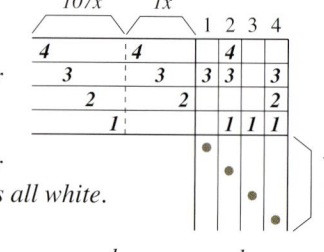

4. Weft joins

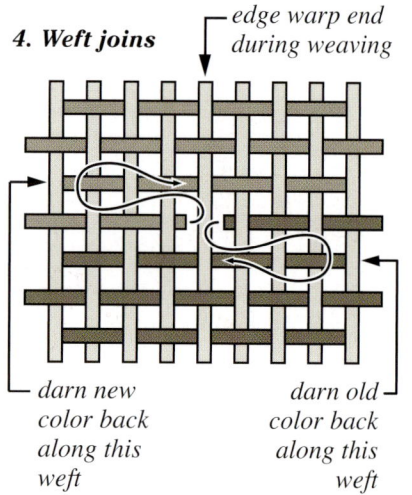

edge warp end during weaving

darn new color back along this weft

darn old color back along this weft

color order. Since the lower cloth color order is 216 White, you'll weave ½ of 216 x 2 = 216 White. Next, weave the upper cloth color order followed by the lower cloth color order two times (this will mean 430 picks for upper cloth color order, 432 picks White, 430 picks again of upper cloth color order, and 432 picks again of White). Finally, weave the upper cloth color order (430 picks) followed by half of the lower cloth color order (216 picks) as at the beginning. Weave 1–2"

in scrap yarn and cut the fabric from the loom. To begin and end new colors, allow 2–3" weft tails to protrude past the edge. Do not work tails back into the fabric until the weaving is off the loom.

- To finish, first darn in weft tails with a blunt needle. Flatten the tube as in *4* so that the selvedge is in the center of the tube. Darn the weft tails across the original selvedge warp thread along the weft path of the same color. Machine straightstitch just inside the scrap-yarn

Here's a very clever use of double weave: a bias-cut wrap in soft wool. You'll weave an 18" seamless tube and end up with a 25" flat shawl with a unique shape. It's very mysterious, very easy, and a lot of fun!

5. Cutting the tube

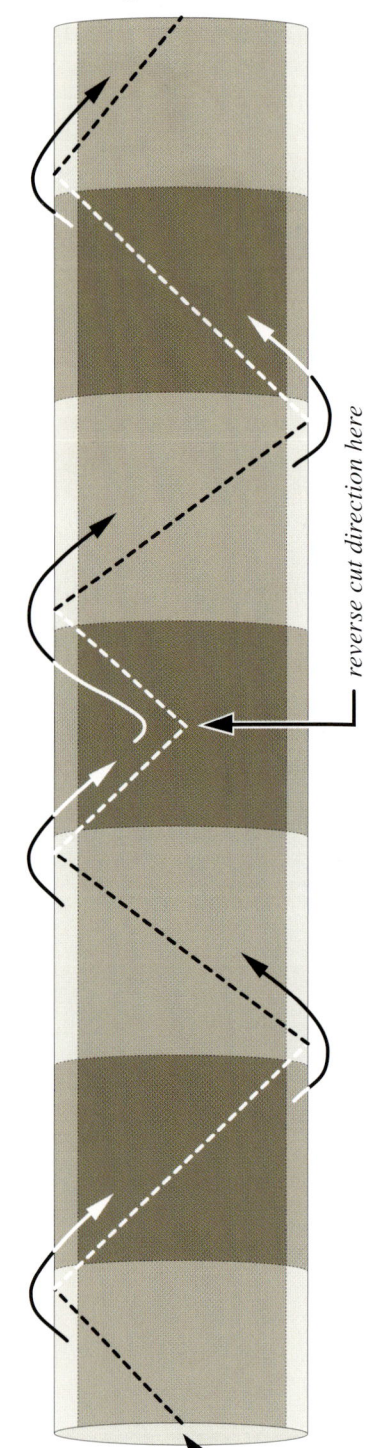

reverse cut direction here

begin cutting here

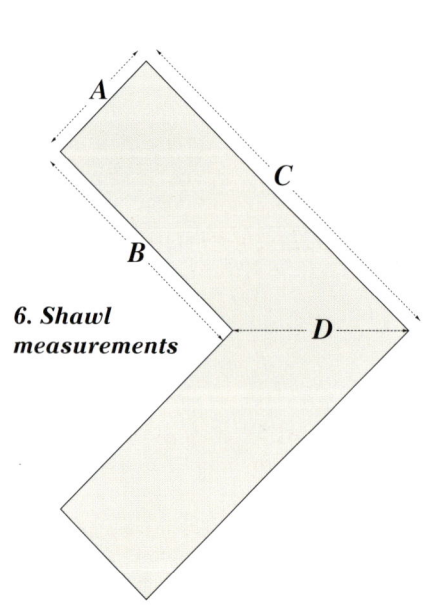

6. Shawl measurements

A *(finished shawl width)*
$= \sqrt{2(\text{width in loom}^2)}$
$= \sqrt{2(18^2)} = \sqrt{648} = 25.46''$
$B = 2(A) = 50.92''$
$C = 3(A) = 76.38''$
$D = 2(\text{width in loom}) = 2(18'') = 36''$

headings and trim along the stitching. Lightly steam press on both sides of the tube. Machine wash (hot/hot) with detergent and fabric softener, full cycle, on a normal setting. Lay flat to dry.

❏ To cut and sew: mark the path of the cut with a disappearing sewing marker as in *5*. Examine the marks—there should be no cutlines through the large upper-layer plaid sections. Take courage in hand and make the cut along the whole length of the tube. Lay out flat and cut off the triangle portions at each end (the 'final cuts' in *7*). Because it is fulled, the finished shawl will not ravel. An applied edge treatment will, however, firm the edges and prevent strain at the inside corner. This shawl has a crocheted edging sewn into place. Other edgings—knitted, blanket stitch, woven bindings, Ultrasuede, etc.—can also be used. This shawl also has a crocheted cord at the inside corner to take up excess strain and to allow a better fit adjustment for the wearer. ✂

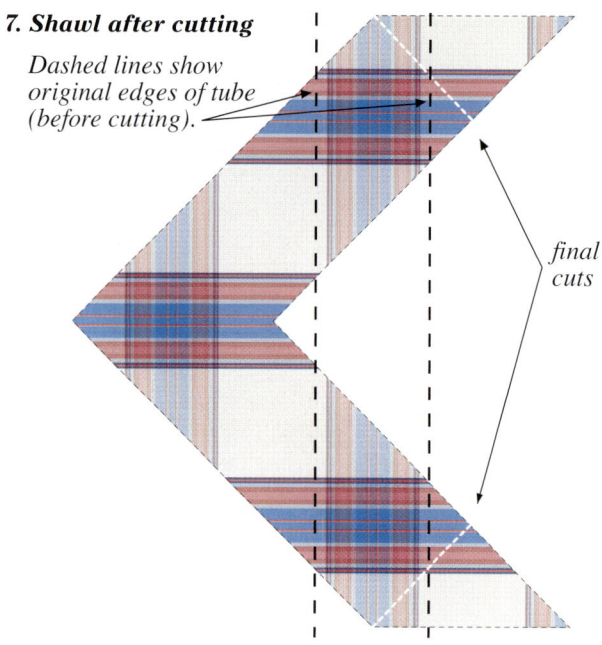

7. Shawl after cutting

Dashed lines show original edges of tube (before cutting).

final cuts

stitched double cloth

ruana in stitched double cloth	22
she fancies plush: two self-lined jackets	24
double tartan with extra-weft stitching	28
designing stitched double cloth	32

ruana in stitched double cloth

Doramay Keasbey

The simple lines and neutral colors of this ruana harmonize easily with other garments. You can choose colors especially suitable for your wardrobe instead—two colors for the striped face cloth, a single color for the back cloth. The draft for the ruana combines 2/2 herringbone twill for the face with 2/2 straight twill for the back. The stitchers are designed by raising back warp threads over face weft threads (see stitching Method 1, pages 33–34). Weaving the ruana is easy! Two shuttles alternate throughout in a straight treadling sequence. The finished fabric is pleasant to work with as it can be cut and handled without fear of excessive raveling.

- Equipment. 8-shaft loom, 26" weaving width; 10-dent reed; 2 shuttles; two #3 knitting needles; sewing machine; blunt yarn needle.
- Materials. Warp and weft: 2-ply wool (1645 yds/lb, Munkagarn, Nordic Studio), 32 oz plum, 20 oz light gray, 12 oz dark gray; matching sewing thread; 2 sew-on snaps; 1 pewter clasp.
- Wind two separate warp chains 6½ yds long each (includes take-up, shrinkage, 24" loom waste, and 24" for sampling). Wind the first chain with 1 dark gray and 1 plum end paired 172x (344 total warp ends) and the second chain with 1 light gray and 1 plum end paired 84x (168 total warp ends).
- Sley the reed with the first chain 2/dent, centered for 25½". Fill eight dents, leave the next four dents empty, and repeat. The last group will fill four dents only. Then sley the second chain 2/dent in all the empty dents. The color order for the face warp is 8 dark gray ends alternating with 4 light gray ends (x 21) ending with 4 dark gray. The back warp is solid plum.
- Thread following the draft in *1* so that all plum threads are on shafts 2, 4, 6, 8, and eight dark gray threads alternate with four light gray threads on shafts 1, 3, 5, 7.
- Weave following the treadling in *1* with one shuttle for each layer, light gray for the face weft, plum for the back weft. The two shuttles alternate 1:1 throughout. Beat to achieve 18 picks per inch (nine picks per inch in each layer) measured under tension. Follow the treadling from top to bottom until you have woven 95" measured under tension. Insert an extra colored weft as a marker; then reverse the treadling direction for 95". This ensures that the herringbone stripes will meet correctly with diagonals in opposite directions when the two panels are cut apart and seamed together.
- Finish by removing the fabric from the loom and machine washing for about five minutes, gentle cycle, cold water, with mild detergent. Check frequently during the wash cycle and turn fabric by hand if necessary to be sure all parts are agitated evenly. Rinse thoroughly; spin to extract water; spread flat to dry. Expect shrinkage of about 7% of woven length and 12½% of width in the reed.
- Knit a bicolored band: cast on four stitches light gray, four stitches plum. Knit in stockinette for 3 yds crossing yarn colors to make vertical stripes. Wash band by hand and hang to dry; then steam press. Also wash and air dry 3 yds each of plum and dark gray yarn (thrums or short pieces totaling 3 yds each color will do).
- To assemble the ruana, work with the fabric relaxed and spread flat on a large table or smooth floor. Cut panels apart along the colored thread at the midpoint of weaving. Trim off the other end of each so the panels measure exactly 80". With gray side up, align the panels side by side so the edges with stripes of four dark gray warp threads meet. Beginning at one end, join these edges by hand for 39". Use the prewashed dark gray yarn to sew through only the gray layer with a figure-eight stitch; turn the panels over and sew with plum-colored yarn through only the plum layer with a figure-eight stitch. At the end of the stitching cut out a 15" circumference oval neck opening (approximately 3½" x 6" wide). Machine staystitch ½" from the cut neck edge.
- Cover all raw edges with knitted binding: Lay the binding face down against the plum side of the fabric with the plum half of the binding ½" from the raw fabric edge; machine stitch through both fabrics as close as possible to the edge of the binding. At the ends, make two rows of machine stitching across the binding; cut off excess binding between the rows of stitching. Turn the binding around the fabric edge so the gray half covers the stitching on the gray fabric surface; stitch down invisibly by hand. Attach clasp at neck. Fold ruana across shoulders so lower edges are even. At each side, sew snaps 18" from shoulder fold. Finished dimensions (opened out flat) = 44" x 80". ✂

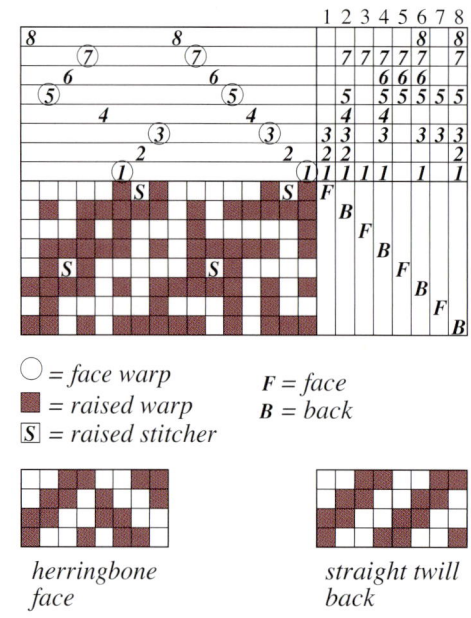

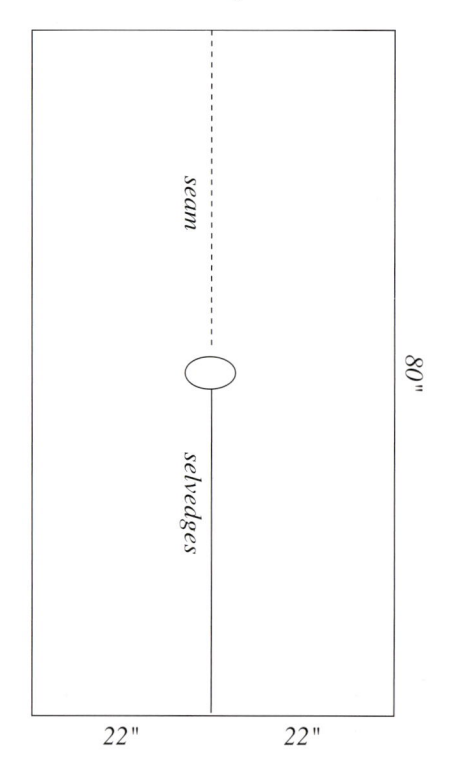

This marvelously warm ruana makes a great winter traveling companion since it can be worn over almost everything, folds flat, and can even double as a snug blanket on an unexpectedly cold night.

she fancies plush: two self-lined jackets
Nish Raymond

a. Face fabric

b. Back fabric

TWILL-PATTERNED JACKET
For a warm and serviceable jacket with an intricate pattern to delight the eyes and a soft surprise inside, try this approach to garment lining: a stitched double cloth. It all happens on the loom and makes sewing a breeze!

- Equipment. 12-shaft loom, 30" weaving width; 2 back beams if available; 6-dent reed; 3 shuttles.
- Materials. Warp and tabby weft for face fabric: 18/2 or 20/2 wool (5040 or 5600 yds/lb), brown, 5000 yds (used doubled in the warp, singly in the tabby weft). Pattern weft for face fabric: 6/2 wool (1680 yds/lb), natural, 840 yds (½ lb). Back warp and weft: cotton chenille (900 yds/lb), natural, 900 yds (1 lb).
- Wind a face warp of 360 doubled 18/2 or 20/2 ends (720 total ends) 4½ yds long. Wind a back warp of 180 chenille ends 4½ yds long.
- Sley 3/dent in a 6-dent reed (2 doubled face ends, 1 back end) in each dent, centered for 30".
- Thread following the draft in *1*.
- Beam the warp on separate beams if possible. Otherwise, beam the face warp only and suspend the back warp in several chains over the back beam and weight each chain.
- Weave the fabric following the treadling in *1* for 125" or length required by pattern (allow 10% shrinkage). Note that pattern and tabby picks alternate for the face fabric; tabby picks are not shown in the treadling draft. Two pairs of pattern and tabby picks are woven for every back pick.
- Finish by removing the fabric from the loom and machine washing in lukewarm water, gentle cycle. Lay flat to dry.
- To sew the jacket, use a favorite simple commercial jacket pattern. Lay out pattern pieces and cut. Serge all cut edges. Front and sleeve edges can be bound by plain-weave bias binding: Weave a tube (1 yd long, 9" wide provides sufficient binding for this jacket) with 18/2 or 20/2 wool used singly at 36 ends and picks per inch (18 ends and picks/layer). Cut the tube in a spiral like that of a cardboard paper towel tube—lay a triangle on the tube and cut a 45° cut (through one layer) to the end of the triangle, move to the new position and cut, and repeat until the 45° cut traverses around the entire tube. The resulting parallelogram can then be cut into six 2"-wide binding strips 50" long each (washed and pressed). The inside seams of this jacket are finished with commercial seam tape.

1. 12-shaft draft for twill jacket

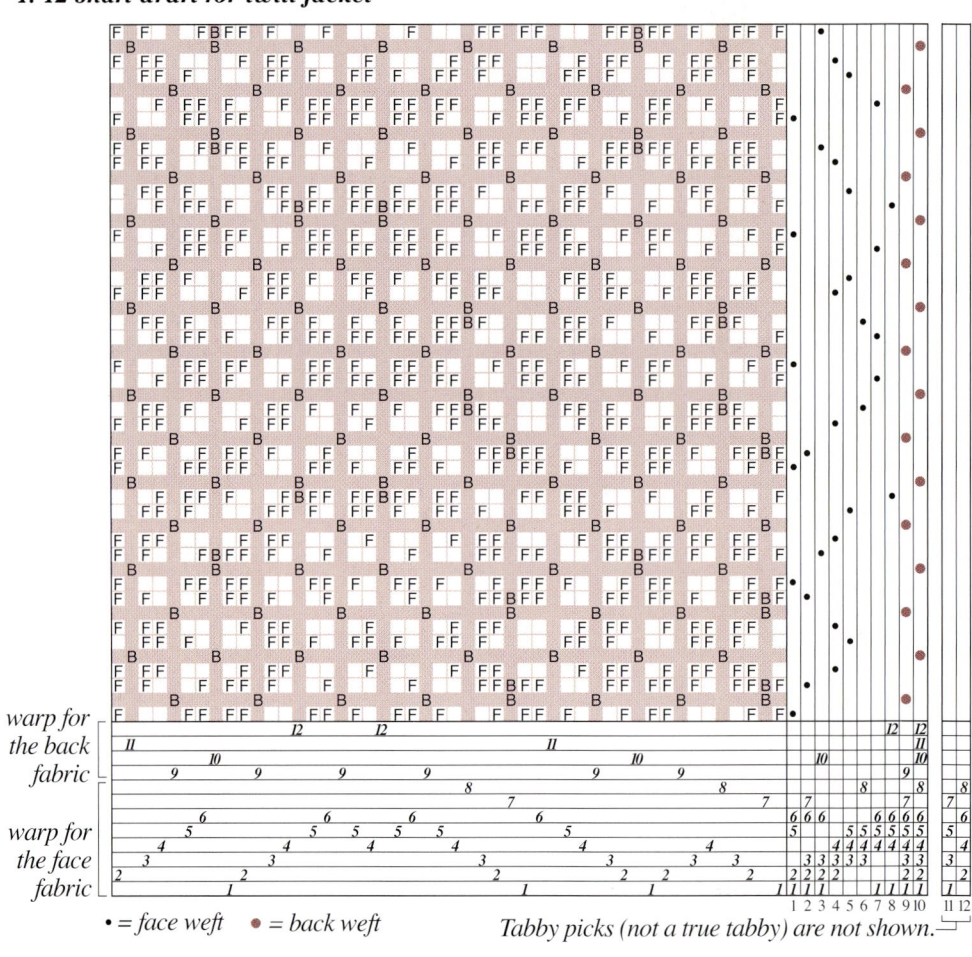

• = face weft   • = back weft

Tabby picks (not a true tabby) are not shown.

This patterned jacket exploits one of the best uses for a stitched double cloth: to provide a self-stitched lining for a garment. Cotton chenille adds to this wool outerwear a soft, plushy surprise inside.

a. Face fabric

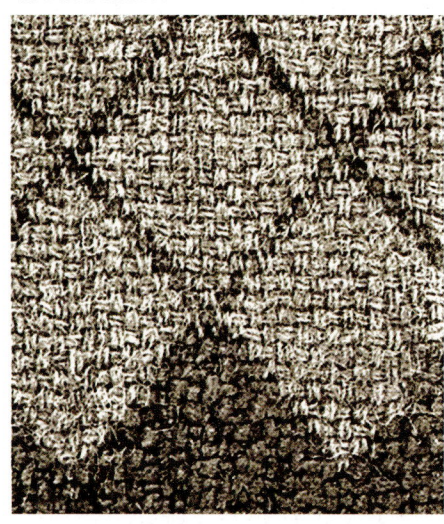

b. Back fabric

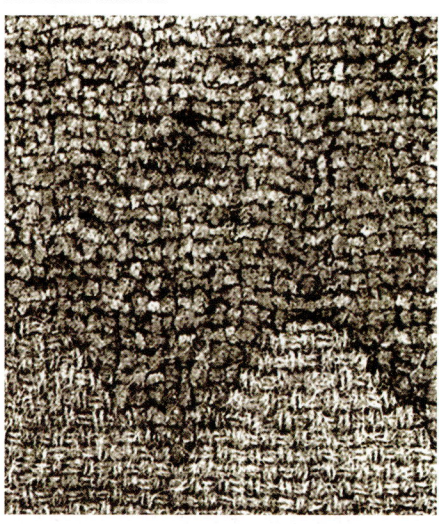

HARLEQUIN JACKET

This jacket is beautiful to look at and to touch—inside and out. To the basic idea of bringing the back cloth to the face as a design element, you can add your own touches and place the shiny diamonds wherever you like.

- Equipment. 12-shaft loom, 30" weaving width; 2 back beams if available; 15-dent reed; 2 shuttles; 34" pick-up stick (optional for weaving diamonds on the surface).
- Materials. Face warp and weft: 20/2 wool (5600 yds/lb, JaggerSpun), Iris, 7400 yds (1 lb, 5¼ oz). Back warp and weft: rayon chenille (1450 yds/lb), green, 3700 yds (2 lb, 4 oz).
- Wind a face warp of 900 ends 20/2 wool and a back warp of 450 ends chenille 4½ yds long each.
- Sley the face warp 2/dent and the back warp 1/dent in a 15-dent reed, centered for 30" weaving width.
- Thread following the draft in *2*; the face warp is threaded on shafts 1–2; the back warp is threaded on shafts 3–12.
- Beam the warps separately if two beams are available. If not, wind the face warp on the warp beam and suspend the chenille warp from the back beam in several weighted chains.
- Weave following the treadling in *2* for 125" using the sequence of face-back-face picks as shown. For green diamonds on the surface, use double-weave pick-up techniques: Pick up the green warp threads to appear on the face in the diamond, weave a blue background pick; pick up the blue background warp threads (all the blue threads except where the green diamond is to show), weave green; pick up the green threads in the diamond as before, weave a blue background pick. Repeat this 3-pick process for one full treadling repeat of a diamond.
- To finish, machine wash fabric in lukewarm water, gentle cycle. Lay flat to dry. Place pattern pieces in this order: one sleeve with cuff facing top edge, two fronts side by side, one back, and then the second sleeve with cuff facing bottom edge. Cut and serge edges to secure. After sewing, the edges for this jacket were trimmed with bias binding (see p. 24) and a separating zipper sewn into the inside front binding seam as a closure. ✂

2. 12-shaft draft for diamond jacket

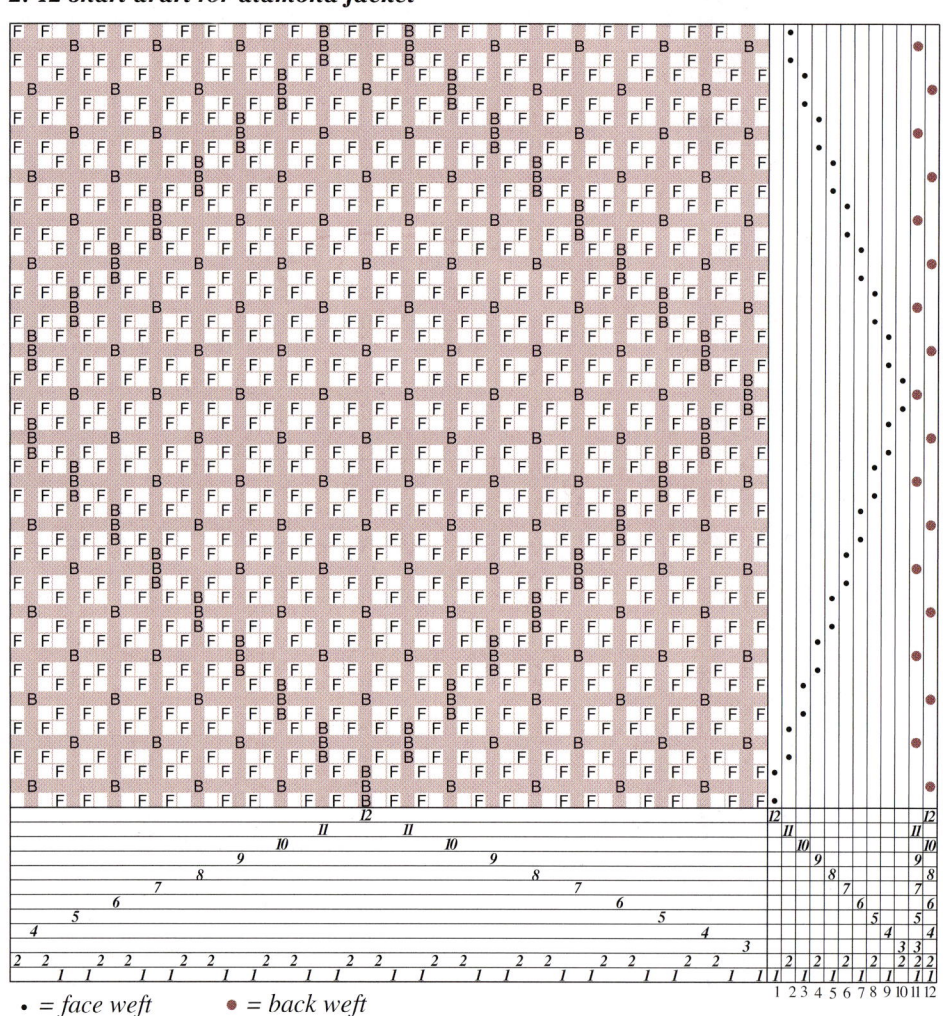

• = face weft   • = back weft

For this jacket, the plushy self-stitched lining is brought to the outside with an easy pick-up technique that adds to the decorative stitching. The stitching is done loom-controlled in an allover diamond pattern.

double tartan with extra-weft stitching

David Xenakis

Tradition need not have been only anciently instituted but can be part of an ongoing creative process for the benefit of the future!

The Scots, we are told, don't mind if the colors in their tartan plaids are sometimes varied. Scarlet, for example, might be used in place of crimson, or gray-blue in place of azure. What *is* important is that the proper number of threads of each color are used. The color order and proportions of each color in both warp and weft are the vital part of the overall design.

Having made this obeisance to tartan orthodoxy, I must tell you that the weaving of a double tartan (two tartans stitched invisibly together so that an entirely different plaid shows on each face) should be considered—especially since the bottom tartan cannot be seen until the cloth is taken from the loom—an exercise in masochism. In fact, it occurs to me that perhaps this is why one often sees pieces of stitched double twill in which a brilliant and intricate plaid is backed by a fabric that resembles an army blanket!

Once it is decided that the goal is an afghan with a brilliant and intricate plaid on *both* sides, the only sane design would be one that aligned the two tartan color repeats. To make this happen, the plaid design in the simpler of the two tartans used for this afghan breaks the aforementioned traditional tartan proportions—quite a few threads in both warp and weft are added to the large background color area. I could simply claim artistic license, but as a true Scot I've decided that tradition need not have been only anciently instituted but can be part of an ongoing creative process for the benefit of the future.

One other note for those tartanophiles in our midst (what a marvelous word... it sounds like an Aegean city of the late Byzantine Empire famous for the manufacture of oxhide temple drums): the more complex of our two tartans is that called *Anderson*. The other bears a strong resemblance to that called *Macbeth*, though, as any Scot could tell you, the colors are all wrong. The bright primary colors of the Macbeth tartan, lovely in themselves, would not easily have harmonized with the room where the Anderson tartan's colors are suitable.

STITCHED DOUBLE 2/2 TWILL

In a 'stitched double 2/2 twill' cloth, two independent 2/2 twill fabrics are woven, one above the other, and stitched together at short intervals with a fine stitching weft. The stitching weft does not show on either face of the fabric but weaves between the two layers as it binds them together.

The warp cross-sections in **4a–4b** (p. 31) show how the stitching weft accomplishes this binding (**4a** in double plain weave on four shafts, **4b** in double 2/2 twill on eight. In both figures, T = treadle, so T1 = treadle 1, T2 = treadle 2, etc.).

DOUBLE CLOTH ADVANTAGES

There are several advantages to be gained from the weaving of a stitched double cloth. The first and most obvious is the fabric's reversibility. Another is that quite a thick fabric can be made without the use of coarse materials or the appearance of coarse cloth. Moreover, due to the nature of the construction, air spaces trapped between the two layers provide additional insulation. Finally, the making of these fabrics is a very neat trick which will knock the socks off weaving and non-weaving friends alike!

1. 8-shaft draft for exta-weft stitched double 2/2 twill

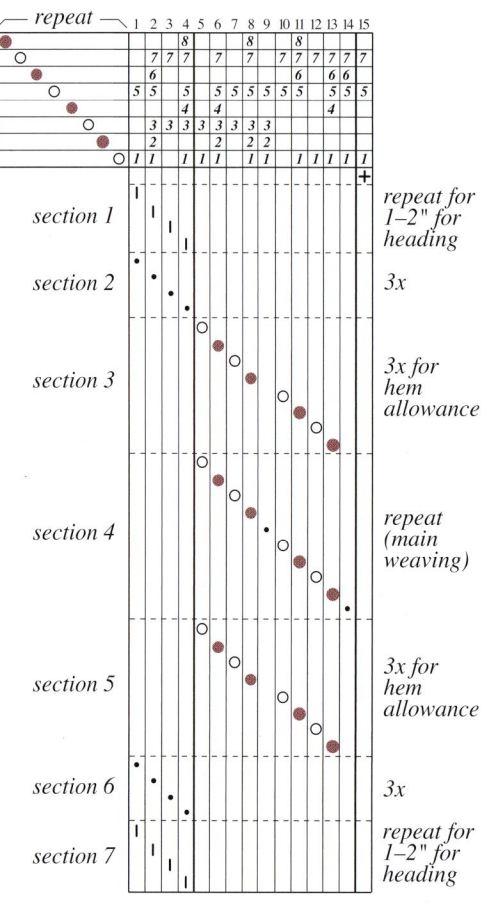

2. 4-shaft draft for extra-weft stitched double plain weave

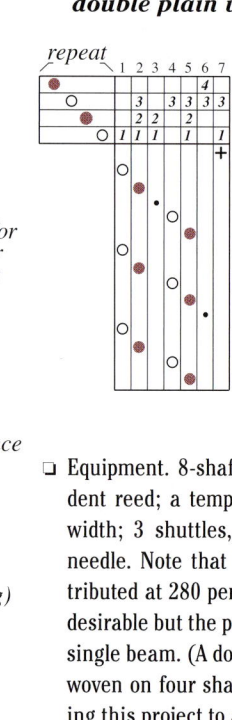

- • stitching weft
- ○ warp or weft of upper cloth
- ● warp or weft of lower cloth
- | weft for heading
- + special treadle

- ❏ **Equipment.** 8-shaft loom, 63" weaving width; 6-dent reed; a temple (stretcher) for 63" weaving width; 3 shuttles, 16 bobbins; 1 blunt tapestry needle. Note that you'll need 2,240 heddles distributed at 280 per shaft. A second warp beam is desirable but the project can also be woven with a single beam. (A double *plain-weave* tartan can be woven on four shafts. See suggestions for adapting this project to a 4-shaft loom, p. 30.)
- ❏ **Materials.** Warp and weft: 2-ply Shetland wool (1800 yds/lb, Harrisville Designs), Plum, 1530 yds (13 oz); Azure, 3075 yds (25 oz); Black, 3075 yds (25 oz); White, 390 yds (4 oz); Begonia, 260 yds (3 oz); Royal Blue, 525 yds (5 oz); Peacock, 2850 yds (23 oz); Teal, 3500 yds (28 oz); Seafoam, 770 yds (7 oz); Pearl, 390 yds (4 oz), Aubergine, 1430 yds (12 oz). Stitching weft: 20/2 wool (5,600 yds/lb, JaggerSpun, Maine Line), Navy, 2100 yd (6 oz).
- ❏ Wind eight warp chains 5 yds long each following the color order in *3*, p. 30 (wind one chain for each color repeat in the top fabric, one for each color repeat in the bottom fabric; add the four edge threads only to the first and last chains in each layer). The 5-yd length allows 15% take-up, hem allowance, and 1½ yds loom waste.
- ❏ Sley the chains for each layer 3/dent in a 6-dent reed (6/dent overall), centering for 62¼".
- ❏ Thread following the draft in *1*.
- ❏ Beam the warp (use one beam for the top layer and the other for the bottom layer if two beams are available), tie the warp onto the cloth-beam apron rod, and adjust the tension.
- ❏ Weave following the treadling in *1*. Use two shuttles, one for the upper cloth and one for the lower cloth. Begin with treadling section 1 to weave a 1–2" heading in scrap yarn. Attach the temple to

Choose colors like these—or plan a reversible tartan with two very different-colored faces. The two plaid designs depend on the color ordering and proportions of both warp and weft threads in each layer.

3. Color orders

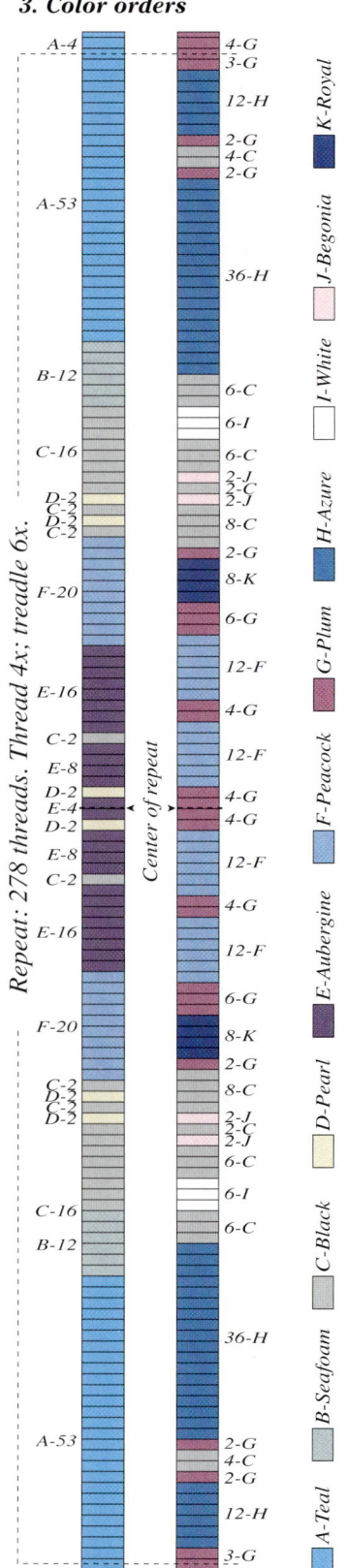

Repeat: 278 threads. Thread 4x; treadle 6x.

Left column (A-Teal layer, top to bottom): A-4, A-53, B-12, C-16, D-2, C-2, D-2, C-2, F-20, E-16, C-2, E-8, D-2, E-4, D-2, E-8, C-2, E-16 *(Center of repeat)*, F-20, C-2, D-2, D-2, C-16, B-12, A-53, F-20

Right column (top to bottom): 4-G, 3-G, 12-H, 2-G, 4-C, 2-G, 36-H, 6-C, 6-I, 6-C, 2-J, 2-J, 8-C, 2-G, 8-K, 6-G, 12-F, 4-G, 12-F, 4-G, 4-G, 12-F, 4-G, 12-F, 6-G, 8-K, 2-G, 8-C, 2-J, 2-J, 6-C, 6-I, 6-C, 36-H, 2-G, 4-C, 2-G, 12-H, 3-G, 4-G

Color key:
- A-Teal
- B-Seafoam
- C-Black
- D-Pearl
- E-Aubergine
- F-Peacock
- G-Plum
- H-Azure
- I-White
- J-Begonia
- K-Royal

---

this heading. With two shuttles and the stitching weft only, weave three repeats of treadling section 2.

Then, beginning at the bottom of the color order chart in *3*, weave using treadling section 3, alternating a shuttle with the weft color for the top layer with a shuttle with the weft color for the bottom layer. (This section begins the double twill but does not include the stitching weft.) Then weave the main portion of the afghan with three shuttles following treadling section 4 and including the stitching weft.

Maintain a 50/50 relationship of warp to Shetland wool weft (18 Shetland wool picks per inch in each layer). Weave the color order six times, but stop using treadling section 4 at 24 picks (12 upper and 12 lower cloth picks) from the end of the last color repeat.

Then weave using treadling section 5. This section concludes the color repeat without the stitching weft. Follow with three repeats of treadling section 6 woven with two shuttles carrying the stitching weft. Conclude with 1–2" of scrap yarn using two shuttles to weave treadling section 7.

- Finish by removing the fabric from the loom. With a blunt tapestry needle and a length of 20/2 wool, hemstitch across the plain-weave areas on both layers (keeping them separate) of both ends of the afghan. Carefully cut away the scrap yarn about 1/8" away from the fine wefts and ravel any remaining scrap yarn. Use a steam iron to press the narrow plain-weave sections to the inside of the unstitched twill sections.

  With a blunt needle and a doubled length of 20/2 wool, blindstitch the two layers together at each end. Blindstitch together the short slits along the selvedges at each side of each end.

- Repair all weaving errors and trim all weft tails.
- Machine wash the fabric in warm water with mild detergent. Be sure to control the amount of time the fabric agitates. Check the cloth often until the desired softness has been achieved. Rinse thoroughly several times. Add ½ cup of fabric softener to the final rinse. Spin to remove excess water. Lay flat to dry. After drying, steam lightly if needed. The finished afghan is approximately 62" x 91".

You don't want double trouble? You haven't woven plaids before? Then it is best to take the plaids one at a time. Choose one of these tartan color orders (or another!) to weave as a single fabric, or you can weave the bottom fabric in a single color and avoid weft color changes in the bottom layer.

ADAPTING THE AFGHAN TO A 4-SHAFT LOOM

Weavers with 4-shaft looms can construct a comparable version of this project using the 4-shaft draft shown in *2*. This draft produces a cloth called 'weft-stitched double plain weave.' The treadling draft in *2* spaces the stitching wefts so that they approximate the frequency used for the double twill.

If the same yarns specified here are used, a sett of 24 epi (12 epi per cloth) can be achieved by sleying 4/dent in the 6-dent reed. (The sett needs to be looser to accommodate plain weave's greater frequency of interlacement.) Changing the sett, however, will change the size of the color repeat from 15.4" width at 18 epi to 23.2" at 12 epi. Thus, three repeats in width and five repeats in length would produce a fabric approximately 70" x 117". Such a cloth is probably too large for most looms, so a solution would be to reduce some of the numbers of threads in the color repeat.

WARPING AND WEAVING NOTES

1. The color key in *3* gives the ordering of the warp colors for each layer and shows the way they line up with each other. Each small rectangle in the key represents 2 threads. The color repeat of 278 ends is threaded 4x. There are four extra threads on each side of each layer (these threads are on the selvedges only and are not used between repeats.)
2. To avoid bulk on the warping board wind a single chain for each 278-end repeat of each layer. Wind the 4 extra edge threads at the beginning of the first chain and at the end of the last chain in each layer.
3. The overall sett for this project is 36 epi (18 epi per layer). The use of the coarse 6-dent reed is suggested to prevent undue abrasion of the warp ends and to facilitate the formation of the sheds in the reed.
4. The size of the yarns used with this sett will make it especially important to wind the warp on the warp beam at a consistent width with even and firm tension, packing the layers with smooth paper. Warp tension and shed formation will both be aided by using two warp beams, if available.
5. If the weft threads are inserted in the directions shown in the drawings in *4*, the selvedge warp threads will bind with all the wefts.
6. The stitching weft should be woven with fairly tight tension and beaten on an open shed. Care should be taken that the stitching weft does not twist around the wefts of the tartans but is allowed to loop up to its next shed between the tartan selvedges.

7. The use of a temple (stretcher) is strongly recommended to prevent draw-in.
8. An extra treadle (#15 in *1*; #7 in *2*) has been added to the tie-up for a very useful purpose. When ending one weft color and/or beginning a new one, allow a 3–4" tail to extend from the selvedge. Beat the weft and then depress the extra treadle. Take the weft tail around the edge warp thread and into the shed for 2–3" and then bring the tail up and out of the shed.

    When the yarn on a bobbin comes to an end, overlap the ends of the old and new yarns for ½" within the shed, beat the weft, depress treadle 15 or 7, and take the tails of each yarn between the two layers for 2–3" before bringing them up and out of the shed. As the weaving progresses those protruding bits of yarn can be trimmed flush with the fabric's surface. Weavers lacking the needed treadle can leave the end of yarn protruding and accomplish the same effect with a blunt darning needle after the fabric is removed from the loom.
9. Treadles 1–4 in *1* are needed only at the beginning and ending of the afghan (treadling sections 1, 2, 6, and 7). Weavers with 10 treadles can tie the first four treadles this way at the beginning of the weaving, retie them as treadles 5–8 for the main weaving, and then re-tie them again as for treadles 1–4 at the end. ✂

4a. Stitched double cloth, two layers of plain weave, stitched with an extra weft, four shafts

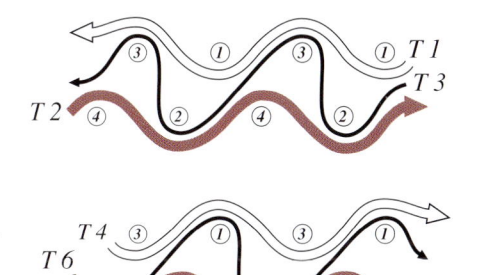

4b. Stitched double cloth, two layers of 2/2 twill, stitched with an extra weft, eight shafts

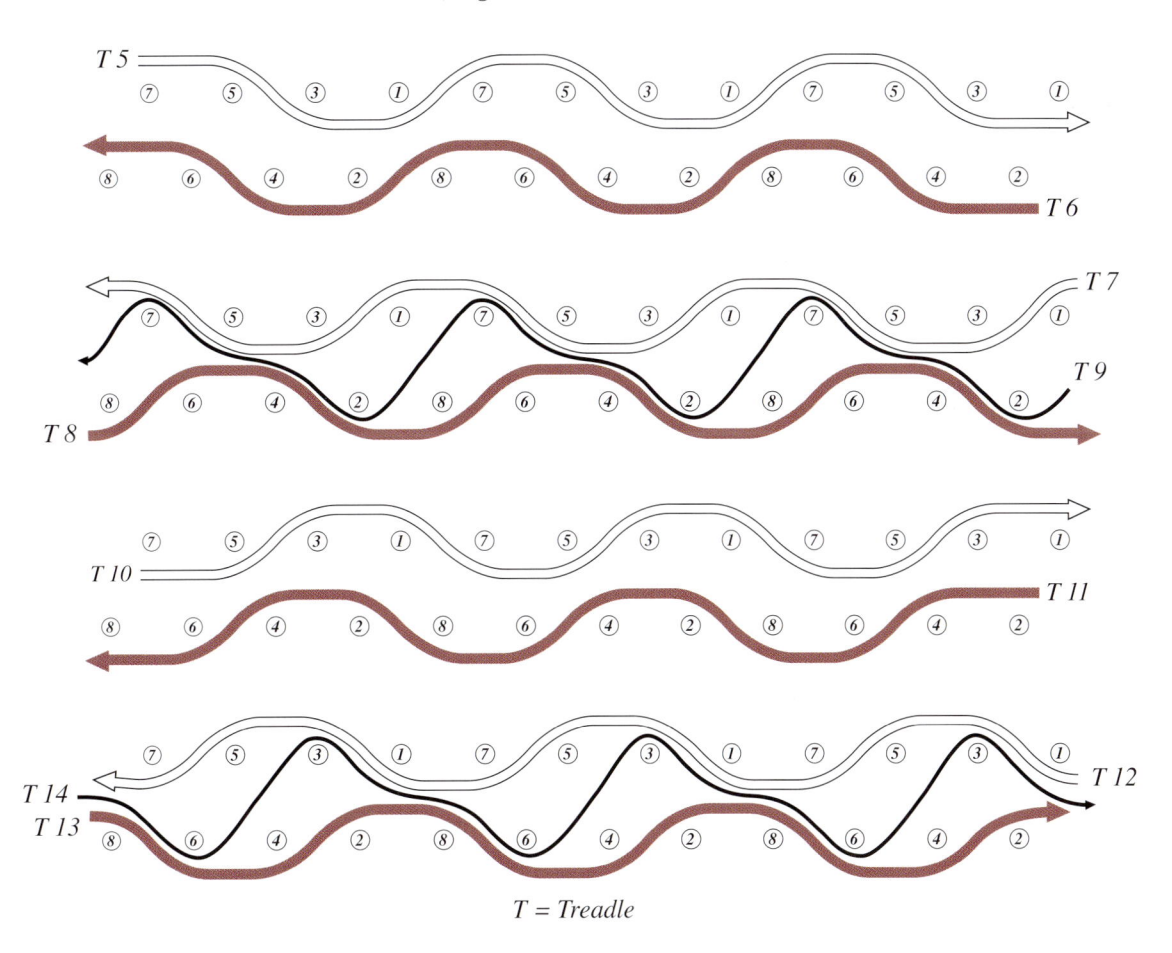

T = Treadle

designing stitched double cloth

Doramay Keasbey

Handweaving is full of surprises and puzzles, and finding solutions is one of the things that makes it so fascinating. A small incident observed early in my weaving experience sparked a puzzle-solving instinct that has had enormous influence on my subsequent progress and delight in weaving.

When asked if a rather unusual, intricately woven fabric might be a kind of double cloth, a respected weaving teacher responded by saying, "Let me see if I can separate the layers" as she pinched opposite sides of the cloth and pulled gently. Her cautious verdict expressed some doubt when nowhere could she find evidence of any space or pocket between face and back even though two quite different weaves appeared to exist, one on each side. The double nature seemed so obvious that my curiosity was aroused. Was separating the components the ultimate test for double cloth? What held those layers together so tightly? If two layers really did exist and were interwoven in some way, why didn't any of the threads from one side show up on the other? And, most nagging of all: how can *I* learn to design two completely different weaves that are mysteriously and invisibly linked?

Since there would be little point in weaving simultaneously two fabrics that would become completely independent after removal from the loom, it follows that the two structures usually *are* connected—in one of several ways. The mysterious cloth that sparked my research is representative of the category called *stitched double cloth*.

The two layers of stitched double cloth, each formed by a distinct warp and weft system, are held together at intervals through the 'stitching' action of a thread from one layer interlacing with a thread from the other or by an added thread interlacing with both layers. Each layer can be quite different in structure, color, texture, and even density of threads. Stitching can be prominent or so subtle that it is not visible. When the layers are loosely connected as, for example, when widely spaced stitching produces a quilted effect, each layer can be fairly easily identified and even pinched apart. When stitching points occur very close together, the two weave systems may become so tightly connected—as in the example that puzzled my teacher—that separating them is impossible.

My search for answers quickly turned up ready-made drafts in numerous sources for simple versions of stitched double cloth, but how they were derived was left a mystery. Then, happily, I found two helpful books: a German industrial weaving text (with instructions for drafting stitched double cloth using a color coding system) and a turn-of-the-century English book for textile industry designers (with symbols to designate specific warp and weft functions); see the Bibliography, p. 34. This article borrows a bit from both to present the drafting process in a series of steps using a letter code with suggestions for shading or coloring for increased clarity.

BENEFITS AND LIMITS

At least four shafts are required for any type of true double weave since a minimum of two are needed for plain weave in one layer and two for the other. When two layers of plain weave are stitched together, the stitching points are difficult to hide completely because there are no long surface floats for them to slide under. Therefore, plain weave is an ideal surface for *intentionally* conspicuous stitching as demonstrated by piqué, for example. To stitch together two layers of plain weave without completely interweaving the two layers, additional shafts are necessary to carry individually controlled stitching threads.

More shafts also make possible the selection of different weaves for one or both layers, and that is where the fun of original designing begins. Some simple structural variations for two stitched layers are possible on as few as five shafts. On eight shafts a wide range of weave combinations becomes possible since any two 4-shaft single cloths can be woven and stitched together without altering the threading of either structure. Individual control of warp threads used for stitching requires more shafts; therefore, looms with 12 or 16 shafts expand the opportunities tremendously for decorative *and* hidden stitching.

The warps for both layers can be wound on the same warp beam when they are similar in thread size and fiber characteristics and when the number of intersections of warp with weft is the same in each layer. When any one of these factors is different, it may be necessary to put the warps on separate beams. If all warp ends of one layer are involved as stitchers an equal number of times, their take-up and tension should remain relatively constant. However, if some warp threads serve as stitchers while others do not, a difference in tension may develop. A solution is to separate the looser warp threads with a sturdy bar near the back beam and to weight the bar to equalize tension.

Stitching two layers of fabric together can produce an especially thick yet supple cloth, make an article dramatically reversible, provide a comfortably smooth lining for a rough or abrasive surface, offset precious or fancy surface yarns with a less expensive backing, increase insulating qualities by forming a multitude of tiny air pockets between layers or by introducing stuffing between them, and provide stability and invisible support for an exceptionally loose or light and airy surface weave.

CHOOSING STITCHING METHODS

There are several ways to stitch two layers together.

Self stitching
I. Raising a warp thread from the bottom layer over a weft thread from the top layer (see pp. 22–23).
II. Sinking a warp thread from the top layer under a weft thread from the bottom layer
III. A combination of 1 and 2

Center stitching
IV. Interlacing both layers with an extra warp that otherwise floats between the layers
V. Interlacing both layers with an extra weft that otherwise floats between the layers (see pp. 28–31).

Although prominent stitching points may be desirable in some textiles as an added design element, often the intention for stitched double cloth is to join the layers as invisibly as possible so the weave structures of front and back are not disturbed. The choice of the most appropriate method depends on a variety of factors. The basic process for *hiding* the stitching effectively depends on two conditions:

A. Stitching is hidden when selected threads from each layer interlace with each other where the structure of their respective layers places them in contact on the inside. For example, where a warp thread of the bottom layer rises over a top-layer weft thread that is floating below the surface, the two will interlace between the layers.

B. Stitching is hidden when it occurs between *pairs* of warp or weft threads that are floating on the surface (face or back).

Some combinations of weaves make it difficult to find the coincidence of ideal conditions for stitching by a particular method. Thus the weave structure for each layer may be a determining factor in the choice of stitching method. When practical, stitching by raising warp ends from the bottom layer over weft threads from the top layer produces more invisible stitching since the warp under tension can pull an upper-layer weft beneath the surface more effectively than a weft from the bottom can pull a warp thread downward. However, this often means raising more shafts, resulting in heavier treadling. Surface yarns that relax and spread during the finishing process also help hide stitching. Sometimes a combination of stitching types is called for to provide a suitable distribution of stitching points.

When self-stitching methods are not feasible, Methods IV or V can be selected. The additional warp or weft stitchers can be thinner than the yarns of either layer, fewer in number, and matching one of them in color for better camouflage. The stitching thread lies passively between the layers except at the points where it rises to stitch a thread from the face or sinks to stitch a thread from the back layer, and it must stitch both layers alternately. Generally this results in looser joining of the layers than by the self-stitching methods. Center stitching by an additional warp also requires additional shafts for their control, and stitching by an additional weft reduces weaving efficiency due to handling an extra shuttle; see the draft on p. 28.

GETTING STARTED

The following directions are for determining the location of stitching points and deriving the threading, tie-up, and treadling for self-stitched double cloth. Proceeding step by step may seem a bit like working a crossword puzzle! Graph paper with four squares per inch is recommended to provide space for legible marking with colored pencils. Use one color for the face or top layer, another for the back or bottom layer. This helps identify the two warp systems at a glance. After the drawdown has been fully marked using a letter code to identify the specific function of each warp thread, dark shading (such as blue) over the marks of the back layer and light shading (such as red) over the marks of the face will help distinguish the two warp systems and make it easier to make changes as you design.

For best results choose a weave for the back layer that repeats on the same number of ends and picks as the weave for the face layer or else is an even factor or multiple of it. Other combinations are possible but more complicated. For hidden stitching, remember that weaves with warp or weft floats over two or more threads will be more successful than those with extensive areas of plain weave.

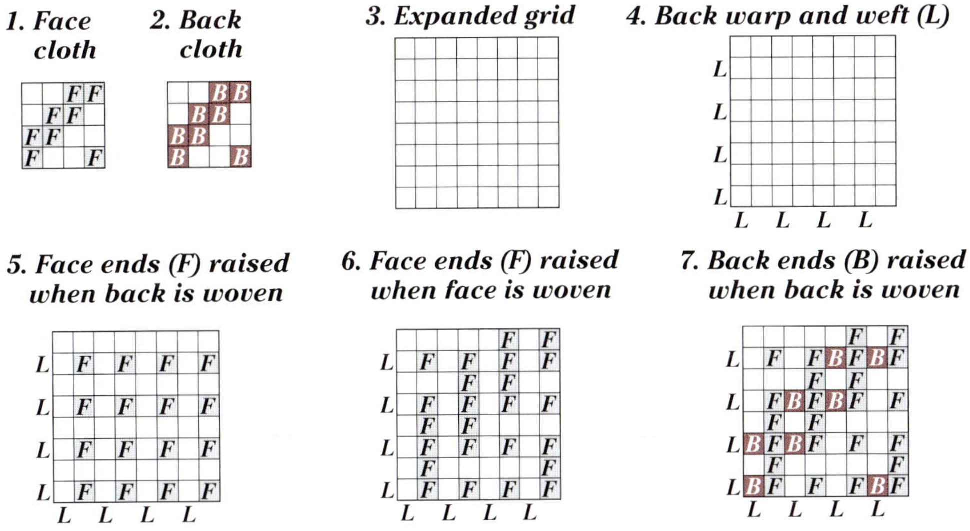

DESIGNING STEPS

Key for the drafts correspond to Steps *1–17*:
L = lower (back) layer columns and rows
F = warp end of the face layer
B = warp end of the back layer
S = stitching point where back warp end rises
X = stitching point where face warp end sinks

Method I: Stitching by raising back warp over face weft

Let's begin by designing s stitched double cloth of 2/2 straight twill in both layers with a warp and weft ratio of 1:1 between the layers (many other structures and ratios are possible). Each step below is illustrated by the corresponding draft (*1–17*).

1. Make a warp drawdown for the face (the top layer). Let F = the position of raised warp threads in the top layer.
2. Make a warp drawdown for the back (the bottom layer). This drawdown is viewed as though the upper layer were removed to expose the bottom layer without turning it over. Let B = the position of raised warp threads in the bottom layer.
3. Make an expanded grid to accommodate both layers on a single plane with as many columns and rows as the grids in *1* and *2* combined. In our example, 4 face columns + 4 back columns = 8 columns in the expanded grid, and 4 face rows + 4 back rows = 8 rows. Leave plenty of room above and beside this grid in order to add threading and treadling (as in Steps *8, 9, 10* on p. 34).
4. Label L the rows and columns representing the warp and weft threads of the bottom (back) layer. Unlabeled rows and columns represent the top (face) layer. Since the two structures in this example contain the same number of threads, the rows and columns alternate face and back in a ratio of 1:1. For different ratios, distribute face and back threads as evenly as possible.
5. Place F on each square where an L row crosses an *unlabeled* column. This marks where face warp threads are raised automatically in order to be above the back layer as it is being woven.
6. Following the drawdown in *1*, mark the position of the raised warp for the face layer with F in the corresponding squares of the unlabeled rows and columns in *1*. For example, in *1*, the first vertical column on the left is marked with an F in the first and second squares. In *6*, the corresponding squares are the first and second blank squares in the second vertical column from the left.
7. Following the drawdown in *2*, mark the position of raised warp threads in the lower layer with B in the corresponding squares of the rows and columns that are labeled L. The *first* vertical column on the left in *7* shows a B in the first two L rows.
8. Mark possible stitching points with S. To meet conditions A and B for hidden stitching, these points should occur in the columns marked L where the square above and the square below is marked B and where the adjacent face warp threads are marked F (to float above to hide the stitching). In other words, the ideal squares for invisible stitching points are those surrounded by squares marked B and F. In the drawdown in *8*, all marked squares indicate warp threads raised;

9. Threading

8. Drawdown
Stitching points are added.

10. Tie-up and treadling

13. Threading

12. Drawdown
Cancelled F's are removed.

14. Tie-up and treadling

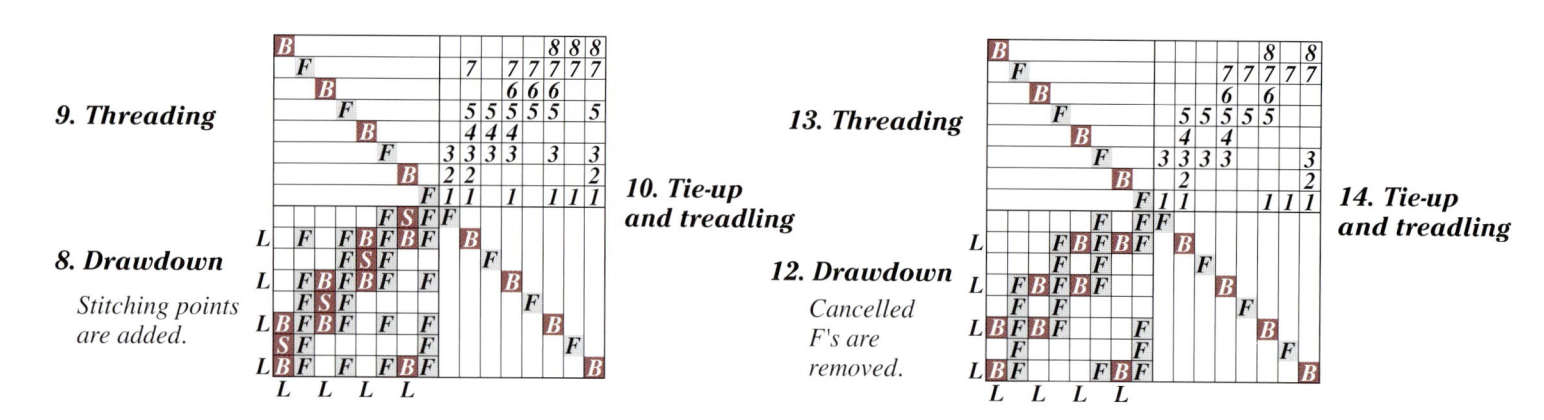

empty squares indicate weft floats. (When the above conditions cannot be met, it is sometimes possible to achieve them by realigning the two layers, that is, by shifting one of the weaves to start on a different warp thread. If it is still not possible, it might be necessary to compromise and allow the stitching to show slightly on the surface or to select one of the other stitching methods.)

9. Determine the threading by placing appropriate symbols (F or B) in the threading grid above the drawdown. For example, starting at the right, place an F above the first thread on the first row (shaft 1). Place a B on the second row (shaft 2) for the second thread. Continue for each column. If any column is identical with a previously examined column, place its symbol on the same threading row as its twin.

10. Determine the tie-up and treadling by examining one row at a time in the drawdown and finding the number of the shaft on which each marked (raised) warp end is threaded. Write the shaft numbers for each different row in a column in the tie-up. Place the symbol corresponding to the layer being woven in each row below its treadle (F for unlabeled drawdown rows and B for drawdown rows labeled L). For example: the top row of the drawdown shows raised warp threads on shafts 1, 2, and 3. These numbers are written in their respective squares in the first vertical tie-up column at the left. The letter F appears directly under this column on the same level as the top drawdown row to indicate a face weft in that shed.

The completed draft can now be used as a guide for weaving stitched double cloth in your choice of yarn colors and sizes, setts, and weave structures. Use stitched double cloth for coat or jacket fabrics, blankets, upholstery, table runners, mats, and more. You'll think of many possibilities as you experiment with this exciting version of double weave!

11. Drawdown
X indicates face not raised for back weft.

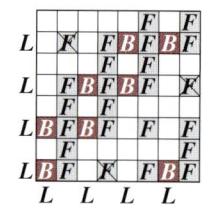

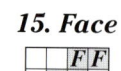

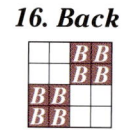

15. Face

16. Back

17. Drawdown
Rising stitchers = S
Sinking stitchers = X

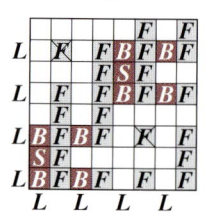

Method II: Stitching by sinking face warp under back weft

This example uses the same two weaves as for Method I. Steps *1-7* are the same as for Method I.

11. Now mark the possible sinking stitching points by crossing out selected F squares on L rows. Choose isolated F squares, that is, F squares surrounded on all sides by empty squares. In these places adjacent back warp threads that are not raised float on the underside to conceal the stitch. The X printed over each F cancels its lift for the back weft.

12. Rewrite the drawdown excluding the squares marked X.

13–14. Determine threading, tie-up, and treadling for the drawdown in *12* by following the same process as for Steps *9* and *10* of Method I.

Method III: Stitching by combining Methods I and II

The same 2/2 straight twills can be used with both Methods I and II (rising *and* sinking stitchers) for a very firm bonding of the two layers. The resulting drawdown will look like *12* but with the rising stitchers (S) added from *8*. In this case all of the warp ends from both layers are used as stitchers.

Designing stitchers for other structures

15–17. Many other structures can be used for stitched double cloth (as well as other ratios than 1:1 between the warp and weft of one layer and the warp and weft of the other). In *15–17*, 2/2 twill is used for one layer (face) and basket weave for the other (back). This combination illustrates a situation in which ideal conditions for inconspicuous stitching occur for only half the warp ends of the back layer by Method I and half the warp ends of the face layer by Method II. By incorporating both methods a better distribution of stitching points occurs within the repeat than by either method alone. Follow Steps *1–7* as before (using basket weave instead of 2/2 twill for the back layer). Follow Step *8* to mark possible rising stitching points S. Then cross out F squares as in *11*. See if you can derive the threading, tie-up, and treadling (not illustrated here).

BIBLIOGRAPHY

Authors' Collective. *Grundlagen der Gewebetechnik*, 2nd edition. Leipzig: VEB Fachbuchverlag, 1968.

Grosicki, Z. J. *Watson's Advanced Textile Design*, 4th edition. London: Newnes-Butterworths, 1977.

double-weave blocks and color

double-weave jacket in interlocking crosses	36
color windows	39
windows coat	40
reversible panel vest with color windows	42
mixed color effects in double weave	44
summer sherbet runner	46
color in loom-controlled double weave	48
patchwork jacket in double-woven twill	54

double-weave jacket in interlocking crosses

Gretchen Romey-Tanzer

Use color effects in three blocks of double weave on twelve shafts to create a subtle design of interlocking crosses. In the fabric for this jacket, the warp colors are sections of neutral gray and black. The colors in the interlocking crosses are created primarily by the weft; the black and gray warp acts only to soften and unify the weft colors.

The interlocking cross design is achieved by a four-color rotation in the weft. Two colors are used for three sets of 20 picks each to form a row of crosses. In the next three sets (of 20 picks each), the first color is dropped. The second color moves into the position of the first color (let's call this position 1) and a new color (3) replaces the second color (in position 2). In this set, the row of crosses is formed by the original second color. In the third three sets of 20 picks each, color 3 moves into position 1, color 2 is dropped, and color 4 is introduced in position 2 (the crosses are now woven in color 3). This is all harder to say than to do! Examine the weft color rotations WXYZ on page 38.

This process can then be repeated with color 4 as the new color 1. The remaining colors can be the same as before, or one, two, or three new colors can be introduced.

Have fun selecting warp and weft colors for your jacket fabric! Sample first to find a pleasing repeating four-color weft sequence or choose a blend of colors from one area of the jacket to the other. Just remember to keep careful track of all color orders so you can repeat them for matching pattern pieces (like the front and back pieces for this jacket).

The double-woven layers of 10/2 cotton in this fabric provide sufficient weight for a jacket that is soft enough to tailor and drape.

- Equipment. 12-shaft loom, 32" weaving width; 20-dent reed or 10-dent reed; 2 boat shuttles.
- Materials. Warp: 10/2 pearl cotton (4200 yds/lb, Halcyon, The Mannings), black and medium gray, (½ lb black, 1 lb gray). Weft: a variety of 10/2 pearl cotton colors. I used about 15 different colors, but you can use fewer, as long as you have at least 1 lb total (the black and gray warp will help blend and soften even very different hues).
- Wind a warp 4 yds long of 260 ends gray, 60 ends black, 220 ends gray, 180 ends black, 220 ends gray, 60 ends black, and 260 ends gray, for a total of 1260 ends (for the pattern layout for this jacket).
- Beam the warp using a raddle with ½" spaces, centered for a width of 31½". Place the lease sticks behind the heddles for threading.
- Thread according to the draft in *1*, p. 38, making sure that after each 20 threads (½") there is a block change. (The three blocks are threaded in a point, A, B, C, B, A.)
- Sley 2/dent in a 20-dent reed or 4/dent in a 10-dent reed, 40 epi (20 epi per layer), centered for 31½" weaving width.
- Tie up the treadles following *1*, p. 38.
- Weave a 2" heading with scrap yarn using treadles 1–12 in a continuous sequence. Begin weaving the jacket fabric using two shuttles, each in a different color (W and X). For example, start with gray (W) and maroon (X). Depress treadle 1, throw the gray shuttle (W); treadle 2, maroon (X); treadle 3, gray (W); treadle 4, maroon (X); and so on for 20 picks. Treadle 5–8 for 20 picks and 9–12 for 20 picks using the two colors in the same way.
- Now, form the interlocking crosses design by dropping out the gray. Use maroon as the first color and add a new color (Y) as the second color,

This double-weave fabric in 10/2 cotton is an ideal weight for a jacket. Plan warp stripes in black and gray to fit a jacket or kimono pattern, and then play with weft colors in this 12-shaft design of interlocking crosses.

say cream. Continue as before, weaving the same three block sequences (20 picks per block). In each new set of three blocks (60 total picks), the color that was color 1 is dropped, color 2 moves to position 1, and a new color is added in position 2. Note that you can weave a fabric with only two weft colors throughout and still create the cross pattern simply by switching the first and second positions of the shuttles after each set of three blocks is completed.

- Weave the jacket body. Keep track of the sequence of colors used in one 29" body section. Repeat this sequence in reverse order to mirror the colors of the first section for the second 29" body section. (When the cloth is finished the body sections are folded over and a triangular piece is cut out for the front and neck.)
- Weave the jacket sleeves in a 28" section with colors that match the center of the two 29" body sections. (When the cloth is finished, the sleeve section is cut down the middle, folded over, and sewn to the body sections to create 14" x 15½" square sleeves.)
- Weave a 36" section for the neckband, alternating only two weft colors. (When the cloth is finished, extra fabric in this section can be used for pockets or other accents.)
- Finish the fabric by hand washing in cool water; dry and iron flat. (The measurements given below are approximate since shrinkage may vary.)
- Prepare jacket pieces. Before cutting, secure all cut lines by machine zigzagging. Begin by stitching and cutting the 56" body section from the fabric; stitch and cut the two 28" x 14" sleeve sections; stitch and cut the two 6" wide neckbands out of the 36" section (use the black band from the middle of the fabric); stitch and cut the neck opening.
- Assemble and sew the garment: With right sides together, sew a seam joining the neckbands at one end with a ½" seam allowance. Fold the piece lengthwise, and sew a seam at both ends with a ½" seam allowance. Sew neckband to garment starting at center back, sewing across shoulder, turning, and sewing down the front with a ½" seam allowance. Repeat on the other side. Slit fabric to seam at the sharp neckline angles. Finish by handstitching inside.

Four weft colors rotate to produce the interlocking crosses design. They can be changed after each 60 picks or the same four colors used throughout.

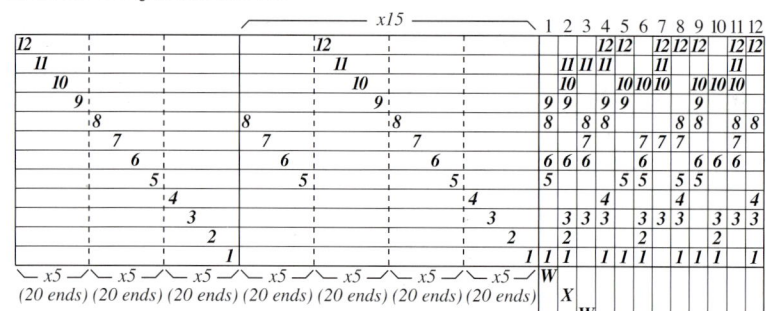

W, X, Y, Z represent any four colors used in the color rotation.

1. Draft for jacket fabric

2. Assembled jacket pieces

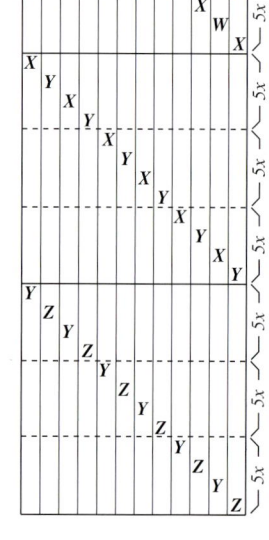

3. Layout for pattern

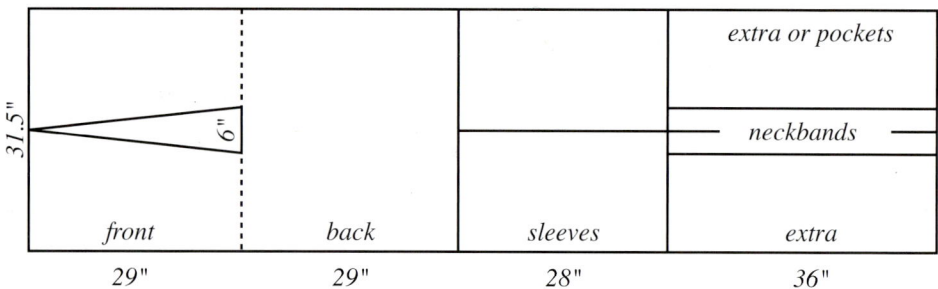

- With right sides together, sew the sleeves on the body, centering the sleeves on the shoulder fold. Sew the bottom seam of sleeves.
- Sew up the side seams of the garment with a ½" seam allowance. Leave a small gap in the underarm to reduce bunching of the fabric. Press all seams. Hem the sleeves and bottom of the garment by hand. Add pockets if desired.
- Many variations of this fabric design are possible. Use any number of weft colors, use non-neutral hues for the warp, or consider other fabric uses, such as placemats or table runners. ✂

color windows

Judie Yamamoto

face   *back*

This started out to be an ordinary sort of color gamp: double-weave window frames of black pearl cotton with windows in Tubular Spectrum colors from the Lunatic Fringe. Ten of the twenty available colors are used for the warp; the weft includes all twenty. The black warp is 10/2 pearl cotton as well, but the black weft is rayon chenille. The chenille creates interesting effects, adding more depth to the colors and shapes. But the best surprise is on the back, where intensely black boxes seem to float on a rainbow ground.

- ❏ **Equipment.** 8-shaft loom, 12" weaving width; 12-dent reed; 2 shuttles.
- ❏ **Materials.** Warp and weft for the colored windows: 10/2 pearl cotton (4200 yds/lb) in 20 color-wheel hues from The Tubular Spectrum color kit by the Lunatic Fringe (kit comes with 1½ oz each color, enough for a 7–8 yd warp). Warp for the black frame: 10/2 black pearl cotton, 2–3 oz for 2 yd warp; add to amounts for longer warp or wider pieces. Weft for the black frame: rayon chenille (1300 yds/lb, Webs), black, 4–5 oz for 2-yd warp.
- ❏ Wind a warp holding 1 end color and 1 end black together using any 10 of the colors in the following order: color #1 35 ends; colors #2–#9 26 ends each; color #10 35 ends; total ends color = 278, total ends black = 278.
- ❏ Sley 4/dent in a 12-dent reed, 48 epi; center for 11½".
- ❏ Thread black 10/2 cotton on odd shafts and colored 10/2 cotton on even shafts following the draft in *1*: Block A 6x, [B 10x, A 3x] 9x; B 10x; A 6x.
- ❏ Weave all-black frame using treadles 1–4 alternating black chenille with selected color weft. Weave the sections of windows (to square) also alternating black chenille with selected color weft using treadles 5–8.
- ❏ Finish by removing fabric from loom; secure ends. Wash by hand in lukewarm water; lay flat to dry. ✄

1. Draft for color windows

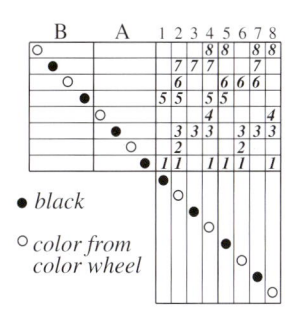

- ● black
- ○ color from color wheel

DOUBLE WEAVE   39

windows coat

Bonnie Luckey

Looking back over the experience of creating the design, dyeing the fibers, and weaving the fabric for the 'Windows' coat, I realize that although I felt prepared when I began, I learned much more as I wove. This is just the beginning of my study of double-woven windows!

- Equipment. 16-shaft loom for a double-weave fabric in two layers of 2/2 twill; 8-shaft loom for two plain-weave layers, 27" weaving width; 10- or 15-dent reed for 16-shaft draft, 12-dent reed for 8-shaft draft; 2 shuttles.
- Materials. 12/2 pearl cotton (5000 yds/lb, Earth Guild), natural, 3½ lbs for petite size coat; Sabracron F dyes from PRO Chemical & Dye; see Dye Formulas chart; supplies required by dye manufacturer; tunic coat pattern; 6 buttons; sewing notions. If you choose not to dye fibers for your coat, you can substitute 10/2 pearl cotton in commercial colors of your choice.
- Wind two separate warps 7 yds long of 768 ends each for the 16-shaft draft, 624 ends each for the 8-shaft draft. One chain will be dyed in the window colors and the other in the frame colors; add more ends for a larger coat.
- Prepare dyes following dye manufacturer's instructions and step-by-step directions given by Linda Knutsen (see the Bibliography).
- Space-dye the warp following steps outlined by Betsy Blumenthal and Kathryn Kreider (see the Bibliography). To achieve the same color gradation from shoulder to hem throughout the garment, paint the warp sections for back, front, and both sleeves identically. (The darkest hue in the windows warp is also used for the shoulder area of the frame warp.) Determine length and sequence of desired hues. Dye skeins of weft yarns in each hue to coordinate with warp color gradations. Calculate take-up at about 10%, shrinkage 3–5%.

   Place a line of masking tape on the tarp covering the surface of the painting table. With permanent marker, mark length of pieces (back, front, sleeves) and then mark color sections within the pieces.

   Place dampened windows warp in a container on the floor at the end of the table. Place a roll of plastic wrap behind the container (next to the table). Starting at the 'cross' end of the warp, pull up together the plastic wrap and amount of warp (after loom waste) required for one piece and spread beside the masking-tape ruler. Pour pre-mixed dye formulas onto the warp in all marked areas. Seal plastic wrap around the dyed length; pull up next length. Paint the frame warp in the same way—the frame warp for this fabric is painted (blue) only in the shoulders area; the rest is natural.
- Sley the frame warp 3/dent in a 10-dent reed or 2/dent in a 15-dent reed for the 16-shaft draft; 2/dent in a 12-dent reed for the 8-shaft draft; center for 25¾" for the 16-shaft draft, 26" for the 8-shaft draft. Place a line of masking tape across the reed above the sleyed warp. Sley the window warp same as the frame warp above the tape; 30 epi/layer 16-shaft draft; 24 epi/layer 8-shaft draft.
- Thread following the 16-shaft draft (for two layers of twill) in *1*: A 8x, *B 3x, A 4x, B 5x, A 4x, B 7x, A 4x, B 9x, A 4x, B 7x, A 4x, B 5x, A 4x* A 4x; repeat between * 3x. Thread following the 8-shaft draft (for two layers of plain weave) in *2*: A 12x, *B 4x, A 6x, B 8x, A 6x, B 12x, A 6x, B 18x, A 6x, B 12x, A 6x, B 8x, A 6x* A 6x; repeat between * 3x.
- Weave all-frame sections using treadles 1–8 for 16-shaft draft at 30 ppi, 1–4 for 8-shaft draft at 24 ppi.
- Weave windows sections with treadles 9–16 for 16-shaft draft, 5–8 for 8-shaft draft. Adjust window and frame sizes and weft colors as desired to coordinate with warp colors. In this coat, eight picks of frame separate each window.

1. 16-shaft draft for Windows coat fabric

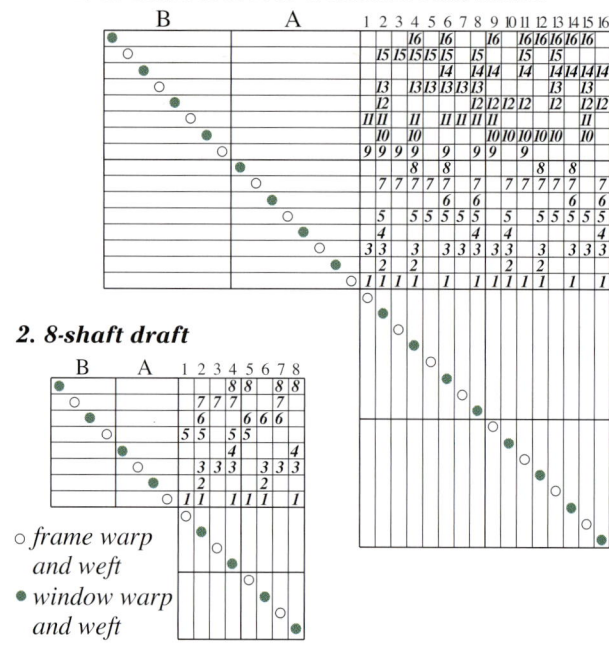

2. 8-shaft draft

○ frame warp and weft
● window warp and weft

Dye formulas for warp

	Gold	Fuchsia	Navy	Depth of Shade
Dark Navy	10%	10%	80%	2%
	Yellow	Scarlet	Blue	
Purple	10%	30%	60%	1%
Rose	30%	50%	20%	1%
Gold	80%	15%	5%	1%
Tan	70%	20%	10%	1%

Dye formulas for weft

	Gold	Fuchsia	Navy	
Dark Navy	10%	10%	80%	2%
Blue-Green	30%	—	70%	.5%
	Yellow	Scarlet	Blue	
Rose	30%	50%	20%	1%
Green	80%	10%	10%	1%
Tan	70%	20%	10%	1%

Window sizes follow a Fibonacci progression times eight picks: 1(8 picks), 2(16), 3(24), 5(40), 3(24), 2(16), 1(8), etc. If warp tends to stick, attach mirrors at sides of loom to check the sheds.

- Finish by removing from loom; secure ends. Wash fabric in cool water; lay flat to dry; steam press. Cut and assemble following pattern directions.

BIBLIOGRAPHY

Blumenthal, Betsy and Kathryn Kreider. *Hands On Dyeing*. Loveland, Colorado: Interweave Press, 1988, pp. 63–65.

Knutsen, Linda. *Synthetic Dyes for Natural Fibers*. Loveland, Colorado: Interweave Press, 1986, p. 120.

In this double-weave coat fabric, twill windows in gently gradated colors contrast with a neutral twill frame. Use warp and weft painting in your favorite colors for coat fabric on eight or sixteen shafts.

reversible panel vest with color windows

Priscilla Lynch

In this vest, windows of warm hues ranging from orange to violet are framed by a layer of solid brown. The warp for the brown layer is threaded on shafts 1 and 3 in Block A and 5 and 7 in Block B. The windows warp (on shafts 2 and 4 in A; 6 and 8 in B) changes from block to block to form rectangles of varying hues.

- Equipment. 8-shaft loom, 12 treadles, 28" weaving width; 12-dent reed; 2 shuttles.
- Materials. Warp and weft: 10/2 pearl cotton (4200 yds/lb, Halcyon), brown (B) (#114) 19 oz, fuchsia (F) (#123) 10 oz, mauve (M) (#124) 3½ oz, orange (O) (#118) 3 oz, violet (V) (#128) 2 oz, gold (G) (#115) 1½ oz; 6¼" of 45"-wide Ultrasuede for trim.
- Wind a warp in three chains each 4 yds long: one chain of 672 ends B, one chain of 336 ends F, and one chain of 36 M, 12 O, 24 V, 12 O, 24 M, 12 O, 24 G, 12 O, 24 V, 12 O, 24 G, 12 O, 24 M, 12 O, 24 V, 12 O, 36 M.
- Sley the brown warp chain 2/dent across warp width, centered for 28". Sley fuchsia warp chain: 2 ends every other dent for 36 ends; [1/dent 12x, 2 ends every other dent for 24 ends] 7x; 1/dent 12x; 2 ends every other for 36 ends. Sley stripe warp chain 2 ends in every other dent alternating with fuchsia except sley orange 1/dent in the same dents as the single-dented fuchsia. Each dent contains 4 ends, 48 epi (2 B ends plus 2 F, M, V, G, or F/O ends).
- Thread following the profile threading in *2* substituting one unit of Block A (1-2-3-4) for every black square on the A row and one unit of Block B (5-6-7-8) for every black square on the B row (brown on shafts 1, 3, 5, 7; other colors on 2, 4, 6, 8).
- Weave following *1*, choosing weft color order 1, 2, or 3 as directed in *2*.
- Finish by removing from loom; secure ends and correct errors.
- Handwash in cool water with mild soap. Since red-hued pearl cottons are notorious for bleeding, add a little vinegar to the water to set colors. Hang to dry. Shrinkage is less than 1%.
- Prepare garment by cutting center front opening, necklines, and armholes as shown in *2*. Machine zigzag or serge all cut edges. Sew shoulder edges together leaving a ¾" seam allowance. Trim off half of back seam allowance and press front seam allowance to the back. Tuck under ¼" of front seam allowance and handsew to create a flat-fell seam. Do the same on the side seams. (Extra width is added to this edge to allow for draw-in during weaving and fitting so that this seam is kept very straight. The seam should look like part of the vertical stripe pattern.)

Trim front neck and armhole edges by cutting five crosswise strips of Ultrasuede each 1" wide (a rotary cutter and ruler work best). Piece the strips together end to end and stitch with ¼" seams. Fold the long strip in half and baste; then sew to encase the cut edges. Holding small, sharp scissors flat and close to the edge, trim the Ultrasuede after sewing if necessary. Ultrasuede stretches on the crosswise grain and therefore acts as a bias trim. Though expensive, it comes in beautiful colors and wears well. Bias tape made from cotton fabric can be substituted. ✂

1. Draft for vest

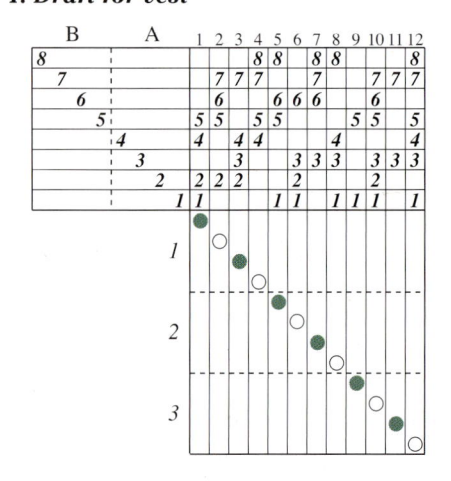

2. Profile threading and pattern layout

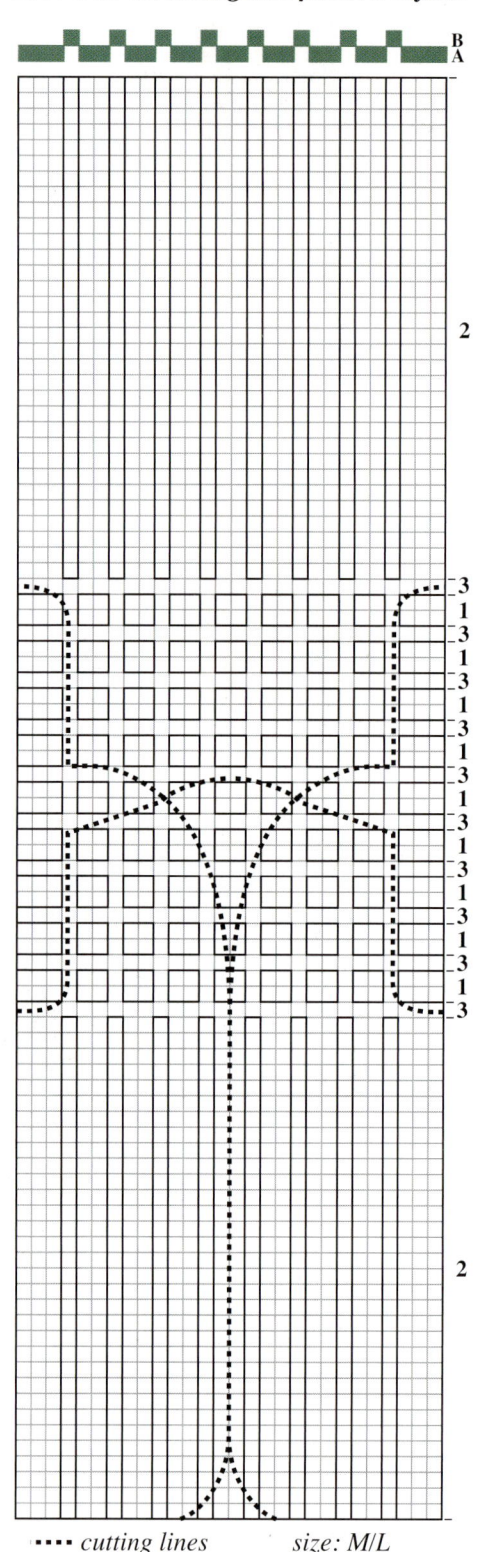

Weft color order:

1. ●B
    ○F
    ●B
    ○F
    ●B
    ○X
    (M 1st x,
    G 2nd x,
    V 3rd x)

2. ●B
    ○F
    ●B
    ○F

3. ●B
    ○F
    ●B
    ○F
    ●B
    ○X
    (M 1st x, G 2nd x,
    V 3rd x)

Warp color order:
Shafts 1, 3, 5, 7 all B
Shafts 2, 4, 6, 8:
2F 2M 18x (= 72 ends)
1F 1O 12x
2F 2V 12x
1F 1O 12x
2F 2M 12x
1F 1O 12x
2F 1O 2G 12x
1F 1O 12x
2F 2V 12x (center; repeat in reverse order)

---- cutting lines
1 square = 1"
size: M/L
1" = 48 picks

Color-and-weave effects add depth and interest to one of the layers in the long panel vest. Since the colors are very close in value, their effects from a distance give an impression of many slightly different colors.

mixed color effects in double weave

Doramay Keasbey

Color interplay between two layers of cloth is a double delight! Intriguing mixtures of warp and weft colors can be made to appear and disappear mysteriously. Discover just a few of the ways that only two colors can be used to form visual patterns in two layers!

Color changes in double weave can occur by varying: the number of colors in the warp and/or weft, the order of colors in the warp and/or weft, the threading order of the shafts, and/or the treadling order of the shafts. To provide a systematic approach and to keep the tempting variety of options within reasonable bounds, for this experiment all of these variables are kept constant except one: the treadling order. Two colors (XYXY) alternate throughout in both warp and weft, and the threading is in straight order on four shafts. This article explores what happens to two colors in two layers of plain weave when only the treadling varies (see also Paul O'Connor, 'Color in Loom-controlled Double Weave,' pp. 48–53).

TREADLING VARIATIONS

Since two shafts are needed for plain weave in a single layer, four shafts are required for plain weave in two layers. The great variety of color effects comes from which two shafts (i.e., which colors) are selected for each layer and which shaft (i.e., which color) rises for which weft color. Can the treadling vary without modifying the weave structure? Although a break may occur between one variation and the next, plain weave is woven in each layer with each shed sequence in this exercise.

Color effects on four shafts

All of the possible color effects produced by varying the treadling orders on a 4-shaft straight threading with warp and weft color orders XYXY are shown in *1*. Odd-numbered warp ends and weft picks are white. Gray represents a single selected color for the even-numbered warp ends and weft picks.

Some of the color effects in *1* look the same on the front of the cloth even though they may be different on the back. The treadling orders from *1* that produce seven distinct color effects on the front are shown in *2a–g*. If the 4-shaft threading in *1* is repeated from selvedge to selvedge, treadling sequences *2a–g* produce a series of horizontal tubes, each with a different color effect.

1. Treadling orders for two layers of plain weave on four shafts

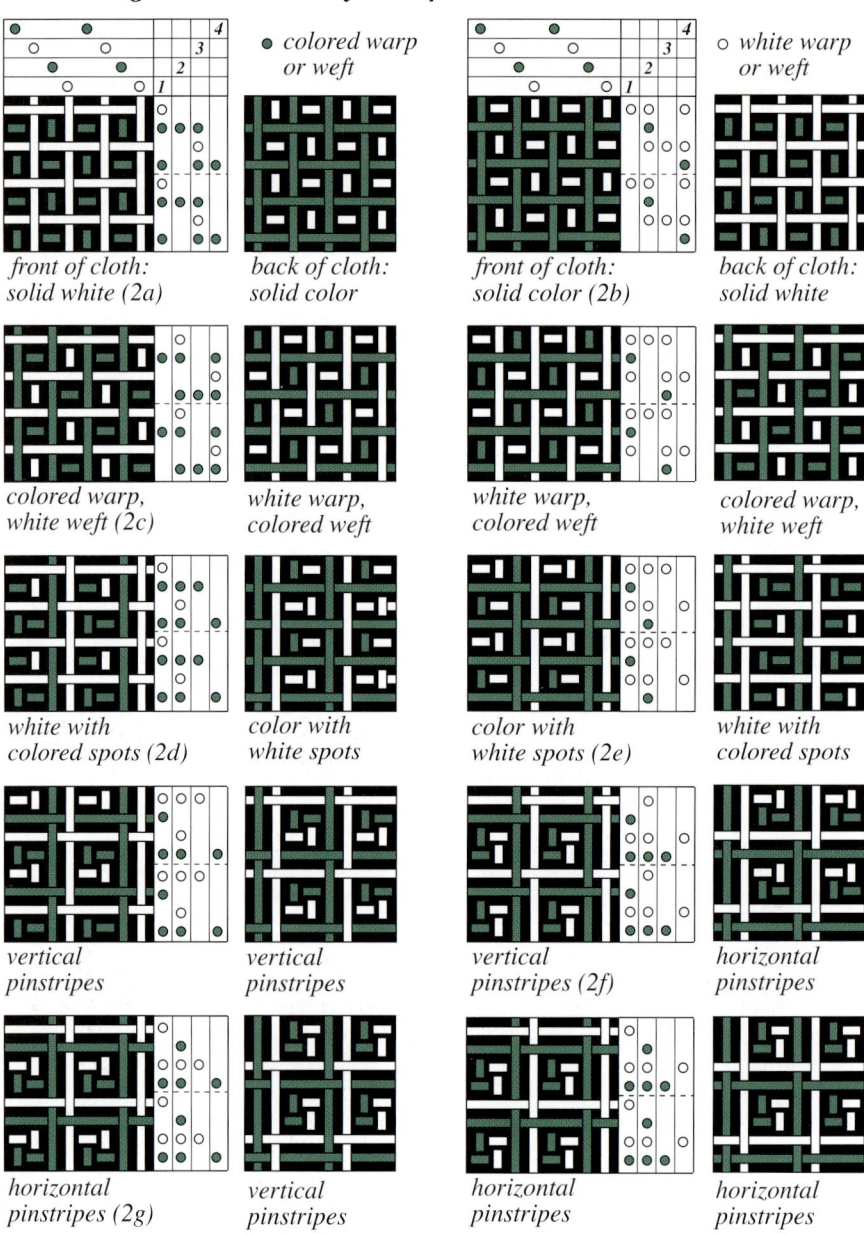

● colored warp or weft
○ white warp or weft

front of cloth: solid white (2a)
back of cloth: solid color
front of cloth: solid color (2b)
back of cloth: solid white

colored warp, white weft (2c)
white warp, colored weft
white warp, colored weft
colored warp, white weft

white with colored spots (2d)
color with white spots
color with white spots (2e)
white with colored spots

vertical pinstripes
vertical pinstripes
vertical pinstripes (2f)
horizontal pinstripes

horizontal pinstripes (2g)
vertical pinstripes
horizontal pinstripes
horizontal pinstripes

2. Selected treadling orders for distinct color effects on the front

a. solid white
b. solid color
c. colored warp, white weft
d. white with colored spots
e. color with white spots
f. vertical pinstripes
g. horizontal pinstripes

44

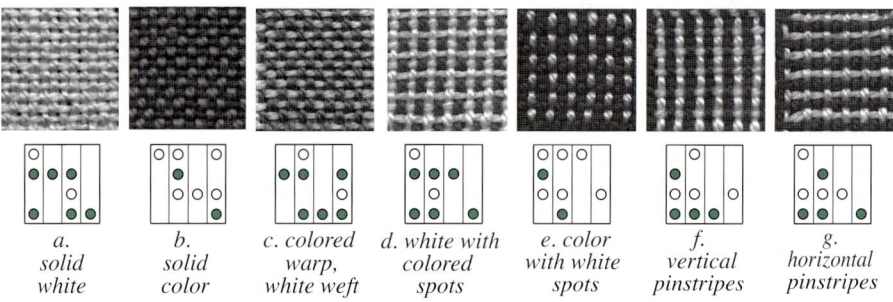

Combining color effects on eight or more shafts

Two or more different color effects can occur independently across the width of the warp if additional sets of four shafts are available. Eight shafts produce two independent blocks (Block A = 1–4, B = 5–8); 12 shafts produce three blocks (C = 9–12), and 16 shafts produce four blocks (D = 13–16). If two colors alternate XYXY in the threading and the weft color order is also XYXY, any of the seven color effects in *2* can be produced in any block independently of the others.

In order to produce a specific color effect in a block, substitute the appropriate 4-shed treadling sequence from *2* for the corresponding set of four shafts. For example, in the first four picks in the 8-shaft draft in *3a*, shed sequence *a* from *2* is used for shafts 1–4 to produce solid white on top in Block A. Shed sequence *f* is used for shafts 5–8 to produce vertical pinstripes in Block B. For the second four picks, shed sequence *g* produces horizontal pinstripes in A while *b* produces solid color on top in B. These shed sequences can be woven as shown in *3a* using a table or dobby loom: read across each horizontal treadling row to see which shafts to raise for each pick. On a treadle loom, the tie-up in *3b* can be used to make the same sheds.

THE DESIGN KEY

A design key (see *3a*) is useful for planning different arrangements of the color effects. Sample design keys for four, eight, and 16 shafts are shown in *4–6*. The letters in the design key squares indicate the corresponding shed sequence from *2*. In *6a–b*, four blocks are arranged in point order on 16 shafts and color effects planned to shade gradually from light at the corners and edges to full strength solid color at the center. The resulting drafts for all three design keys are shown in *7–9*.

The clearest color effects for solid color (*a*, *b*), mixed plain weave (*c*), and pinstripes (*f*, *g*) occur when the same pair of colors is used in both warp and weft. When warp and weft feature completely different colors, the result can become jarringly 'busy' unless carefully controlled. A solution is for one of the two colors to be the same in both warp and weft. An effective fabric design (as for this runner) is to thread each repeat using a different second color and to change the second color for each full treadling repeat in the same way.

In the 'Summer Sherbet' runner, p. 47, one of the colors is white in both warp and weft throughout.

3a. Two blocks

a, b, f, g = sheds from 2

3b. Full tie-up for *3a*

A: solid white
B: vertical pinstripes
A: horizontal pinstripes
B: solid color

4. Design key for four shafts
Shafts 1-4 are threaded XYXY.

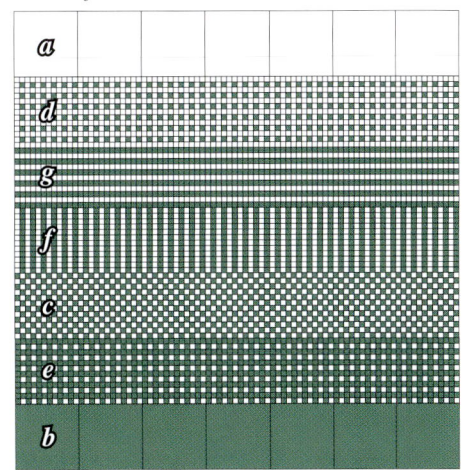

5. Design key for eight shafts

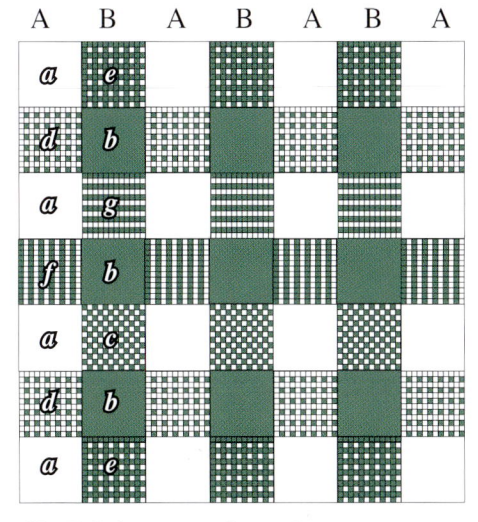

6a. Design key for sixteen shafts

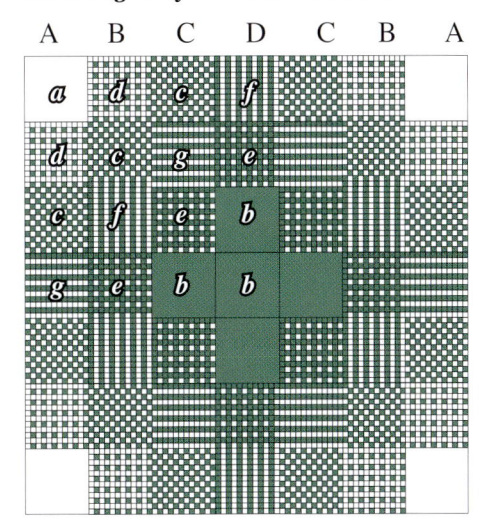

6b. Fabric woven from *6a*

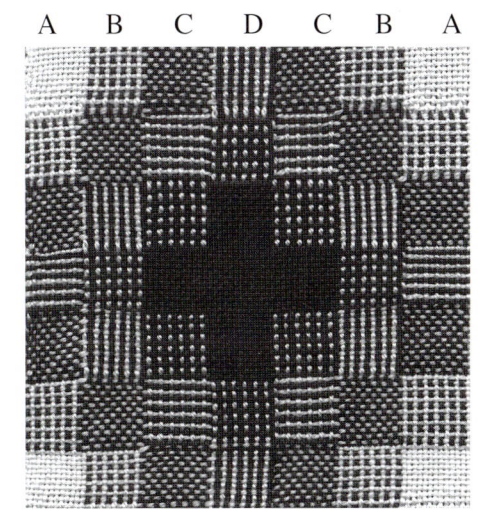

The second color is changed for each repeat of the full design in both threading and treadling.

You can weave a 'Summer Sherbet' runner on four shafts (the stripes of color effects weave as tubes), eight shafts, or 16 shafts (like the one on p. 47). The 8-shaft version of the runner requires a table loom or a dobby loom to form the many sheds required for all of the effects. Only two combinations of effects can be produced using a full tie-up that has only eight treadles. ✂

summer sherbet runner

Doramay Keasbey

Explore the mysterious interaction of colors in two layers of plain weave and at the same time make a decorative centerpiece for your table. The bright light of summertime—white in this runner—blends with colors evocative of fruit flavors to produce a perfect backdrop for servings of cool, pastel-colored sherbet. For an autumn table runner, replace the white threads by deep browns or rusts.

- Equipment. 4-shaft loom, 8-shaft (table or dobby) loom, or 16-shaft (table or dobby) loom; 12-dent reed; 2 shuttles.
- Materials. Warp and weft: 10/2 pearl cotton (4200 yds/lb): 2¼ oz white; ½ oz each of cherry red, lemon yellow, blueberry blue; about 40 yds each of dark blue, grape, orange, pineapple yellow, lime green, kelly green, blue-green.
- Wind a warp of 504 warp ends as follows: [1 white, 1 cherry] 84x; [1 white, 1 lemon] x84; [1 white, 1 blueberry] 84x (252 total white ends and 84 ends of each of three colors).
- Sley 4/dent in a 12-dent reed, 48 epi; center for 10½".
- Thread following the 4-shaft draft in *7* (21x); the 8-shaft draft in *8* (10x, balance with Block A 1x); or the 16-shaft draft in *9* (3x), alternating white and colored ends so white is on odd-numbered shafts and colors on even-numbered shafts.
- Weave following the treadling sequence in the selected draft, alternating one pick white and one pick of selected weft color for each full repeat in the following order: white with dark blue for first repeat; change blue to grape for next repeat; then use orange, pineapple yellow, lime green, kelly green, and blue-green for subsequent repeats.

To read the treadling sequences, for each weft raise all of the shafts marked with 'o' in the corresponding horizontal row. For example, following the 8-shaft draft, for the first pick (white), raise 1, 5, 6, 7. Shaded circles indicate picks with colored weft. Use two feet to make the required sheds with the 4-shaft draft. Beat firmly to produce a balanced plain weave in each layer. Begin and end the runner with hemstitching. Leave about 2" for fringe at each end.

You may notice that occasionally at the change to a new shed sequence the last pick of one sequence is the same as the first pick of the next. This is difficult to prevent without complicated modifications in portions of the lifting plan, depending on the sequence of color effects in individual blocks. The overall effect of the duplications is not objectionable and so can be ignored (also see 'Design tips' below). With the 4-shaft draft, duplicate picks can simply be eliminated.

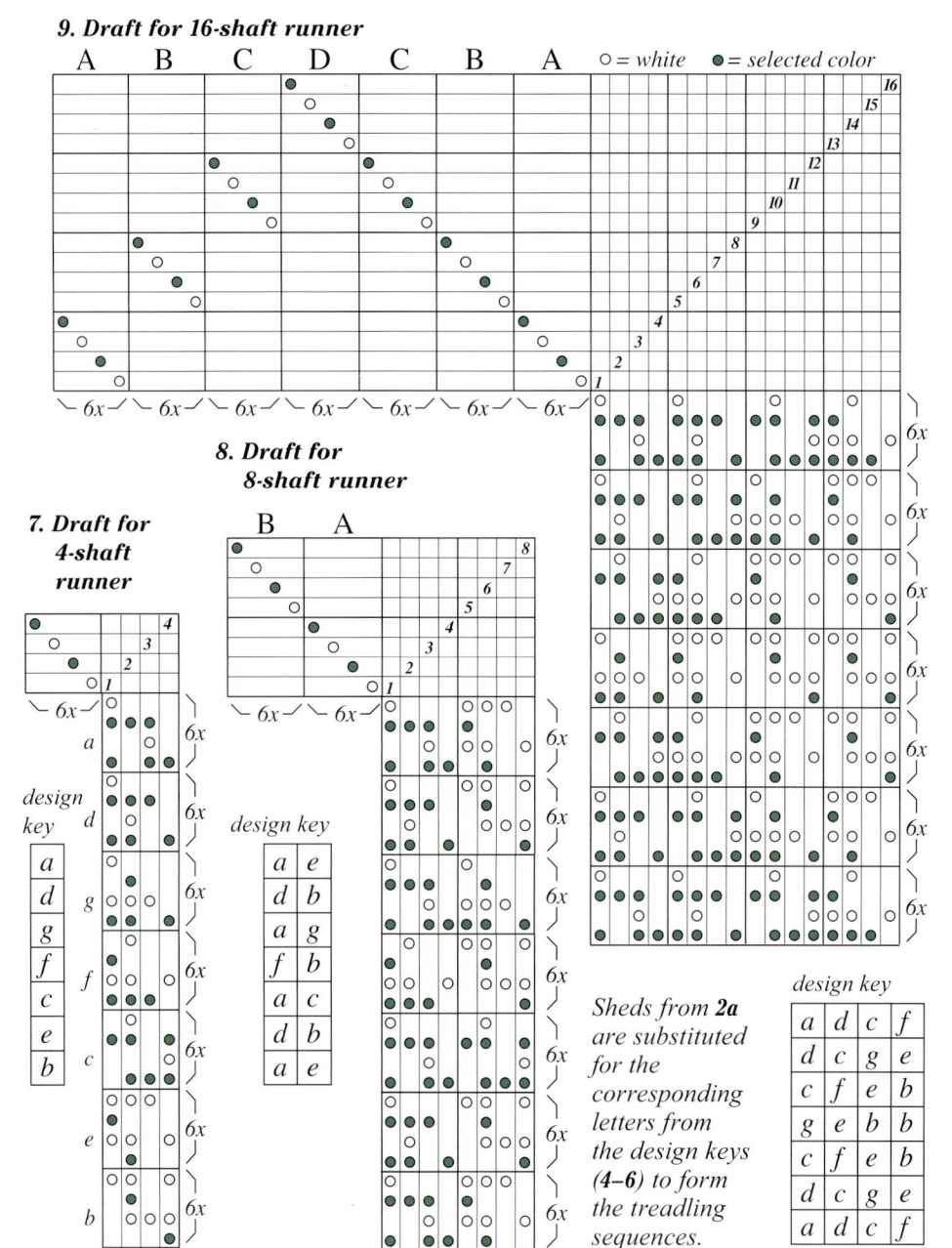

- Finish the fabric by washing gently in warm water; dry flat or hang over a bar; steam press lightly. Trim fringe evenly to about 1½".
- Design tips. For 8-shaft designs try varying the sizes of Blocks A and B in threading and treadling directions. For 16-shaft designs, use a computer graphics program to arrange design-key squares representing the color effects, or cut squares of paper and mark with design-key letters to represent the seven effects and experiment with their placement in the four blocks.

If you wish to try to avoid doubling identical sheds when changing sequences, just remember: a change that produces a smooth transition in one block may require further changes to accommodate the blocks that follow.

Strawberry, blueberry, lemon, or lime
Sherbets are favorites for summertime.
Delightfully cool with a delicate tint

Choose raspberry, pineapple, orange, or mint.
No matter which flavor or mixture you choose
Serve it with style on this mat of pure hues.

color in loom-controlled double weave

Paul O'Connor

1. 4-shaft threading in two colors, A and B

4			B	
3	A			
2			B	
1	A			

2. Six possible shaft combinations for each layer

top layer	12	13	14	23	24	34
bottom layer	34	24	23	14	13	12

3. Deriving tie-ups to weave warp pairs 12, 14, 13, 23 on top

a. Shafts 1, 2 weave on top (warp color pair AB)

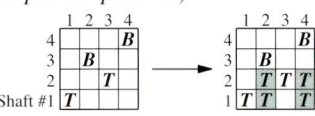

b. Shafts 1, 4 weave on top (warp color pair AB)

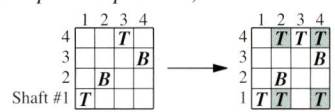

c. Shafts 1, 3 weave on top (warp color pair AA)

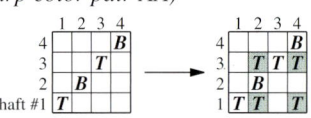

d. Shafts 2, 3 weave on top (warp color pair BA)

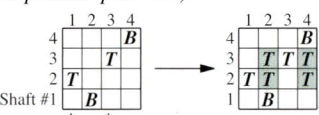

4. Skeleton tie-up

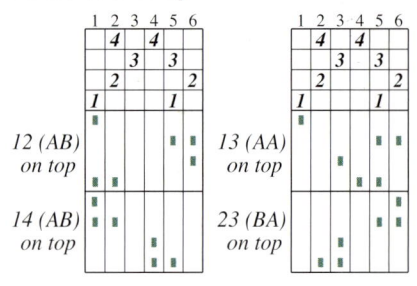

12 (AB) on top
13 (AA) on top
14 (AB) on top
23 (BA) on top

All types of weavers have long been fascinated with the color blending made possible when warp and weft colors change layers in double weave. It is not surprising that weavers who are colorists love double weave—they can mix colors like paints yet achieve strong contrasts. But weavers who are mathematicians and technicians also love double weave—they can play with the endless permutations and combinations that only increase geometrically with the addition of more shafts.

This article presents the basic theory for designing with four colors on four and eight shafts. Practice with a sampler following the instructions given here. Once you're hooked, you'll want to learn more ways to manipulate color with double weave (for more information; see the Bibliography, page 52).

But for now, let's start at the beginning. Did you know that you can choose among six warp pairs for the top layer when you are weaving double weave on four shafts? Varying warp and weft color orders and selecting different combinations of these shaft pairs can lead to some very exciting color possibilities in loom-controlled double weave.

4-SHAFT DOUBLE WEAVE: STRUCTURE

The first step is to review some of the basic principles of double weave using a straight-draw threading and alternating two colors, A and B. Any pair of shafts can be used for weaving the top layer while the complementary pair of shafts forms the bottom layer. Note the 4-shaft threading in *1*. The six possible pairs of shafts that can produce the top (and bottom) layers are shown in *2*.

Derive the tie-up

The principal challenge in designing and weaving double weave lies in the tie-up. The basic principle of double weave is that the top layer must be raised in order to weave the bottom layer. A tie-up for double weave can be formed in two stages, a preliminary tie-up and a final tie-up (see *3a–d*). The symbols 'T' and 'B' indicate raised shafts in the top and bottom layers. In the preliminary tie-up in *3a*, for example, shafts 1 and 2 are designated to form the top layer and shafts 3 and 4 the bottom layer. For treadles 2 and 4 in the final tie-up, shaded T's are added for shafts 1 and 2 to show that they must be raised (the top layer) when the bottom layer is woven. In this example, the treadles are used in succession (alternate picks are used for top and bottom layers; one shuttle is used for each layer).

After weaving the color pairs 12/34 for awhile, you may want to change to a different color pair, say 14/23. All you need is a new tie-up, and the tie-up for this pair is shown in *3b*.

Some changes from one color pair to another can produce weaving errors. Changing from 12/34 to 23/14, for example, causes shaft 2 to be raised at the end of the first section of weaving in the top layer and then again at the beginning of the next section of weaving in the top layer, placing two adjacent threads in the same shed in the top layer. There is a simple way to avoid that kind of error. Reverse the treadling order in the second tie-up so that the change is from 12/34 to 32/14 (reverse the treadles marked * in *3d*; i.e., begin weaving in the top layer by raising shaft 3 first, followed by shaft 2).

Use a skeleton tie-up

You may find yourself crawling under the loom every five minutes if you want to make many changes in the warp pair used for the top layer! Fortunately a skeleton tie-up is possible on four shafts that avoids that problem if you are willing to use two feet in treadling. The skeleton tie-up in *4* allows all the necessary combinations of shafts to be lifted for the warp pairs given in *2*.

The treadling sequences in *4* produce the same interlacements as the full tie-ups in *3a–d*. Note that two symbols (I) on the same horizontal row in a skeleton treadling sequence indicate that both treadles are depressed at the same time.

With that introduction behind us, now let's talk more about color.

4-SHAFT DOUBLE WEAVE: COLOR

The warp pairs in *2* can be represented in a slightly different manner by replacing shaft numbers with the colors A and B. Notice that there are three kinds of pairs: AA, AB, and BB. (BA does turn out to be different from AB, which we'll see later, when weft colors are discussed.) The weft colors can, of

Women of Rajasthan *Homage to Agam #II* *Theme and Variations*

With eight shafts, use one layer for a neutral background and the other for blending colors (as in the full-page fabric). Sixteen shafts provide more blocks and color combinations (see the fabrics in the insets).

5. Warp color combinations in 4-shaft, 2-color double weave

top layer	AB	AA	AB	BA	BB	AB
bottom layer	AB	BB	BA	AB	AA	AB

6. Suggested threading sequences for two colors on four shafts

$(ABAB)_x$
$(AAAA)_x (BBBB)_y (AAAA)_x$
$(ABAB)_x (BABA)_y$
$(ABAB)_x (AAAA)_y (ABAB)_x$

7. 4-shaft threading in four colors: A, B, C, D

```
    1 2 3 4
1       D
2     C
3   B
4 A
```

8. Warp color combinations in 4-shaft, 4-color double weave

top layer	AB	AC	AD	BC	BD	CD
bottom layer	CD	BD	BC	AD	AC	AB

9. Suggested threading sequences for four colors on four shafts

$(ABCD)_x$
$(A_1 A_2 A_3 A_4)_x$
$(AAAA)_x (BBBB)_x (CCCC)_x (DDDD)_x$
$(A_1 B_1 A_2 B_2)_x$
$(ABCD)_x (BCDA)_x (CDAB)_x (DABC)_x (ABCD)_x$

course, be anything you choose, but for now let's consider only colors A and B in the weft as well as in the warp. We'll also limit the weave structure to balanced plain weave, where warp and weft colors are of equal importance.

The 4-shaft sampler in **Photos a** and **b** shows both the top and bottom layers as they appear when the six possible warp pairs are combined with the possible combinations of two colors in the weft.

There are many interesting 2-color threading sequences that can be explored in 4-shaft double weave. Only a few possibilities are given in **6**. (The subscripts x and y indicate threading repeats of any desired width.) In the second threading sequence in **6**, for example, thread AAAA for the desired width, thread BBBB for a different width, and then repeat AAAA for the same width as previously.

4-SHAFT, 4-COLOR DOUBLE WEAVE

With more colors in the warp, more color combinations become available to the weaver. In **7**, a straight-draw threading is given with four colors in the warp and **8** gives the six possible combinations of warp pairs (compare **8** with **2** and **5**).

The four colors A, B, C, and D might be four value gradations of one hue; or four neighboring hues such as green, turquoise, blue, and purple; or light and dark values of two hues. **Photos c** and **d** show two different checkerboard patterns using different weft colors. **Photo e** illustrates the 'log cabin' color-and-weave effects also shown in **Photo a**. **Photo f** gives a more complex checkerboard design, where the warp threads rotate from one section to the next, where the weft colors change, and where the six different shaft pairs are used for the top layer. To experiment: select a warp threading scheme from **9** and weave a sampler varying weft color pairs.

For your sampler, choose 5/2 pearl cotton at a sett of 15 ends per inch per layer or 10/2 pearl cotton at a sett of 24 ends per inch per layer. Wind the warp so that the color orders change from section to section (plan sections about ½" wide, each in a different color order, such as ABAB, ABCD, BACD, CDAB, DABC, ABCB, etc.). Use a skeleton tie-up and experiment with changing the colors in the top and bottom layers—it's easier than it sounds!

COLOR IN 8-SHAFT DOUBLE WEAVE

With an 8-shaft loom, two blocks are available for double weave, presenting many more options for using color. Block A is threaded on shafts 1–4 and Block B on shafts 5–8. Six different combinations of warp pairs are possible in Block A, *and* six different combinations are possible in Block B. In the tie-up in **10a** and the warp cross section in **10b**, shafts 1 and 3 weave the top layer in Block A and 5 and 7 the top layer in Block B.

Note that for each block there are two choices for the behavior of the warp, to be in the top or in the bottom layer, and two choices for the behavior of the

10a. 8-shaft tie-up; warp pair 13 on top in A, 57 on top in B

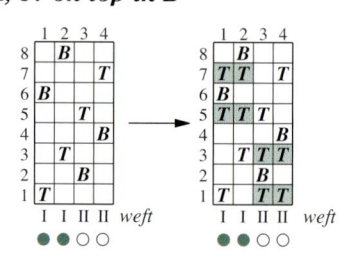

10b. Cross section of interlacement produced by tie-up in 10a

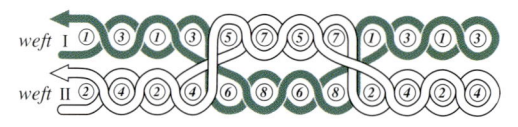

10c. Skeleton tie-up

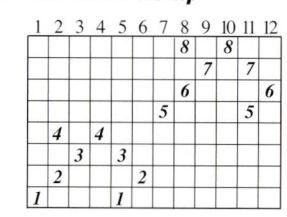

weft, again to be in the top or in the bottom layer. This means there are 2 × 2 choices for weaving Block A and 2 × 2 choices for weaving Block B, for a total of 16 different color arrangements.

Each choice requires four treadles (such as those in **10a**). An 8-shaft loom with 10 treadles requires changes in the tie-up to produce a wide variety of combinations of warp pairs. A skeleton tie-up with 12 treadles (see **10c**) can produce *all* of them but requires that *both* feet depress more than one treadle to produce some of the sheds.

TRY AN 8-SHAFT SAMPLER

In the 8-shaft threading in **11a**, four colors are used in the warp. Each color is threaded twice in each block; the combinations are varied (from left to right: AB, CD, BD, AC, DA).

❑ Thread a sampler varying the widths of the two blocks and changing the pairs of colors in any chosen order. Choose 5/2 pearl cotton at 15 epi per layer (30 epi overall, 2/dent in a 15-dent reed)

4-shaft sample book

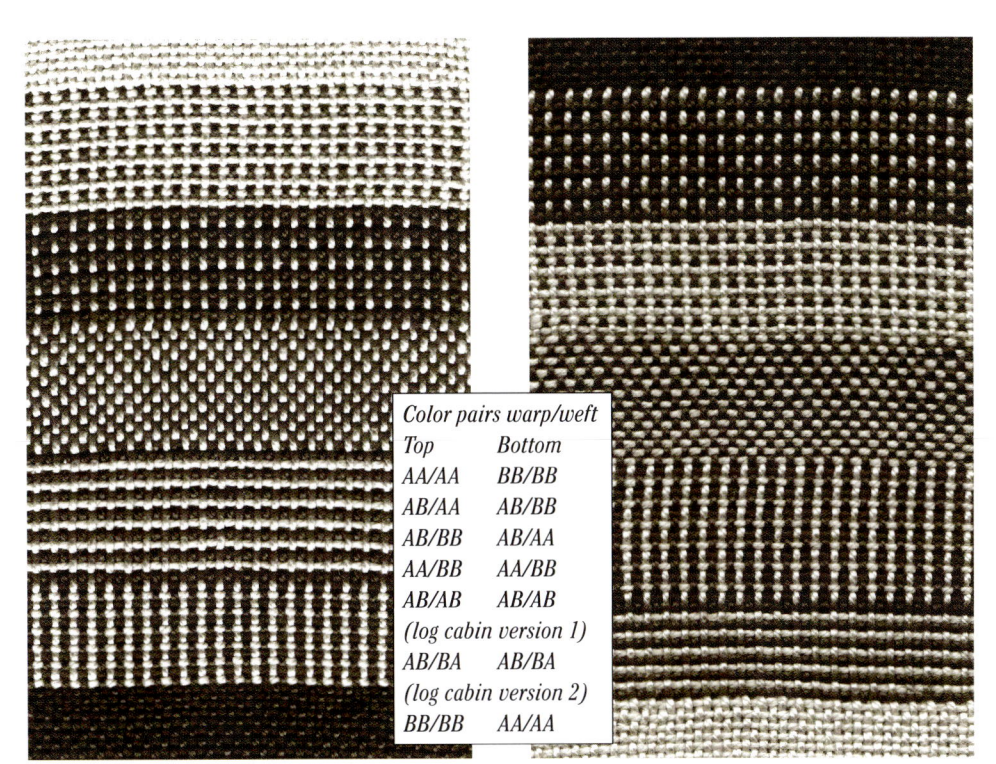

Color pairs warp/weft
Top	Bottom
AA/AA	BB/BB
AB/AA	AB/BB
AB/BB	AB/AA
AA/BB	AA/BB
AB/AB	AB/AB
(log cabin version 1)	
AB/BA	AB/BA
(log cabin version 2)	
BB/BB	AA/AA

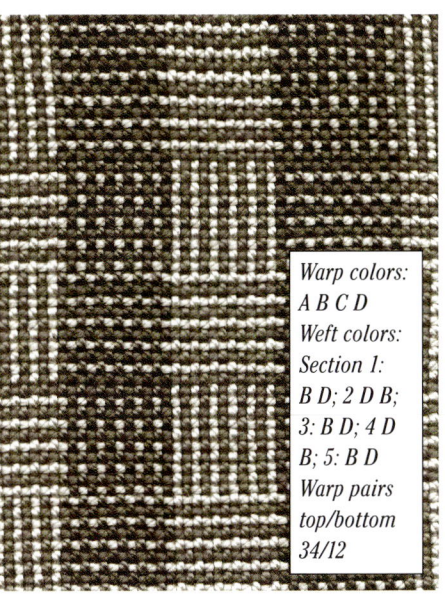

a. *4-shaft, 2-color double weave, top*

b. *4-shaft, 2-color double weave, bottom*

Warp colors:
A B C D
Weft colors:
Section 1:
B D; 2 D B;
3: B D; 4 D
B; 5: B D
Warp pairs
top/bottom
34/12

e. *4-shaft double weave, four warp colors, two weft colors*

Warp colors (in alternate sections): A B C D; B A D C. Weft color: C
Warp pairs top/bottom: 24/13; 13/24; 24/13

Warp colors same as c. Weft colors: section 1: A; section 2: B; section 3: A.
Warp pairs top/bottom: 13/24; 24/13; 13/24

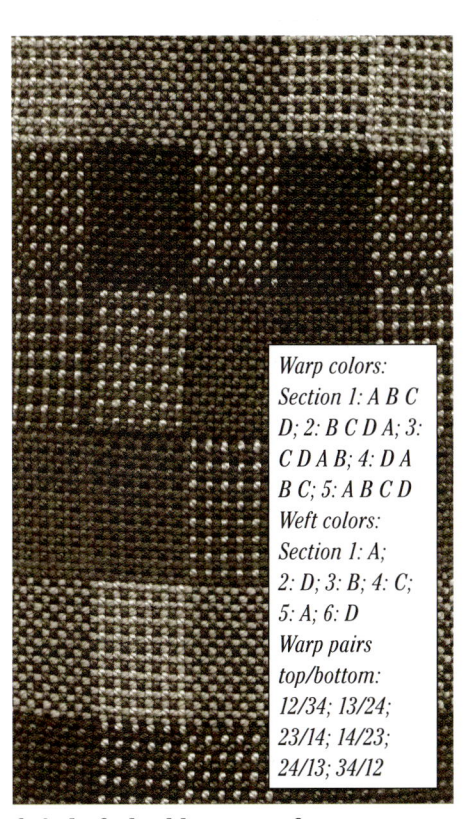

Warp colors:
Section 1: A B C
D; 2: B C D A; 3:
C D A B; 4: D A
B C; 5: A B C D
Weft colors:
Section 1: A;
2: D; 3: B; 4: C;
5: A; 6: D
Warp pairs
top/bottom:
12/34; 13/24;
23/14; 14/23;
24/13; 34/12

c. *4-shaft, 2-color double weave, log-cabin effect*

d. *4-shaft, 2-color double weave, different log-cabin effect*

f. *4-shaft double weave, four warp colors, four weft colors*

DOUBLE WEAVE

11a. 8-shaft, 4-color threading

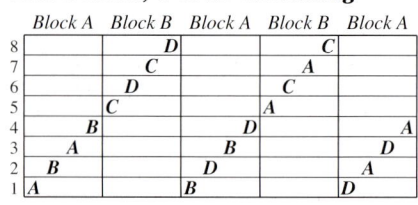

	Block A	Block B	Block A	Block B	Block A
8		D			C
7		C		A	
6		D		C	
5	C			A	
4	B		D		A
3	A		B		D
2	B		D		A
1	A		B		D

Derive the final tie-ups for an 8-shaft threading using the same method as for a 4-shaft threading. Write 'T' or 'B' for the chosen position of the warp pairs. Then add 'T's for the top-layer shafts wherever a 'B' shaft is lifted.

11b. Warp pairs 24 on top in A, 57 on top in B

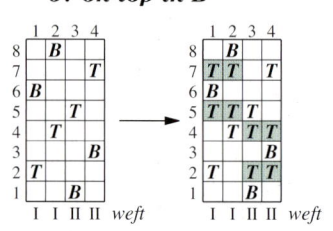

11c. Warp pairs 13 on top in A, 68 on top in B

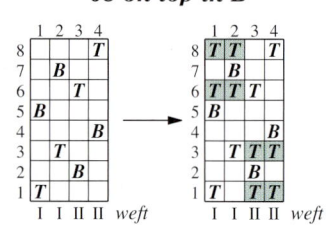

11d. Warp pairs 23 on top in A, 58 on top in B

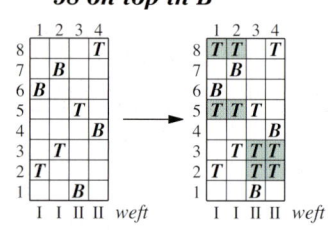

11e. Warp pairs 14 on top in A, 67 on top in B

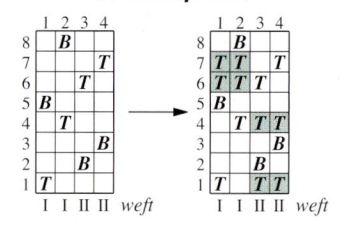

11f. Partial treadling sequence for weaving 11a 'as drawn in'

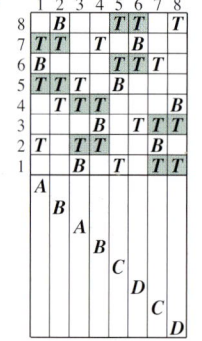

12a. 8-shaft 'Windows' threading

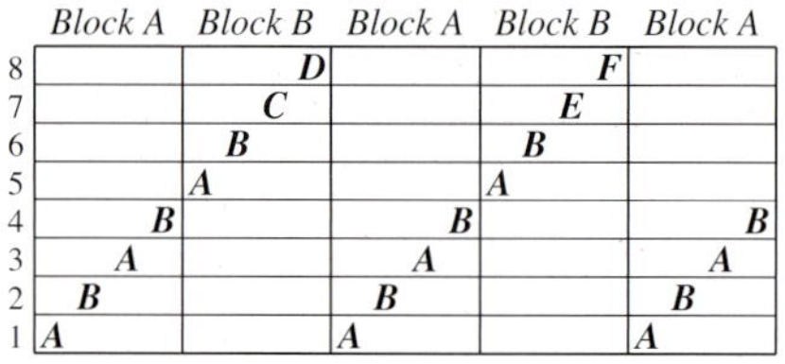

	Block A	Block B	Block A	Block B	Block A
8		D		F	
7		C		E	
6		B		B	
5	A		A		
4	B		B		B
3	A		A		A
2	B		B		B
1	A		A		A

12b. Warp pair 12 on top in A, 56 on top in B

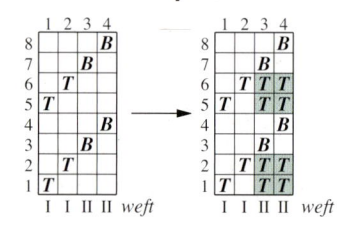

12c. Warp pair 12 on top in A, 78 on top in B

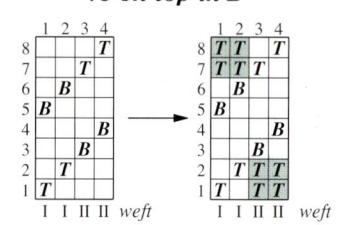

or 10/2 pearl cotton at 24 epi per layer (48 epi overall, 4/dent in a 12-dent reed).

- Derive an 8-treadle tie-up by selecting a pair of shafts for the top layer in each block for the first four treadles and then reversing their positions for the second four treadles as in **11b–c** and **11d–e**.
- Treadle 'as drawn in.' *Photos g* and *h* show two samples in which a similar threading is woven 'as drawn in,' (i.e., the weft color order matches that of the threading) with two different 8-treadle tie-ups. Compare the two treadling sequences in **11f** with the threading of the first two blocks in **11a** (read **11a** left to right). A consequence of weaving as drawn in is the symmetry along the diagonal from the top left to the bottom right of the samples in *Photos g* and *h*.

A second way to weave with this threading is shown in *Photo j*. The blocks are all woven the same length, but the warp pairs are changed in one block while in the second they stay the same; then the warp pairs are changed in the second block while in the first they stay the same (this requires 16 treadles or four different treadling orders using the 12-treadle skeleton tie-up in **10c**).

8-shaft 'Windows' sampler

A second threading 'Windows' is shown in **12a**. Block A is the 'background' block, Block B the 'pattern' block. Two colors are used in Block A and four colors in Block B, two of which must be the same as those in Block A. To weave the background, the two colors common to both blocks are woven in the top layer; see **12b** (weft I is in the top layer, weft II in the bottom layer, for both blocks).

To weave the pattern block or the 'windows,' the tie-up for Block A stays the same while the tie-up for Block B makes use of any of the six warp color pairs that are possible (pair 78 in **12c**). *Photo i* shows the top layer of this weaving, the 'windows' side, and *Photo l* shows the plaid design that forms in the bottom layer. The sample shown in *Photo k* is woven on the same 'Windows' warp, with all six warp color pairs developed in the long pattern rectangles.

BIBLIOGRAPHY

O'Connor, Paul. *Loom-Controlled Double Weave: from the Notebook of a Double Weaver.* St. Paul, Minnesota: Paul O'Connor, 1996.

___. *More Loom-Controlled Double Weave: from the Notebook of a Double Weaver.* St. Paul, Minnesota: Paul O'Connor, 2001.

8-shaft sample book

g. Four colors, woven 'as drawn in'

h. Four colors, woven 'as drawn in,' different tie-up from g

i. 'Windows' threading, top layer (see tie-ups 12b–c)

j. Same threading as in g and h; blocks change pairs in staggered fashion, requiring 12 treadles.

k. 'Windows' threading; all six possible color pairs are used in B

l. 'Windows' threading, bottom layer

patchwork jacket in double-woven twill

Doramay Keasbey

A double-woven 'patchwork' of one-inch blocks using a multitude of warp and weft colors is a perfect project to clear out at least part of a weaver's ever-burgeoning yarn collection. Selecting colors is easier than you may suppose since the small size of the blocks and the frequent interchange of the layers combined with the blending effect of warp and weft interlacement help to harmonize almost any number or combination of colors.

It may be advisable to limit other variables by keeping the yarns all the same type—such as all cotton or all wool of the same size and degree of smoothness. The finer the yarn, the smoother the visual blend of the interlaced colors. Yet even fairly coarse yarn can produce pleasing blends with a lively and coordinated appearance within this small twill-block format. A key to the patchwork effect is combining a variety of colors—bright and subdued, light and dark. It's time to raid the yarn bin!

SELECT A VARIETY OF YARNS

To integrate a collection of seemingly disparate colors, choose some unifying feature and let it predominate. For example, select a particular color family as the main theme and add small amounts of others that seem compatible. The multicolored jacket shown here is an example of a solution for making a needed garment while also reducing yarn inventory. The color arrangement is partly the result of serendipity and partly of conscious effort.

First, sort the available yarns into piles that seem to 'go' together and eliminate any discordant skeins or cones. The majority of the selected yarns in this jacket are subdued modifications of blue—several pale blue pastels and a variety of similar slate or steel shades of blue—with no pure hue. The soft blue-green, a near neighbor to the blues, brightens the mix, and a dark heathery burgundy provides a hint of the green's complement in keeping with the generally muted tones.

If your own yarn collection tends toward more intense, pure hues, then a bolder, brighter result can be expected. Try making your selections around a dominant color theme such as warm colors with a few deep values added for richness and contrast, or choose a set of analogous shades and tints or maybe a palette of pastels. Once you start pulling skeins and cones from your shelves, you'll find that decisions are easy.

DESIGNING WITH COLOR IN 2-BLOCK DOUBLE WEAVE

A simple checkerboard effect can be produced in double weave by alternating two structural blocks both vertically and horizontally. When the blocks are fairly small (one inch in our example), the exchanging of the layers at frequent intervals produces a thick essentially integrated textile suitable to be cut and sewn into a jacket.

Colors in two alternating blocks can be controlled in a number of different ways to produce fascinating effects (see Paul O'Connor, 'Color in Loom-controlled Double Weave,' pp. 48–53). Even if limited to only two colors, the scope for a variety of color arrangements is surprisingly broad. When several colors are available, it may be possible to create a completely unique color sequence throughout the piece without the appearance of any exact repeat—the goal for this jacket fabric. Different colors are paired for each block and the order of the pairs is scrambled sufficiently to avoid obvious repetition.

Eight shafts, two blocks of plain weave

Now consider the possibilities for placing just four colors (W, X, Y, Z) in two blocks (A and B) on eight shafts—two colors per block. In each block, one of the two colors will appear in the top layer and the other color (hidden) in the bottom layer. In the alternate treadling sequence the colors exchange layers.

To illustrate how this works, let's assign capital letters to the colors that appear in the top layer and lower case letters to the colors in the bottom layer. Suppose that three of the colors are similar (like the cool blues and green in this jacket), but that one color (Z, underlined to distinguish it) supplies a contrasting accent (like the burgundy in this jacket).

Here is a sample of how four colors might appear if threaded alternately and selected randomly in the two blocks (threaded A B A B A B A B A B). In actual practice, you might use many colors, substituting a different shade each time W or X or Y is encountered.

Wx Y$\underline{z}$ Xy Yw $\underline{Z}$y Xw Wy Yx X$\underline{z}$ Yw Wx

When the treadling changes to the opposite block, the colors will appear like this:

wX y$\underline{Z}$ xY yW $\underline{z}$Y xW wY yX x$\underline{Z}$ yW wX

Small squares and many warp and weft colors produce the patchwork effect.

Now imagine how the crossing of different-colored wefts affects the apparent color of each block. When weft of a particular color interlaces with the *same* color in the warp, a solid color appears. When warp and weft are different, a blend appears. Simply by pairing different colors and varying the order of the pairs for each block in sequence, you can achieve a wonderfully random patchwork effect.

Twelve shafts, two blocks of 2/1 twill

This method for controlling color in two blocks of double cloth works for any suitable weave structure. The simplest is plain weave in each layer as in our previous example, requiring eight shafts, four for each block. Balanced plain weave blends warp and weft colors equally—one color crossed by another produces the same effect whether it is warp or weft.

Twelve or more shafts provide more options for color blending through the use of unbalanced structures (longer floats in one direction than in the other). The jacket fabric is composed of blocks of 2/1 twill. (It was woven as 1/2 twill for lighter treadling, and the fabric was turned to the other side to emphasize the vertical threads on the outside of the jacket.) Because the 2/1 structure shows more warp than weft, the weft color has less influence on each blend. This means that the same two colors can be present in two different blocks, but if their roles are different, two different blends result. For example, X as warp with Z as weft shows X more prominently, but Z as warp and X as weft in another block emphasizes Z.

Enjoy watching colors blend randomly in each one-inch square while you weave! Choose a range of colors in similar yarns and include accent threads of a strongly contrasting color or texture for added interest.

1. Draft for patchwork jacket fabric

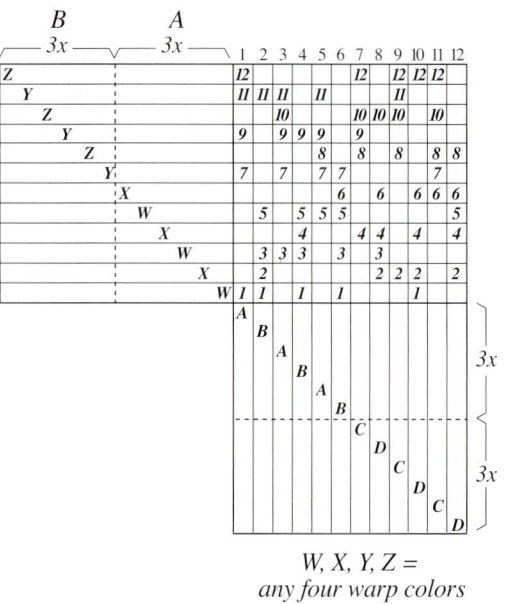

W, X, Y, Z = any four warp colors

A, B, C, D = any four weft colors

THE PATCHWORK JACKET

Use this 12-shaft draft for 2 blocks of double-woven twill and produce a colorful fabric for a unique jacket in your own choice of warp and weft colors. This draft produces one-inch square 'patchwork' blocks after finishing.

- Equipment. 12-shaft loom, width appropriate for your jacket pattern; 8-dent reed; 2 shuttles.
- Materials. Warp and weft: a variety of smooth wool yarns 1500–2000 yds/lb, suitable jacket pattern, sewing notions. (This jacket uses 2-ply Munkagarn, 1645 yds/lb, from Glimåkra Looms 'n Yarns; Harrisville Shetland at 1800 yds/lb would make a good substitute.) Select a simple commercial jacket pattern without darts or complicated shaping. Calculate yarn amounts according to pattern requirements.
- Wind on the warping board the selected pair of colors (these can be any two colors) for each inch: WXWXWX, etc. for the first inch; YZYZYZ for the next, and a new pair of colors for the next, etc. For this jacket, 18 total ends are threaded in each inch (note that whatever the width of each block, the number of ends per block should be a multiple of six). Determine the width and length of the warp required by the selected pattern. Plan the width of the warp in the reed to accommodate the widest pattern piece plus allowance for drawing in and shrinkage. Estimate 20% shrinkage in the length and a minimum of 10% in the width.
- Sley 4/dent in an 8-dent reed, 32 epi (16 epi/layer), for yarns comparable in grist to the Munkagarn (close to twice the normal density of plain weave for each layer). This slightly loose sett for twill assures a flexible yet coherent garment fabric when woven in two exchanging layers.
- Thread following the threading draft in *1*.
- Weave following the treadling sequence in *1*, changing weft colors as desired. Wash the woven fabric by hand gently to full slightly; rinse well; steam press. Secure edges of cut pieces, tailor to your satisfaction, and wear happily. ✄

overshot-patterned double weave

4-block, 4-shaft double weave	58
shamrock table runners	60
mug rugs	62
'colonial' double-weave table runner	64
symmetrical turning blocks	68
overshot-patterned double-weave coverlet	70
network solutions: overshot to double weave	74

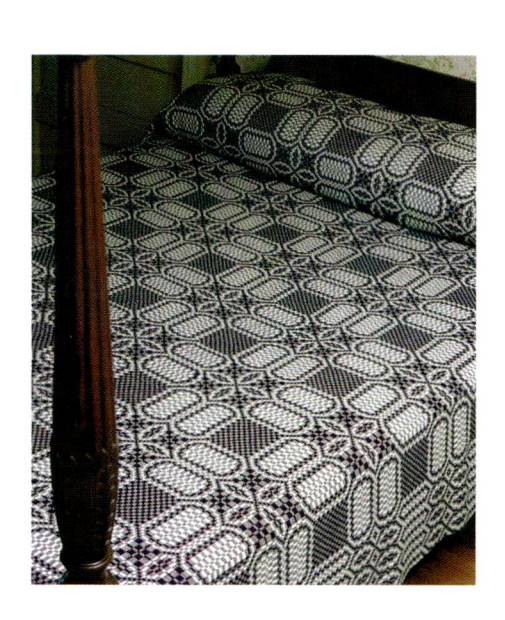

4-block, 4-shaft double weave

Madelyn van der Hoogt

1. From overshot draft to double weave

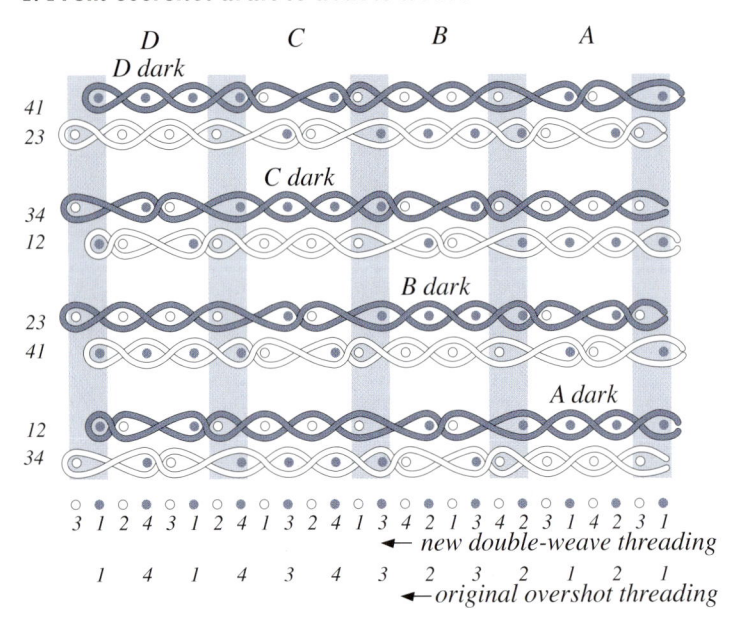

2. From profile draft to double weave

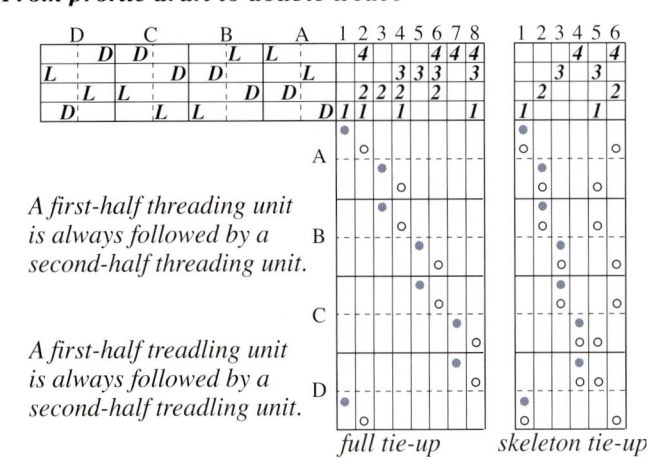

A first-half threading unit is always followed by a second-half threading unit.

A first-half treadling unit is always followed by a second-half treadling unit.

full tie-up   skeleton tie-up

A number of projects in this volume show double weave with overshot patterning. This method of designing blocks in double weave and its several variations have been called 'colonial' double weave (deriving from the term 'colonial' overshot); 4-block, 4-shaft double weave; 4-block, 8-shaft double weave; and overshot-patterned double weave. The good news is, whatever it's called, overshot patterns can be easily translated into double weave on four or eight shafts.

Gain the pattern potential of overshot and the durability and smooth texture of double weave on only four shafts with this little-known drafting technique. One block weaves solid light (or dark); the other three blocks form two kinds of halftones. The weaving is easy—this 4-block, 2-layer miracle can be woven with only one shuttle!

Clotilde Barrett introduces this technique in 'Four-block Double Weave on Four Shafts,' *The Weaver's Journal*, Summer 1983, Issue 29, p. 72. The most effective (and simplest!) way to apply the concept is to begin with an overshot draft. Dark ends (or one colorway) are threaded according to the overshot draft. After every dark end, a light end (or a second colorway) is threaded on the opposite shaft: a dark end (D) on shaft 1 is followed by a light end (L) on shaft 3, D on 2 by L on 4, D on 3 by L on 1, and D on 4 by L on 2. Examine a simple overshot threading converted to double weave in *1*.

The resulting double-weave threadings can also be thought of as block threadings in which Block A = 1-3-2-4, Block B = 2-4-3-1, Block C = 3-1-4-2, and Block D = 4-2-1-3 (all threaded DLDL). Note that all four shafts appear in every block. A different pair of shafts is selected to weave in the top layer (the opposite pair in the bottom layer) to produce pattern in each block: 1-2 (A), 2-3 (B), 3-4 (C), 4-1 (D).

Examine the four picks that weave pattern in Block A in *1*. If a dark weft is used for the top layer and a light weft for the bottom layer: Block A weaves dark on top; Blocks B and D weave ¾ dark halftones (dark weft; ½ dark, ½ light warp); Block C weaves a ½ dark, ½ light halftone (light warp, dark weft). If a light weft is used in both layers (and therefore only one shuttle!), Block A weaves ½ dark, ½ light halftone; Blocks B and D weave ¾ light halftones; Block C weaves all light. The same pattern-block/halftone-block relationships occur for each of the other sequences (pattern in Block B, C, or D).

To use this technique with any overshot draft, thread as described above. Follow the original overshot threading draft as a guide for the treadling: for the top-layer pick, raise the shaft indicated in the threading. If that shaft is an even shaft (2, for example), raise it for the corresponding bottom-layer pick with the two odd shafts (2 with 1 and 3); if it is an odd shaft (1 for example), raise it with the two even shafts (1 with 2 and 4).

DRAFTING FROM A PROFILE DRAFT

The block threading in *2* can be used with any 4-block profile draft that produces pattern in one block at a time (the results will look much like overshot, however, but with one solid-color block and two types of halftones). Certain restrictions must be observed. For example, in the threading, a 1-3 (or 3-1) pair must always alternate with a 2-4 (or 4-2) pair. In the treadling, a pair of picks using the first two treadles of a block must always alternate with a pair of picks using the second two treadles of a block. Transition pairs must therefore be added (or a pair of shafts subtracted) to maintain these orders. Since one of the pairs in each block is also a pair in the two adjacent blocks, blocks overlap just as they do in overshot—the overlap is indicated by the gray areas in *1*. (Note that drafts converted to double weave on eight shafts—as opposed to four—allow solid-color dark *and* solid-color light blocks on the same surface.) ✂

These runners, woven by Norma Smayda, are designed with the drafting principles described on page 58, but the draft is then turned to use eight shafts and four treadles instead of four shafts and eight treadles.

shamrock table runners

Bobbie Irwin

1. Draft for Shamrock runners

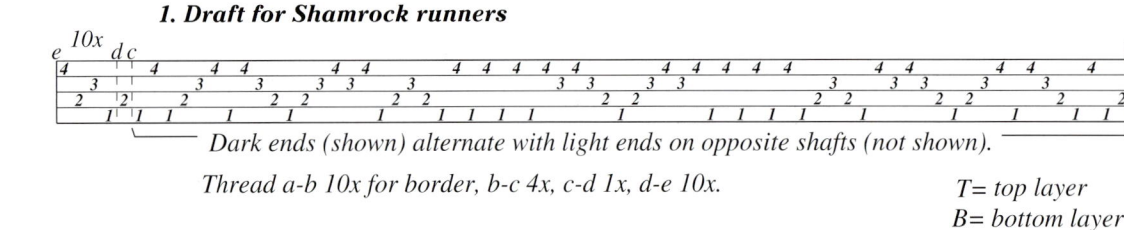

Dark ends (shown) alternate with light ends on opposite shafts (not shown).
Thread a–b 10x for border, b–c 4x, c–d 1x, d–e 10x.

T = top layer
B = bottom layer

Tie-up 1   Tie-up 2

Overshot-patterned double-weave fabrics are as practical as they are beautiful. They look complex (other weavers will marvel at your expertise) but require only four shafts! For a runner with two light sides, use only one shuttle. For a runner with a dark side and a light side, use two.

A 4-shaft double-weave draft can easily be derived from any 4-shaft overshot draft! I've become an enthusiastic convert to this technique—pioneered by Clotilde Barrett and refined by Manuela Kaulitz (see the Bibliography and see also Madelyn van der Hoogt, pp. 58–59).

The overshot draft for the Shamrock runners is an original 'name' draft derived from the words 'overshot-patterned double weave.' No need to adjust for floats since there *are* no floats!

As with any double weave, overshot-patterned double weave is heddle hungry; always check before threading. For this draft, the same number is required on each shaft (152).

- Equipment: 4-shaft loom, 16" weaving width; 10-dent reed; 2 shuttles.
- Materials: 10/2 pearl cotton (4200 yds/lb), Natural #79 (UKI), 10½ oz; Dark Green #26 (UKI), 5½ oz; amounts provide two runners 35–36" long each.
- Wind a warp of 610 total ends 3½ yds long in the following order: 40 ends Natural, 530 ends alternating 1 Dark Green and 1 Natural; end with 40 ends Natural.
- Sley 4/dent in a 10-dent reed, 40 epi; center for 15¼".
- Thread following the threading draft in *1*. The draft shows all ends in the 10x border sections (where all ends are Natural) but *only* the Dark Green ends in the pattern section (b–c): in this section, thread the Dark Green ends as instructed by the draft, but after each Dark Green end thread a Natural end on the opposite shaft (Dark Green on shaft 1 followed by Natural on shaft 3, Dark Green on 2 by Natural on 4, Dark Green on 3 by Natural on 1, Dark Green on 4 by Natural on 2).
- Weave with one shuttle and Natural weft for a runner that is light on both sides (on both sides, the 'dark' blocks will be ½ dark, ½ light; halftones will be ¾ light, ¼ dark; and 'light' blocks will be all light; see the runner on p. 61). Weave with two shuttles, one Natural (top layer), one Dark Green (bottom layer), for a runner that is light on the top side, dark on the bottom side. On the bottom side, 'light' blocks will be ½ dark, ½ light; halftones will be ¾ dark, ¼ light; and 'dark' blocks will be all dark; see the inset on p. 61 (the top 'light' side will look like the runner in the photo). For hems, follow a–b in the draft in *1* for 1" using two shuttles. For fringed ends, hemstitch and leave 6" unwoven warp at each end.
- Weave each runner for about 39" following the treadling in *1*: b–e, d–c; end with c–b to balance. When treadling in the reverse direction, weave the top-layer pick (T) before the corresponding bottom-layer pick (B).

In the treadling, a single shaft is raised for the top layer. For the bottom layer, the same shaft is raised + the odds (1-3) if the shaft is even or + the evens (2-4) if the shaft is odd. Use both feet, one for raising the single shaft and the other for raising the odd or even pairs. To avoid confusion, keep your foot on the single-shaft treadle after weaving the top pick.

Note that the treadling draft is derived from the threading draft—the single shaft that is raised follows the threading of the dark ends. This is easiest to see in Tie-up 2 (ignoring the Bs), but Tie-up 1 is easier to use since it places the treadle for the pairs opposite the corresponding single-shaft treadle. Square the pattern with a relatively gentle beat. When weaving with two shuttles, start the shuttles from opposite sides and make sure the wefts wind around each other at the selvedges by placing the shuttle you just used closest to you (with this draft, the layers don't actually join until the third pick).

You'll discover that the treadling produces a slight asymmetry, more noticeable in large blocks than in small blocks, but this is not an error. Notice also that this draft is woven 'as-drawn-in,' or 'star fashion.' To weave a draft 'rose fashion,' substitute rose-fashion treadling blocks as required by the overshot draft.

- Finish by cutting the fabric from the loom and securing fringe ends with waterproof tape. Machine wash and dry (or hand wash without taping and hang to dry). Take-up and shrinkage are about 13% in width and length when machine-washed (hot wash, cold rinse). Trim fringes to 4" (discarding tape). For hems, zigzag or serge top layer of hem allowances, trim off bottom layers, turn under and machine- or hand-sew top layer.

BIBLIOGRAPHY

Barrett, Clotilde. 'Four Block Double Weave on Four Shafts.' *The Weaver's Journal*, Summer 1983, pp. 72–77.

Kaulitz, Manuela. 'Overshot Patterns in Color-and-Weave Effect Double Weave.' *Handwoven*, January/February 1994, pp. 62–65.

When reversing the treadling direction, weave T before each corresponding B. Use Tie-up 2 for easier treadling.

Choose to weave a runner with a dark and a light side—or one with two light sides; fringe or hem the ends. An overshot name draft ('overshot-patterned double weave') was used to create the draft for this runner.

mug rugs

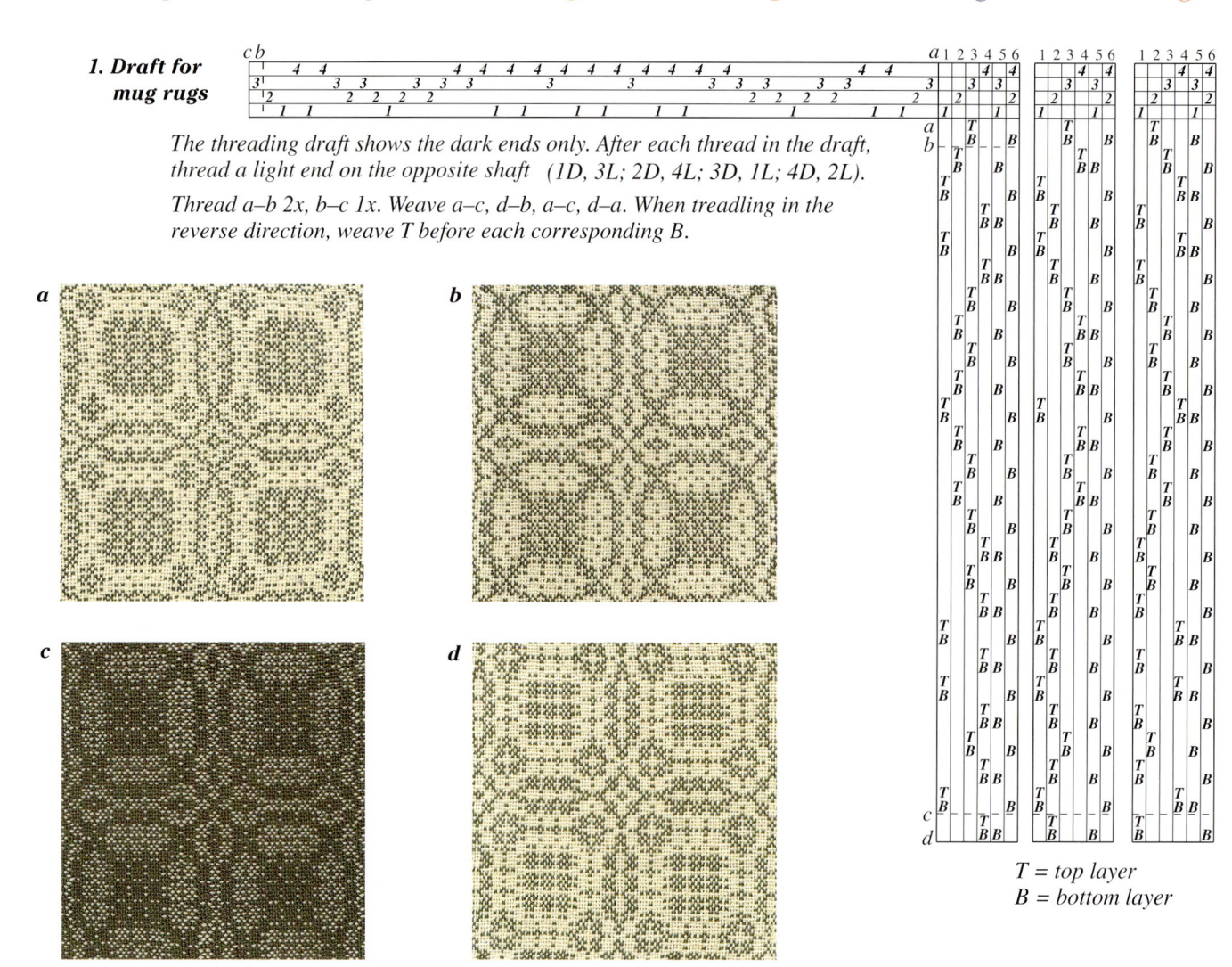

Judie Eatough

1. Draft for mug rugs

The threading draft shows the dark ends only. After each thread in the draft, thread a light end on the opposite shaft (1D, 3L; 2D, 4L; 3D, 1L; 4D, 2L).

Thread a–b 2x, b–c 1x. Weave a–c, d–b, a–c, d–a. When treadling in the reverse direction, weave T before each corresponding B.

T = top layer
B = bottom layer

Tired of weaving those endless samples that hide in your drawers or notebooks? Here's another idea. Thread a narrow warp and play with treadling variations and color orders for many different effects. Make the results into mug rugs to use and enjoy—you'll continue to learn from them at the same time. The double-weave mug rugs on page 63 are all woven using treadlings 1, 2, or 3: (clockwise from cup rug) treadling 1 back, 2 back, 3 back, 3 front, 2 front, 1 back, 1 back (all green weft).

For the mug rugs above: a (treadling 2 back), b (1 front), c (1 front, green weft), d (3 front). See how many designs you can create!

Use the overshot draft in *1* or choose an overshot draft of your own. Here's a handy design tip: to see how an overshot design will look in double weave, enter the overshot threading in a computer weaving program, enter a direct tie-up, and choose 'as-drawn-in' for the treadling. A warp drawdown shows the effect of a light weft in the top layer; a weft drawdown shows the effect of a dark weft.

❏ Equipment. 4-shaft loom, 6" weaving width; 10-dent reed; 1 or 2 shuttles.
❏ Materials. 10/2 pearl cotton (4200 yds/lb, UKI), Mountain #98 (green), 2 oz; Natural #79, 3 oz.
❏ Wind a warp of 202 ends (101 ends each color) 2½ yds long, holding one end Mountain, one end Natural separated by a finger to prevent twisting.
❏ Sley 4 ends/dent in a 10-dent reed, 40 epi; center for 5" weaving width.

❏ Thread Mountain ends as shown in *1*; after every Mountain (D) end, thread a Natural (L) end on the opposite shaft (1D3L, 2D4L, 3D1L, 4D2L).
❏ Weave each mug rug following treadling drafts 1, 2 or 3 using: one shuttle with Natural weft (for mostly natural-colored mats), one shuttle with Mountain weft for mostly green mats, and/or one shuttle with Mountain (top layer) and one shuttle with Natural (bottom layer) for mostly green-on-top, natural-on-bottom mats. Begin and end each mat with a 1" tubular section for turned-in hems using one shuttle with Natural: 1, 124, 2, 123.
❏ Finish by removing from loom. Wash fabric by hand in warm water, Ivory liquid. Hang to dry. Cut apart mats in the center of hem sections. Turn ends of hems to inside and slip stitch to close. Press firmly. ✄

Overshot-patterned double weave invites experimentation with weft color and treadling orders. Weave a set of mug rugs or coasters (or thread a wider warp for placemats) for samplers you can study and enjoy.

'colonial' double weave table runner

Madelyn van der Hoogt

Commercial double-weave upholstery fabric, face and back

'But it looks just like overshot!' I was tantalized by the commercial upholstery fabric on Mary Pflueger's colonial wing chair. What a good idea: double weave for stability and endurance with the traditional look of overshot, perfect for table linens, upholstery—even clothing! But how to produce a fabric that looks like overshot instead of the usual four-block double weave, and even more important, how many shafts would it take?

A basket full of crumpled graph paper and several threading attempts later, here is the answer: four blocks of double weave on only *eight* shafts! You can create double-weave drafts from a wealth of available 4-block overshot drafts, choose any 4-block profile draft, or design your own to fill your house with patterned fabrics.

TWO BLOCKS ON EIGHT SHAFTS

To understand the structure, first review 2-block double weave on eight shafts (*1*). Two layers of plain weave (light and dark) are woven in each of the two blocks. Pattern occurs when one plain-weave layer (hence one color) appears on the face in one block and the other plain-weave layer (the second color) appears on the face in the second block. The layers in the two blocks can be exchanged as desired to produce any 2-block design. Four shafts are required for each block, two for each of the plain-weave layers. (Dark and light ends alternate; in A, dark ends are on 1 and 3, light on 2 and 4. In B, dark ends are on 5 and 7, light on 6 and 8). Twelve shafts provide three blocks; sixteen shafts provide four.

The only actual interlacements that take place are plain weave of the darks and plain weave of the lights. The position of the layers in each block is determined by lifting or lowering (i.e., not lifting) the warp ends of the color *not* weaving. Examine the cross sections in *1*. When dark wefts weave plain weave with dark warp ends, light warp ends are held above or below the dark wefts (in this example, below in A and above in B). When light wefts are weaving plain weave, dark warp ends are held above or below the light wefts (in this case, above in A and below in B). Reversing the positions of these non-weaving ends exchanges the positions of the layers and therefore the colors on the face.

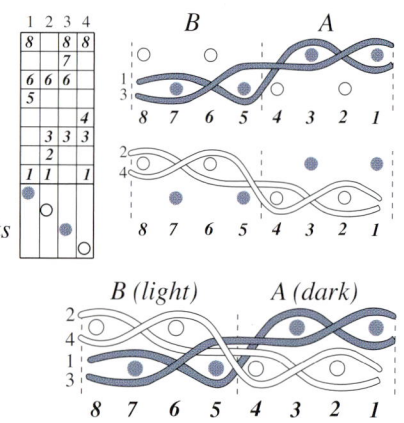

FOUR BLOCKS ON EIGHT SHAFTS

Now examine the threading below the cross sections in *2*. In Block A, a dark-light pair is threaded on 1, 2 and a dark-light pair on 3, 4. In C, a dark-light pair is threaded on 5, 6 and a dark-light pair on 7, 8 (the B block of our former 2-block threading). In B (of our new threading) a dark-light pair is threaded on 3, 4 and a dark-light pair on 5, 6. In D, a dark-light pair is on 7, 8 and a dark-light pair on 1, 2. Notice that each of the blocks shares a pair with two other blocks (similarly to the way that each block shares shafts with two other blocks in 4-shaft overshot). As a result of these shared pairs, when dark weaves on top in A, the pair of warp ends shared with A in B (3, 4) and the pair of warp ends shared with A in D (1, 2) also produce dark on top. When at the same time light weaves on top in C, the pair of warp ends shared with C in D (7, 8) weave light on top and the pair of warp ends shared with C in B (5, 6) weave light on top. B and D therefore

1. 8-shaft double weave: two blocks

In these four picks, dark is on top in A; light is on top in B. The warp ends not weaving in each pick determine the positions of the layers: light warp ends in B are raised for dark picks (light ends in A are down); dark warp ends in A are raised for light picks (dark ends in B are down).

2. 8-shaft double weave: four blocks

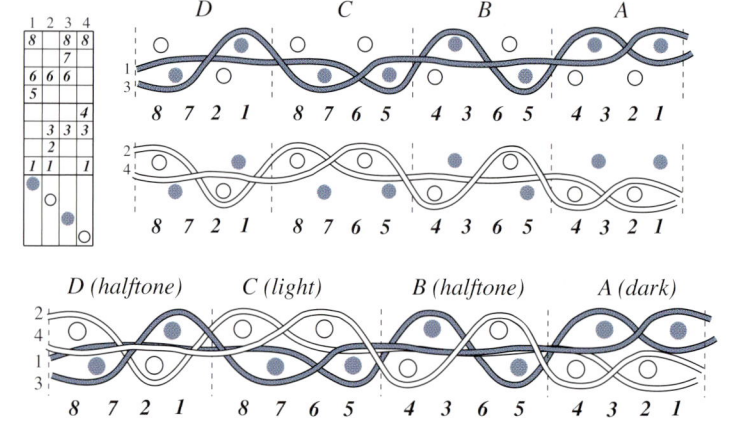

To determine the position of the layers, light warp ends are held above or below dark weft picks; dark warp ends are held above or below light weft picks. In these four picks, A forms dark on top; C forms light on top; B and D form halftones.

Here's a table runner that looks like traditional overshot but has the durability of double weave—no floats! You can take any 4-shaft overshot draft and convert it into double weave on eight shafts.

form halftones. B and D also form halftones when A weaves light on top and C weaves dark. When B or D weave dark or light respectively (see the full tie-up in *4*), A and C form halftones.

Threading restrictions

Dark and light ends alternate. Plain weave of the darks is produced by alternating 1, 5 vs 3, 7, and plain weave of the lights by alternating 2, 6 vs 4, 8. Any selected threading must provide these plain-weave sheds (that is, a 1 or a 5 must alternate with a 3 or a 7 in the dark warp, and a 2 or a 6 alternate with a 4 or an 8 in the light warp).

To avoid interruptions in the plain-weave sheds *and* ensure that blocks on all sides of a symmetrical motif are symmetrical in size, follow the threading instructions given in *4* and begin *and* end each block with the same pair (A on 1, 2; B on 3, 4; C on 5, 6; D on 7, 8). If these transitional pairs are not added, two threads may weave together in each layer and blocks may not be symmetrical within a motif.

Note that every dark thread appears on the right side of every light thread. Halftones on either side of a symmetrical motif are therefore not precisely mirror-image symmetrical. The finer the materials the less apparent is the slight halftone asymmetry.

A limitation of this structure shared with overshot is that pattern is produced in only one block at a time. In every 4-pick sequence one block weaves light on top, one weaves dark on top, and two form halftones (with one exception; stay tuned).

Threading advantages

An advantage to translating overshot drafts into double weave is that block width is no longer restricted by float length. Some interesting effects can be achieved by threading large areas of a single block. Furthermore (the exception to the one-block-light, one-block-dark, two-blocks-halftones rule), all dark or all light can be woven on top at any time to produce horizontal bands of solid color.

Selecting a draft

Happily, the wonderful myriad of existing overshot drafts can be used for this structure. To change an overshot draft into double weave, first write the overshot draft and circle the blocks so you can see the threading order and relative size of each block. Then determine the number of double-weave ends to substitute for circled overshot ends (this depends on the materials, sett, and scope of the design) and thread substituting 'units' in *4*. For example, if every two threads of overshot are to equal one 4-thread unit in double weave, four overshot threads of Block A would become 1-2-3-4 1-2-3-4 1-2—remember always to end with a transitional pair, 1-2 for Block A. (For an easier method for translating overshot drafts into double weave, see Doramay Keasbey, pp. 74–75.)

To convert 4-block profile drafts to 8-shaft double weave, consider each square in the profile threading/treadling equal to four threads (or a multiple of four). Each time the threading changes to a new block, however, add a transition pair (this structure is therefore not a true unit weave). When estimating a total count of warp or weft threads, first count the number of squares and multiply by four. Then count the number of block changes and multiply by two. The sum of these two numbers is the total number of threads. In this threading: 110 squares x 4 = 440; 45 changes x 2 = 90; total warp ends 530.

A Handweaver's Source Book (Marguerite Davison, 1953), *Of Coverlets* (Sadye Tune Wilson and Doris Finch Kennedy, 1983), *The Shuttle-Craft Book of American Hand-Weaving*, (Mary Meigs Atwater, 1928), *Keep Me Warm One Night* (Harold B. and Dorothy K. Burnham, 1972), and *The Coverlet Book* (Helene Bress, 2003) are all excellent sources for overshot drafts to convert to double weave.

3. Profile draft

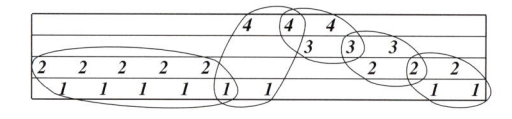

4. Block threading for 'colonial' double weave

Substitute the 4-thread 'unit' for Blocks A, B, C, or D on a 4-block profile threading draft. When changing to a new block, add the pair of threads after the dashed line (t). These transitional pairs ensure tabby in both layers.

A(d); C(l)
B(d); D(l)
C(d); A(l)
D(d); B(l)

full tie-up   *skeleton tie-up*

5. Full profile drawdown of the runner

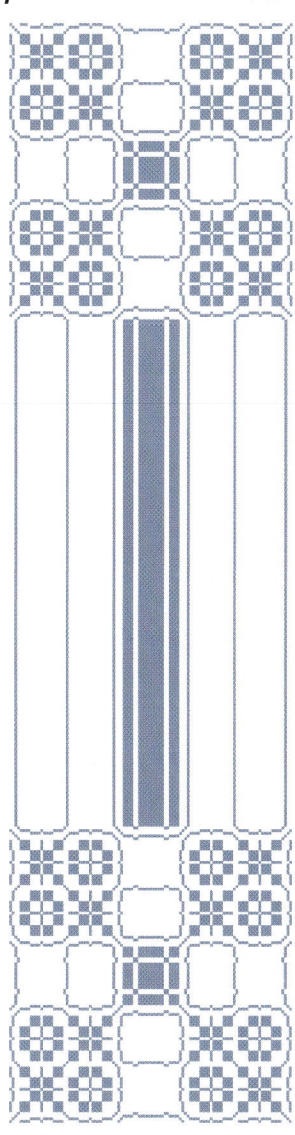

'COLONIAL' DOUBLE WEAVE TABLE RUNNER

- **Equipment.** 8-shaft loom, 18" weaving width; 12 or 16 treadles (two temporary treadles can be added to most 10-treadle looms for this project; see below and **Photo b**, p. 69); 15-dent reed; 2 shuttles; temple (stretcher) for 18" weaving width, if available.
- **Materials.** Warp and weft: 12/3 worsted wool (2100 yds/lb, Nehalem, Oregon Worsted), rust and white, 1850 yd (14 oz) each color (you can substitute Harrisville Shetland, 1800 yd/lb or 5/2 pearl cotton, 2100 yd/lb).
- Wind a warp 4 yds long of 530 total ends holding 1 strand of rust and 1 strand of white together as you wind, keeping a finger between them. (Warp length produces a runner 65" long and allows 1 yd loom waste + 1 yd sampling and warp take-up).
- Sley 2/dent (1 rust/1 white) in each dent of a 15-dent reed, 30 epi; center for 17¾".
- Thread substituting the four ends of the appropriate block (see **4**) for each filled-in square on the profile threading draft (**3**). Add the pair of transition ends ('t' in **4**) before changing to a new block. For example, where a single square occurs in a block, six ends are threaded, four for the square and two for the added pair. When four squares appear in a block, 18 ends are threaded, four for each of the squares and two for the added pair.
- Wind the warp on the warp beam.
- Tie up the treadles as shown, following either the full tie-up or the skeleton tie-up.

The skeleton tie-up presents several advantages: there are fewer shafts to tie, treadling sequences are easier to find with the feet, lifts are lighter since both feet are used, and designing at the loom is easier to do.

If your loom is limited to 10 treadles, two treadles can usually be added; see **Photo b**, p. 69. To add treadles to jack looms with lamms, such as the Baby Wolf, first tie up all of the treadles except 11 and 12. The two extra treadles can be placed between two existing treadles (mine are on the right side) and hinged from the back instead of the front. Use two pieces of wood 27" long and about the same thickness as the existing treadles. Drill two 3/16" holes in the back footrest at selected location for treadles. Drill a vertical hole at the end of each of the two new treadles. Halfway between the existing holes, drill holes in the lamms for shafts 4 and 6 at the 11th treadle position and for 1 and 7 at the 12th. Drill corresponding holes in the treadles and tie cords from lamm holes to treadle holes; tie the treadles to the footrest of the loom. If you prefer not to drill into the loom, tie cords from treadle holes around lamms and footrest (they may occasionally slip from place).

- Weave a heading; insert temple set to the width in reed; weave 2" all light on top for hem (with skeleton tie-up, lift 1-3-4, 2, 2-3-4, 4). Weave following the profile treadling draft in the following order: one complete profile sequence, Block D 1x, Block C for 30", Block D 1x, one complete profile sequence; end with 2" light on top for second hem.

(Each square on the profile treadling draft theoretically represents the 4 picks producing dark on top in the designated block. Experiment, however, to determine the number of picks required to square the design. You can change to a new block after any *pair* of picks. When changing in the middle of a block, however, use the second two treadles of the 4-pick sequence in the new block to maintain plain-weave order of the two layers.)

- To finish, remove the fabric from the loom, machine zigzag 1" from the pattern at each end, cut close to stitching line, turn ends under, and blind stitch to close. Finished size is 16¾" x 65". ✄

symmetrical turning blocks

Madelyn van der Hoogt

1. Part of profile draft for the 'colonial' double weave runner, pages 64–67.

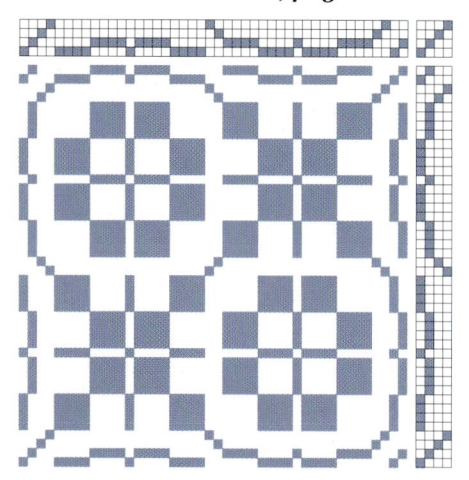

a. Center block in left motif is wider than center block in right motif.

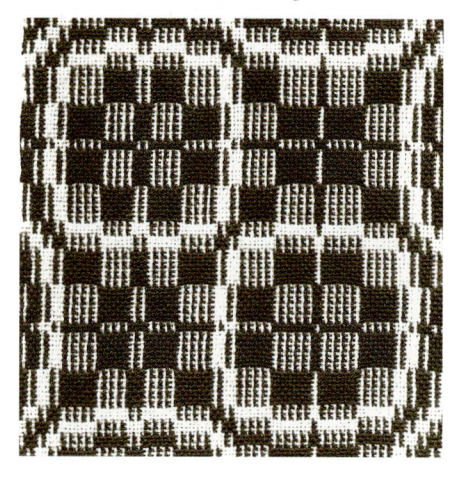

2. Overshot turning blocks

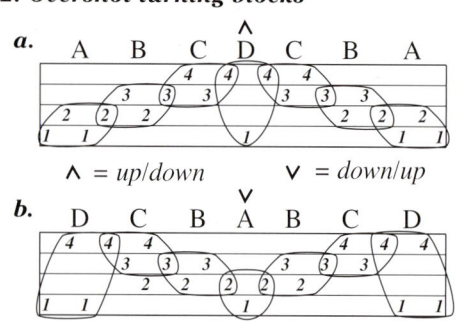

a.   A B C D C B A
          ∧

∧ = up/down   ∨ = down/up

b.   D C B A B C D
            ∨

These two overshot drafts both show point threadings of the blocks: one point that turns from 'up' to 'down' (2a), and one point that turns from 'down' to 'up' (2b).

I wove my first overshot coverlet without even noticing that the threading draft was not 'balanced' (i.e., symmetrical motifs were not mirror-image symmetrical). Then along came this special form of double weave. Surely, I thought, since it has what look like threading 'units,' it should be easy to create drafts with perfect symmetry. Wrong! It didn't take long to discover a problem: not all turning blocks with the same number of ends in the threading look like they have the same number of ends in the woven cloth. Compare the left and right motifs in the drawdown in **1** with the corresponding motifs in Photo a.

TURNING BLOCKS

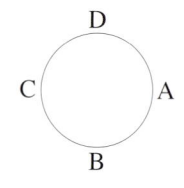

To identify turning blocks, think of the blocks as arranged in a circle. Threading can proceed around the circle in either direction, A-B-C-D or D-C-B-A. Whenever the direction changes, the block on which the direction pivots is a 'turning' block. In the overshot threading draft in **2a**, blocks are threaded in a clockwise direction—'up'—until reaching D, a turning block; they then move counterclockwise—'down.' In **2b**, blocks are threaded counterclockwise,—'down'—to A, a turning block, then clockwise—'up.' The two kinds of turning blocks (up/down in **2a** and down/up in **2b**) are marked by symbols in the drafts.

Circling the blocks in an overshot threading draft identifies all the warp threads that belong to each block; the circles, and therefore the blocks, overlap. Both types of turning blocks (up/down and down/up) show the same number of ends, an odd number (three in this case); compare D and A in **2a–2b**.

Turning blocks in overshot-patterned 4-block, 8-shaft double weave

Though not a true unit weave, 8-shaft, 4-block double weave can be threaded using a profile draft. Each square in the profile threading represents four threads, A = 1-2-3-4; B = 3-4-5-6; C = 5-6-7-8; D = 7-8-1-2 (see **3**). To balance block size and maintain true plain weave in each layer, add a pair of transition threads to the end of one block when changing to a new block, marked 't' in **3**.

The threading draft in **4** shows double-weave blocks arranged in the same point orders as the overshot blocks in **2**. Circling the threads that actually weave in each double-weave block reveals an unexpected difference between the numbers of warp ends in the two turning blocks. Notice that six threads appear in the up/down turning block (C-D-C), and ten threads appear in the down/up turning block (B-A-B). This difference is the source of the discrepancy between the left and right star/rose motifs in **Photo a**.

Adjust for turning-block size

Because Block B's transition threads, on shafts 3 and 4, are also in Block A, when Block A is flanked on both sides by Block B, four threads are added to Block A's apparent size. Since Block A shares threads with Block D and Block C does not, no threads are added to Block D when Block D is flanked on both sides by Block C. Notice that when blocks are threaded in succession, a pair of threads from a succeeding block (going up) or from a preceding block (going down) are added to each block.

To summarize: the effective size of each block is +2 for blocks threaded in succession, +0 for up/down turning blocks, and +4 for down/up turning blocks.

The simplest way to guarantee symmetry and proportion when creating drafts in 8-shaft, 4-block double weave is to subtract four threads from all down/up turning blocks.

Examine **5a**. When the rose is threaded BABAB, warp ends on shafts 3 and 4 are added to both sides of the two Block A 'down/up' turning blocks, giving them four more ends than the outside B blocks. If four ends are removed from each of the A blocks, they become the same size as the B blocks.

Examine **5b**. When the rose is threaded ABABA, the down/up center turning Block A, gains four ends from the adjacent B blocks; see the rose motif in **6a**. The small turning blocks in the table motif in **6a** do not gain threads (these are up/down turning blocks). To adjust the small block in the rose to match the small block in the table as in **6b**, remove four ends from Block A as in **5b**. (The larger blocks in both the rose and the table in **6a** and **6b** have not been adjusted for size.)

These steps are necessary only when you are deriving double-weave drafts from profile drafts by substituting threading 'units.' When you are translating a 'balanced' overshot draft, use Doramay Keasbey's 'network' method, pp. 75–75.

3. Double weave threading units

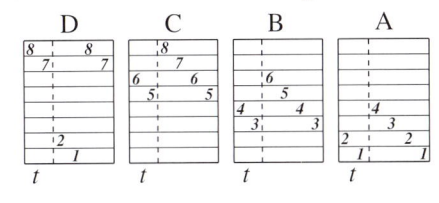

4. Double weave turning blocks

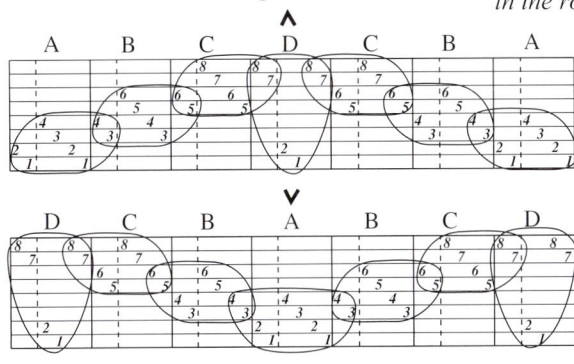

Threading 'units' for 8-shaft, 4-block double weave are shown in **3**. Point threadings of the four blocks (ABCDCBA and DCBABCD) are shown in **4**. In the threading drafts in **5a** and **5b**, ends are subtracted from Block A (a down/up turning block). Drawdowns in **6a** and **6b** show a rose and table: in **6a** no threads are removed from the turning block in the rose; in **6b** four threads are removed.

TREADLE TIP (Photo b)
Tie-ups for 4-block, 8-shaft double weave require at least 12 treadles. Attach temporary treadles to your loom by a cord through a hole in the treadle and a hole in the bottom bar at the back of the loom. Then pass a length of cord through holes in the designated lamms and in the corresponding treadles.

5a. Four ends are subtracted from two Block A down/up turning blocks

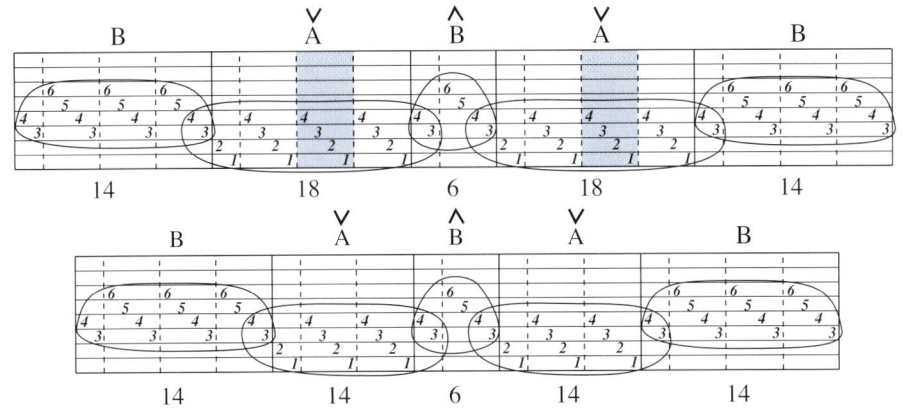

5b. Four ends are subtracted from Block A, a down/up turning block

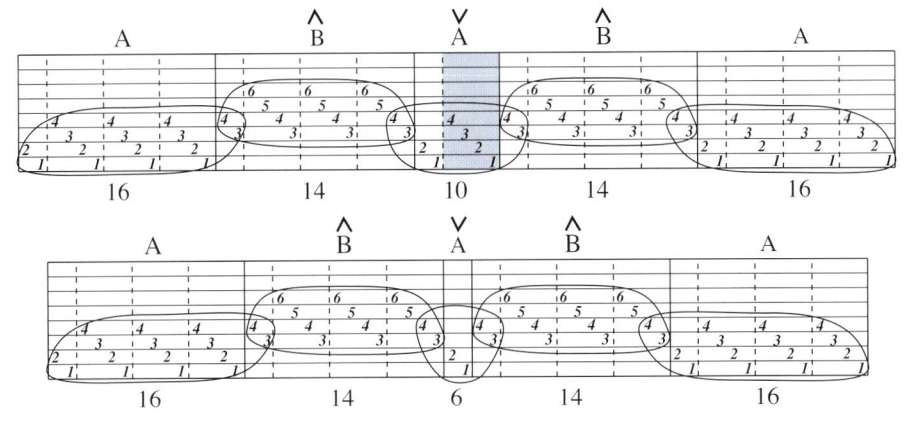

6a. Rose turning block: not adjusted

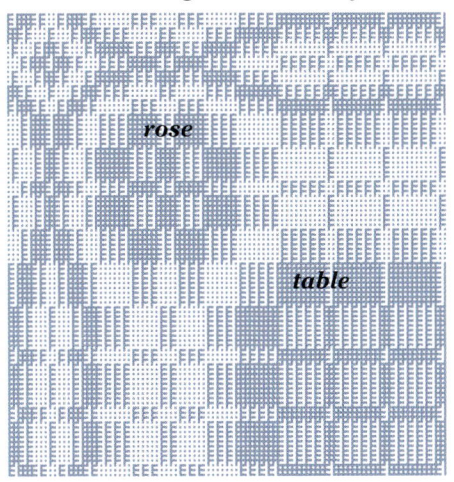

6b. Rose turning block: adjusted

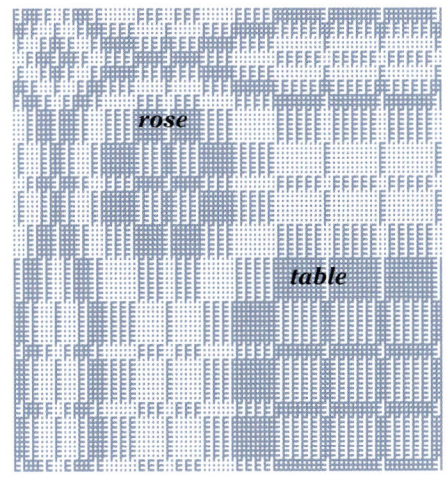

b. Adding treadles to a 10-treadle loom

DOUBLE WEAVE

overshot-patterned double-weave coverlet

Helen Jarvis

a. Sample from an asymmetrical draft

b. Sample from a symmetrical draft

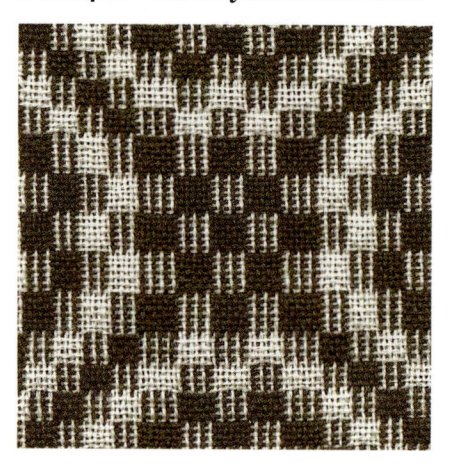

This sturdy 8-shaft double weave creates designs that look like overshot but avoid the liabilities of overshot's long floats. Review Doramay Keasbey's steps in 'Network Solutions: Overshot to Double Weave,' (pages 74–76 and outlined below), for an easy way to derive a double-weave draft from an overshot one.

The overshot pattern 'King's Flower,' from *Of Coverlets* by Sadye Tune Wilson and Doris Finch Kennedy (see the Bibliography), is used to design the double-weave draft for the heirloom coverlet shown in this article.

Drafts for this double-woven overshot look-alike (first introduced by Carol Strickler; see the Bibliography) can be derived directly from block profile drafts, but special steps must be taken to ensure perfectly symmetrical motifs (compare **Photos a** and **b**; also see Madelyn van der Hoogt, "Symmetrical Turning Blocks," pp. 68–69). The easiest way to produce a successful draft, however, is to begin with a symmetrical overshot draft and follow Doramay Keasbey's method as outlined below.

Choose an overshot draft of your own to interpret—or jump right in and weave a 'King's Flower' double-weave coverlet. Instructions are also included (p. 72) for using pick-up to add the recipient's name, your name, and the date to a coverlet border.

STEPS FOR PREPARING SYMMETRICAL DOUBLE-WEAVE DRAFTS FROM DORAMAY KEASBEY

1. Write out a symmetrical overshot draft on graph paper. (A symmetrical draft is one in which the threading for all symmetrical motifs is mirror-image symmetrical.)

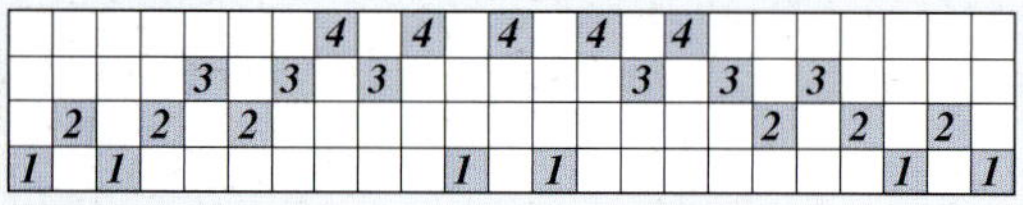

2. Prepare a grid for the double-weave draft that is twice as many squares high and twice as many squares wide as the overshot draft and fill with marks as shown below. All marks on odd rows will represent dark warp threads; all marks on even rows will represent light warp threads.

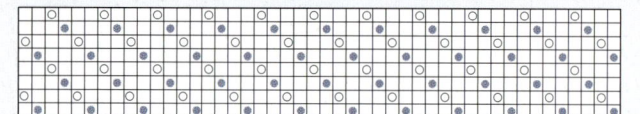

3. With a pencil, shade in two horizontal squares and two vertical squares on the double-weave grid for each marked square in the overshot grid. The original marks within the shaded squares represent the new threading; note that a dark thread always alternates with a light thread.

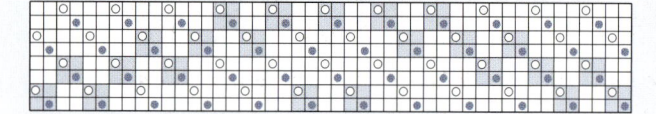

4. To derive the tie-up, for each overshot pattern treadle (below) substitute four double-weave treadles (upper right).

5. To derive the treadling, make a grid like the threading grid under the tie-up (lower right): marks under odd treadles represent dark picks; marks under even treadles represent light picks. For each pattern pick in the overshot draft, shade in four horizontal and two vertical squares under the corresponding block. Marks inside the shaded squares are the double-weave treadling sequence.

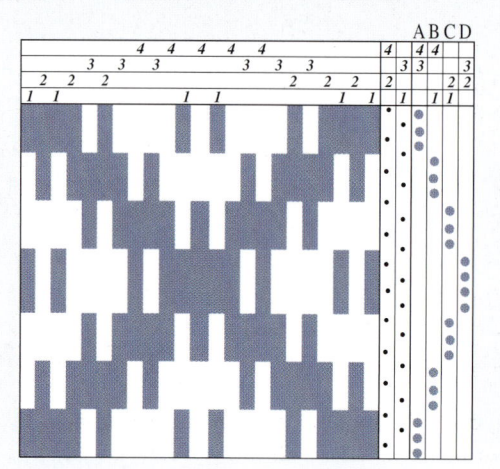

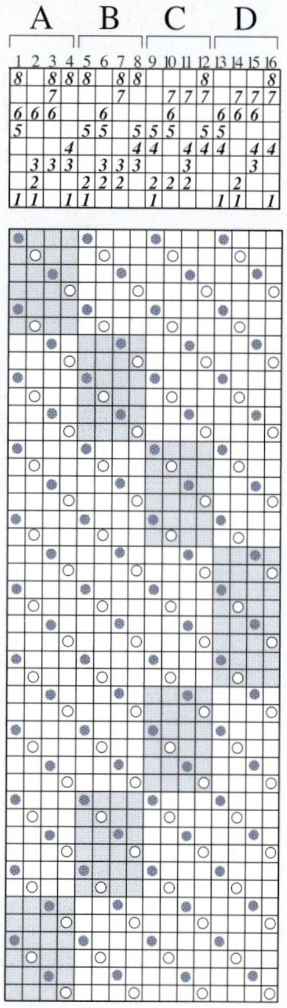

70

Use this 4-block, 8-shaft double weave as the ideal structure for a coverlet. It looks like overshot, but has no floats to catch or wear out. This durable pattern weave is also suitable for outerwear and upholstery.

PICK-UP INSTRUCTIONS FOR NAMES AND DATE

If you have a dobby, program it to make the sheds indicated in the tie-ups in *3* and *2a*. If not, you can use the 12-treadle tie-up in *2b* (if you don't have 12 treadles, you can weave the coverlet without names and date using the tie-up in *2c*). These instructions refer to the pick-up treadles in *2a*. See *2b* for treadle substitutions if you are using the skeleton tie-up. As you do the pick-up, weave the pattern adjacent to the pick-up using the appropriate sheds from *3*. 'Open pattern shed' means to depress the treadle in *3* (or *2b*) that weaves pattern as required in these areas.

Determine where you want to place the pick-up (in the border, corner, etc.). Graph your name(s) and date as in *1*: each (vertical) column represents four warp threads, two dark and two light; each (horizontal) row represents four weft picks, two dark and two light. Graph the letters and numbers so that a few rows of background (light) separate the letters and numbers (dark) from the coverlet pattern. Mark the first and last warp threads of the pick-up area with loops of a contrasting-color thread.

To weave a background row (no letters or numbers are picked up):

Dark weft: (1) open pattern shed; throw shuttle to the first contrasting-color thread; bring shuttle out of the shed to the surface. (2) Depress treadle 23 from *2a*; throw shuttle to the second contrasting-color thread; bring shuttle to surface. (3) Depress same treadle as in 1; weave to opposite selvedge.

Light weft: (4) depress second treadle for appropriate block (2, 6, 10, or 14 from *3*); weave to marker; bring shuttle to surface. (5) Depress treadle 20 (*2a*); pass shuttle to second marker; remove. (6) Depress same pattern treadle as in 4; weave to selvedge.

Repeat above steps: for dark weft with treadles 3, 7, 11, or 15 in pattern area, treadle 24 (*2a*) in pick-up area; for light weft with treadle 4, 8, 12, or 16 in pattern area and treadle 22 (*2a*) in pick-up area.

To weave the letters and numbers, for each row:

Dark weft: (1) open pattern shed; throw shuttle to marker; bring to surface. (2) Depress treadle 23 (*2a*); pass shuttle through short plain-weave background area to first letter or number; bring shuttle to surface. (3) Raise light threads (treadle 18, *2a*); pick up on a stick one pair of light warp threads for each blank square; leave pick-up stick in place. (4) Depress treadle 19 (*2a*); pull up on the pick-up stick to clear shed; carefully pass shuttle through area with letters or numbers. Bring shuttle to surface; leave pick-up stick in place. (5) Transfer all of the light picked-up threads from stick to the flexible knitting needle; leave needle in place and bring it close to the web. (6) Same as 2; weave to second marker; bring shuttle to surface. (7) Same as 1; weave to selvedge; leave knitting needle in place.

Light weft: (1) open pattern shed; throw shuttle to marker; bring to surface. (2) Depress treadle 20 (*2a*); pass shuttle through background area to first letter or number; bring to surface. (3) Put white threads from the knitting needle back on the pick-up stick. Remove needle. Raise all the dark threads (treadle 17, *2a*); pick up on a second stick all dark threads between the light threads on the first pick-up stick. Remove the first stick. (4) Depress treadle 20; pull up on the stick to clear shed; pass shuttle through area with letters or numbers; bring to surface. (5) Transfer all dark threads on the pick-up stick to the knitting needle and bring the needle close to the web. (6) Same as 2; weave to second marker; bring shuttle to surface. (7) Same as 1; weave to selvedge. Leave knitting needle in place.

Dark weft: repeat seven steps above but substitute treadle 24 for treadle 23 and treadle 21 for treadle 19 (see treadling sequence in *2a*).

Light weft: repeat as above but substitute treadle 22 for treadle 20. (Transfer pick-up from stick to needle to stick as above.)

You have now completed one graph paper row and four picks. Repeat these sequences to complete the pick-up design. Finish with an area of all background before returning to weaving the coverlet pattern alone.

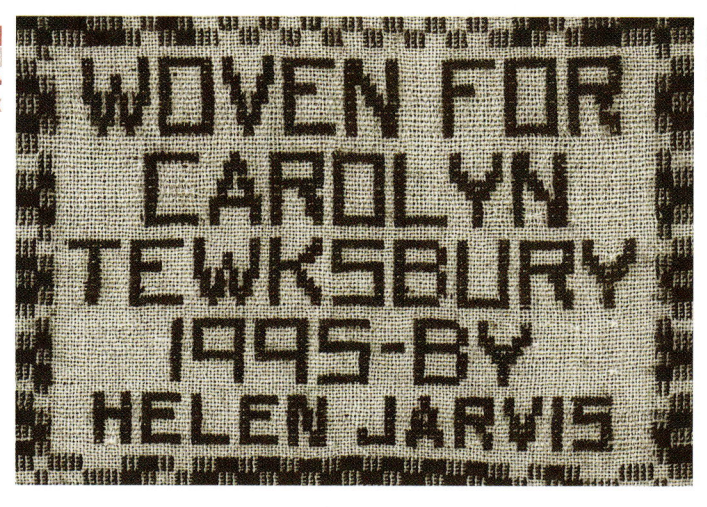

1. Graph for pick-up design

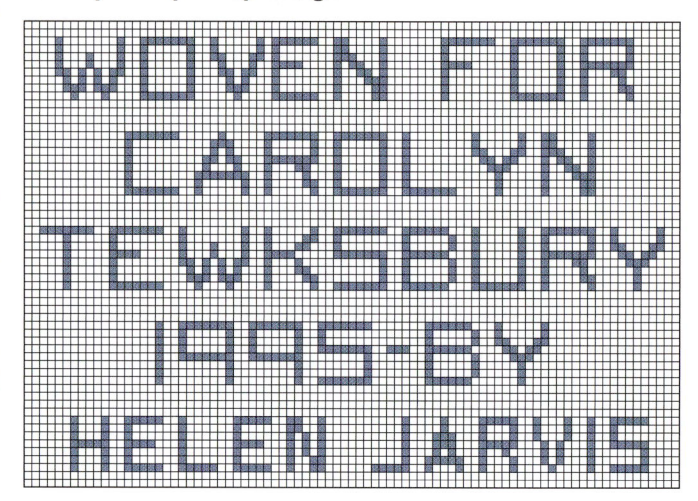

2. Pick-up and skeleton tie-ups; see full coverlet tie-up in 3

a. Full tie-up for pick-up

b. Skeleton tie-up for coverlet and pick-up

c. Skeleton tie-up for coverlet without pick-up

P = shed for pick-up
B = shed for background
I = shed for letters and numbers
● = dark weft
○ = light weft

P = treadle 17
P = treadle 18
I = treadle 19
I = treadle 20
B/I = treadle 21
B/I = treadle 22
B = treadle 23
B = treadle 24

Using skeleton tie-up *2b*, substitute treadles 1–4 for treadles 17–24 in tie-up *2a*.

3. Draft for 'King's Flower' coverlet

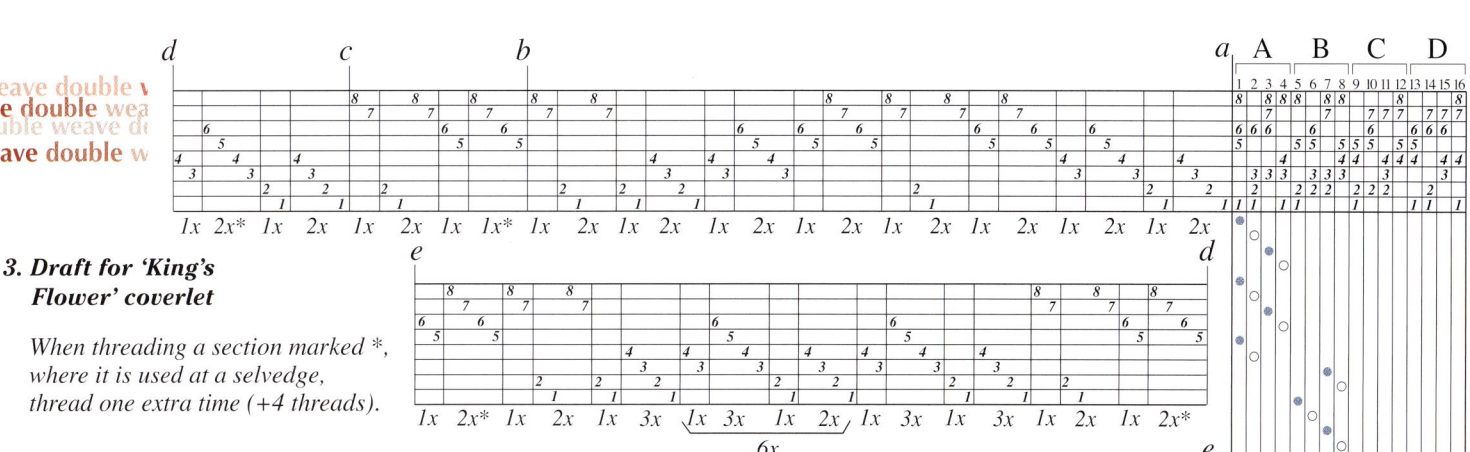

When threading a section marked *, where it is used at a selvedge, thread one extra time (+4 threads).

For side panels: thread b to c 1x (20 ends; note *); a to c 3x (288 ends); c to f 2x (1032 ends), c to d 1x (24 ends; note *). Total: 1364 ends.

For center panel: thread d to f 1x (500 ends; note *); c to f 1x (516 ends); c to e 1x (250 ends; note *). Total: 1266 ends.

'KING'S FLOWER' IN DOUBLE WEAVE

- **Equipment.** 8-shaft loom equipped with either *a)* a computer-aided dobby, *b)* 12 treadles for a skeleton tie-up that can produce the coverlet pattern and the picked-up names and date (see **2b**), or *c)* with 10 treadles for a skeleton tie-up that can produce the coverlet without the pick-up (see **2c**), 35" weaving width; 10-dent reed; 2 shuttles. (If you have 16 treadles, you can use the tie-up in **3** for the pattern without the signature.)
- **Materials.** 20/2 wool (5600 yds/lb, JaggerSpun), navy blue and natural, 3¼ lbs each (for a finished coverlet 89" wide x 108" long); 2 smooth pick-up sticks; 1 flexible, double-pointed, circular knitting needle.
- Wind a warp of 1364 ends (682 ends dark alternating 1/1 with 682 ends light), 12 yds long. This amount produces three panels, 112" long each plus 1–2 yds loom waste and sampling.
- Sley 4/dent in a 10-dent reed, 20 epi/layer; center for 34".
- Thread following the instructions for the side panels in **3**. After weaving the two side panels, cut them from the loom and rethread following the instructions for the center panel.
- Weave the blocks 'as-drawn-in' by substituting the four treadles for Block A (1-2-3-4) for the four warp threads in Block A (1-2-3-4), the four treadles in Block B (5-6-7-8) for the four warp threads in Block B (3-4-5-6), the four treadles in Block C (9-10-11-12) for the four warp threads in Block C (5-6-7-8), and the four treadles in Block D 13-14-15-16 for the four warp threads in Block D (7-8-1-2). The first 100 picks are shown in **3**. Adjust numbers of picks in a block to square the design if necessary, but when changing blocks if ending with the second treadle of one block, begin with the third treadle of the next.
- Follow the pick-up instructions to place names and date in either the beginning or the ending border—in a corner or in the center panel as desired. The directions given here are an adaptation of Jean Scorgie's excellent double-weave pick-up instructions; see the Bibliography. Wool can be sticky and pick-up sheds difficult to clear. If the yarns stick, try misting the pick-up area with water fairly frequently as you weave.
- For each panel, weave the first and last blocks for an extra ½" for hems. Weave the pattern repeat 9x. On the last repeat, weave the table (b–e); then weave 10 picks each in Blocks B, A, D, C.
- Remove the fabric from the loom, cut panels apart, turn raw ends under twice, and sew hems by hand. Wash panels in lukewarm water; lay flat to dry. Butt panels together, matching blocks. Sew panels together, catching matching weft loops at each edge. Press. Finished size is 89" x 108".

BIBLIOGRAPHY

Jarvis, Helen. *Weaving a Traditional Coverlet.* Loveland, Colorado: Interweave Press, 1989.

___. "Old and New: an Old Coverlet Pattern in a New Way." *Handwoven*, January/February 2000, p. 26.

Keasbey, Doramay. "Network Solutions: Overshot to Double Weave." *Best of Weaver's: Double Weave.* Sioux Falls, South Dakota: XRX, Inc., 2006, pp. 74–76.

Scorgie, Jean. "Easy Doubleweave Pick-up." *Handwoven*, January/February 1988, pp. 41–46.

Strickler, Carol. "Four Blocks on Eight Shafts: Overshot-Inspired Doubleweave." *Handwoven* May/June 1992, pp. 58–60.

van der Hoogt, Madelyn. *The Complete Book of Drafting.* Petaluma, California: Shuttle-Craft Books, 1993, pp. 98–99.

___. "'Colonial' Double Weave Table Runner." *Best of Weaver's: Double Weave.* Sioux Falls, South Dakota: XRX, Inc., 2006, pp. 64–67.

___. "Symmetrical Turning Blocks." *Best of Weaver's: Double Weave.* Sioux Falls, South Dakota: XRX, Inc., 2006, pp. 68–69.

Wilson, Sadye Tune and Doris Finch Kennedy. *Of Coverlets*, Nashville, Tennessee: Sadye Tune Wilson, 1983, p. 163.

network solutions: overshot to double weave

Doramay Keasbey

1. 4-block overshot

Using overshot designs for 4-block, 8-shaft double weave presents a world of very exciting design opportunities. Here's an easy way to get from overshot to double-weave drafts.

A balanced overshot threading draft appears in *1*. Keeping the following principles in mind, we can place this threading directly on a network suitable for double weave.

- In overshot, each block is threaded on two adjacent shafts. By allowing blocks to overlap by half their height, there are four sets of two adjacent shafts on four total shafts: 1-2, 2-3, 3-4, and 4-1. Even and odd threads alternate throughout.
- In double weave, each block is threaded on a set of four adjacent shafts. By allowing blocks to overlap by half their height, there are four sets of four adjacent shafts on eight total shafts: 1-2-3-4, 3-4-5-6, 5-6-7-8, and 7-8-1-2. Even and odd shafts alternate, and the first pair of threads in a unit always alternates with the second pair of threads in a unit both within and between blocks.

THE THREADING

Since double weave with plain weave in both layers requires 4-end units, the double-weave network is based on a 4-end straight initial as in *2*. Each end in the threading in *1* becomes two squares wide and two squares high on the network: a thread on shaft 1 in overshot (O) becomes 1-2 in double weave (D), shaft 2 (O) = shafts 3-4 (D), shaft 3 (O) = shafts 5-6 (D), and shaft 4 (O) = shafts 7-8 (D).

Each 2 x 2 square to be shaded must contain two marks. The first overshot thread on the right in *1* is on shaft 4, which becomes 7-8 on the double-weave network. Since the first pair of columns on the right in the network in *2* does not contain marks for 7-8, start with the next pair of columns. Thereafter the corresponding marks will be in the right position. When you are finished, rewrite the new threading as in *4*, p. 76. (Remember that in double weave, dark ends alternate with light ends; in this draft, dark is threaded on odd shafts; light on even shafts).

THE TIE-UP AND TREADLING

In the tie-up in *3*, treadles 1–4 weave dark on top in A, light on top in C, and halftones in B and D. Treadles 5–8 weave B dark, D light, A, C halftones; 9–12: C dark, A light, B, D halftones; 13–16: D dark, B light, A, C halftones. To convert an overshot treadling to double weave, each pattern treadle in overshot becomes four pattern treadles in double weave. Each pattern pick in overshot becomes two pattern picks in double weave, one dark and one light.

Draw a rectangle on the network treadling grid four squares wide and two squares high for each overshot pattern pick. For example, the first three pattern picks in the overshot treadling in *1* are in Block C (the weft floats over 3-4). In the double-weave treadling in *3*, the first rectangle is in the Block C section (treadles 9–12) and is three times two squares high. Compare the overshot treadling for the first motif with the corresponding treadling in *3*. Rewrite the full treadling as in *5a*, p. 76.

2. Overshot threading plotted on a double-weave network

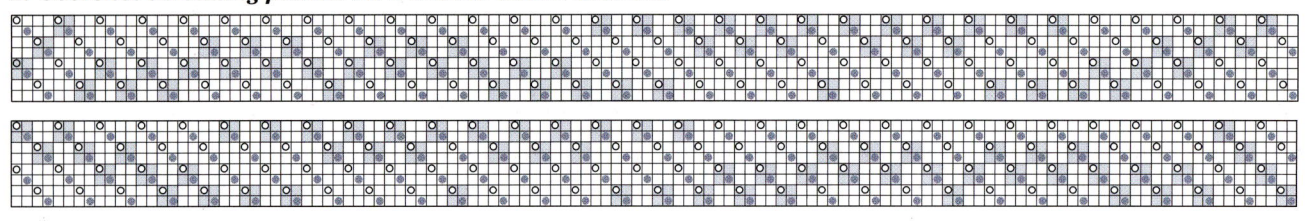

For more about network drafting and double weave, see Alice Schlein, pp. 86–99.

double weave

3. Treadling network

Use this easy method to translate overshot drafts to double-weave drafts. Weave table runners, pillow covers, upholstery, and other decorative household textiles in a multitude of available overshot designs!

TABLE RUNNER

Materials and directions are for a finished runner 16½" x 48".

- **Equipment.** 8-shaft loom, 19" weaving width; 8-dent reed; at least 10 treadles, 12–16 preferred (or table or dobby loom).
- **Materials.** Warp and weft: 8/2 unmercerized cotton (3360 yds/lb), rose (dark) and natural (light), 6 oz each color (or choose any two contrasting colors.
- Wind a warp 2½ yds long holding one dark/one light end together for a total of 586 warp ends (293 ends each color). Keep a finger between the strands to prevent twisting.
- Sley 4 ends/dent in an 8-dent reed, 32 epi; center for 18⅓".
- Thread as in *4* with dark ends on odd shafts and light ends on even shafts. Starting at the right, thread the border (*b*) 2x, then the main pattern (*a*) 2x, and finally the left border (*c*) 2x.
- Tie-up the treadles according to *5b*. If you have only 10 treadles and a jack loom, use the tie-up in *5c* and plan to use both feet as shown to produce the equivalent sheds. Note that sometimes you will need to step on two or even three treadles with one foot, so this method works best if the treadles are placed fairly close together.
- Weave following the treadling sequence in *5a*: 2x the beginning border; 5x the main repeat; 2x the ending border. After the first half inch, hemstitch the beginning of the runner in groups of four ends. When you finish the runner, hemstitch as at the beginning, and cut off the runner to leave approximately 3" fringe at each end. Ply the fringe by pairing hemstitched groups and secure each twisted pair with an overhand knot.
- Finish by washing in hot water and mild detergent, rinse well, spin out excess water, and steam press. ✂

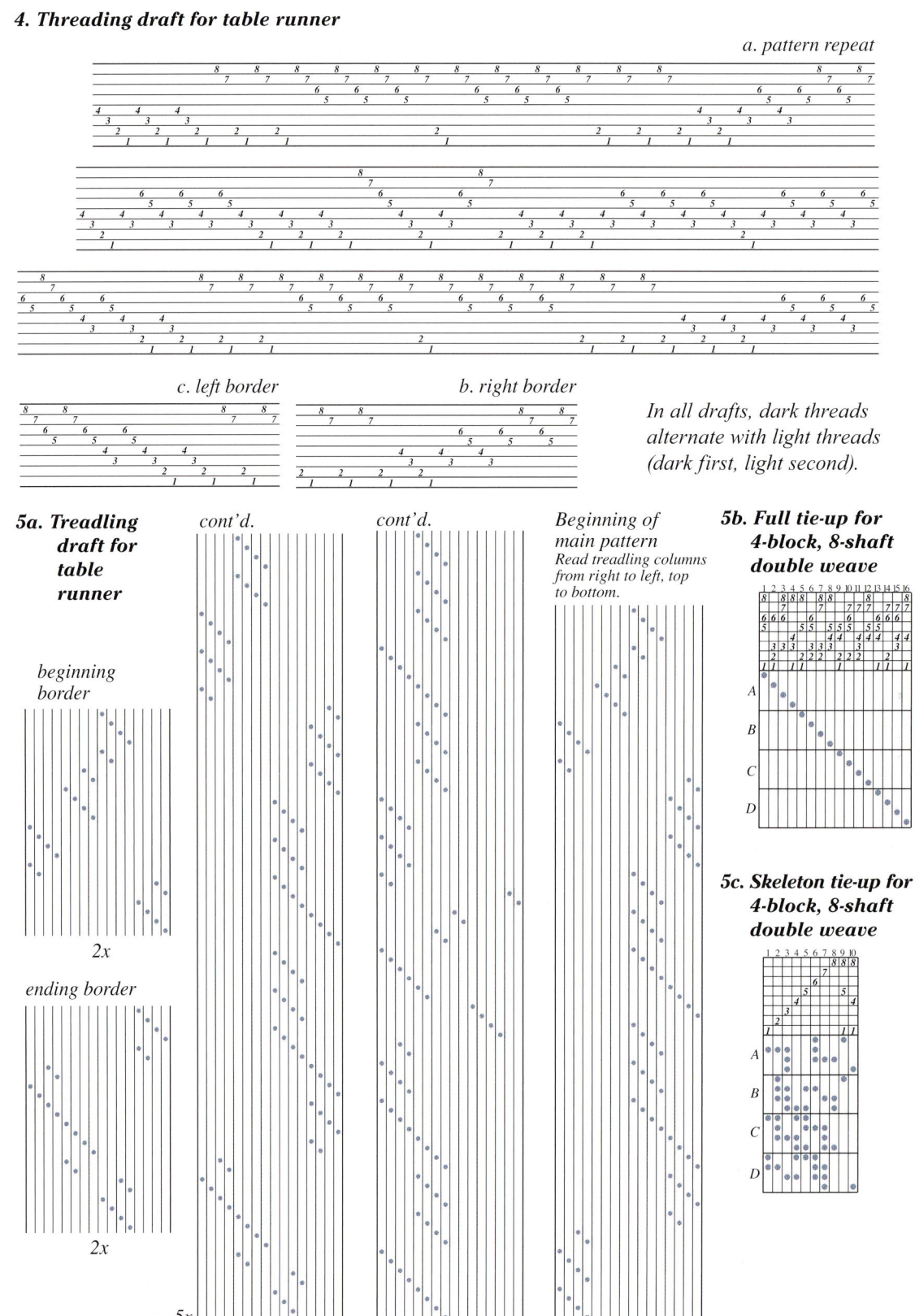

4. Threading draft for table runner

a. pattern repeat

c. left border *b. right border*

In all drafts, dark threads alternate with light threads (dark first, light second).

5a. Treadling draft for table runner

beginning border 2x

ending border 2x

cont'd. cont'd. *Beginning of main pattern* Read treadling columns from right to left, top to bottom.

5x

5b. Full tie-up for 4-block, 8-shaft double weave

5c. Skeleton tie-up for 4-block, 8-shaft double weave

playing with texture and design

grandma's game bags	78
sequins and silk: camisole and skirt	80
baffle weave: mixing layers on the loom	82
'double, double toil and trouble' runner	84
network drafting: double weave	86
double weave a la carte	92
raising eyelashes	95
eyelash vest	98
unconventional double-weave shawl	100
playing with double weave	103

grandma's game bags

Diane Ferguson

My Grandma loved chocolate and always had some to share. She was not an avid housekeeper. Her approach was that dishes could wait but freshly baked biscuits couldn't. She picked the dandelions in her yard only because she enjoyed eating them as she went along.

For fun, we played games. Mostly calm quiet games so that we didn't bother Great Grandma, who was always asleep in the back bedroom. Tick-tack-toe was a favorite with me, but I only won when I played with Grandma.

When I weave these fanciful bags, I like to remember my days with her. You can use your bags like she did to store candies or checkers or cards—or they can be a special place for any favorite treasure. The little bags will delight a visiting child, who'll quickly run to find the surprises you've put inside.

- Equipment. 8-shaft loom (seven shafts are used), 8" weaving width; 10-dent reed; 1 shuttle; 1 tapestry needle. If you don't have eight shafts, not to worry! You can weave a version of the bag on three shafts without pockets in plain weave, placing the navy, ribbon, and bouclé yarns as described below. The sequins can be positioned on the surface of the bag after the fabric is removed from the loom and then enclosed by darning them on with needle and thread to imitate the woven pockets.
- Materials. 8/2 pearl or unmercerized cotton (3360 yds/lb), navy, 6 oz; metallic bouclé novelty yarn (3000 yds/lb, Astra-Glow metallic, Halcyon), 20 yds; ⅛" wide glittery gold ribbon (80% metallic, 20% nylon; Create-a-Craft Ribbon, Wal-Mart, 7 yds/roll), 10 yds or 2 rolls (you can use any fancy gold ribbon); navy sewing thread; 4 glass beads with large holes (these are navy with gold accents); fabric glue or Fraycheck™; 18 sequins/bag: for one bag, ¾" round gold palettes, 9 left as circles and 9 cut into x's; for the other bag, 16 star sequins, 2 round ones cut like the 'man in the moon' (or choose other shapes in a similar size).
- Wind a warp 2 yds long (for two bags) of 146 ends in color order: 10 navy, 2 bouclé, 40 navy, 1 ribbon, 40 navy, 1 ribbon, 40 navy, 2 bouclé, 10 navy.
- Sley 2/dent in a 10-dent reed; except sley the ribbon 1/dent. Center for 7⅖" weaving width.

1. 7-shaft draft for game bags

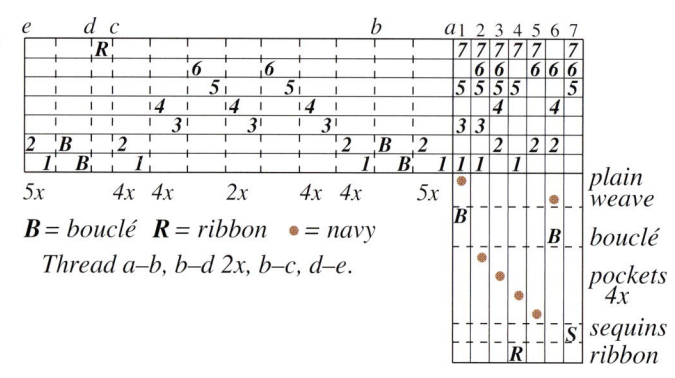

B = bouclé **R** = ribbon • = navy
Thread a–b, b–d 2x, b–c, d–e.

- Thread following the threading draft in *1* or *2*.
- Weave plain weave in scrap yarn. Weave three picks navy and hemstitch over these wefts including four warp threads in each stitch. Weave ¼" navy, leaving a ¼" space for the ribbon drawstring to be inserted later (insert ¼" cardboard strip to maintain space). Weave another ¼" of navy, then two picks of gold bouclé, ½" navy.

  Weave the pockets following the treadling order in *1* or *2*. Open the pockets using treadle 7 and stuff a sequin in each pocket (omit this step on three shafts). Weave ½" navy plain weave and then lay in a piece of ribbon cut about 12" long. Use treadle 4 in the 7-shaft draft and treadle 1 in the 4-shaft draft and handpick from the raised warp ends a number on each side of each ribbon that matches the number of weft threads that just covered the ribbon in the warp (this will be four or five warp threads on each side).

  Continue, placing navy, ribbon, and bouclé following the warp color order. After you finish one bag face, weave 1" navy plain weave to allow ½" navy bottom border on each face. Complete the back bag face in the same way as the front, leaving the space for the drawstring ribbon at the other end of the bag; hemstitch as for the first face. Leave 2" unwoven (or weave 2" with waste yarn) between the two bags.

- Remove the bags from the loom; remove the scrap yarn and spacers; trim fringes evenly at the top opening. It is easiest to place and sew on the sequins for the 3-shaft fabric before constructing the bags. Use several covering stitches in the warp direction and many in the weft direction to secure the sequins in place. Interlace the 'weft' threads with the 'warp' threads as though you were weaving a cloth.

2. 3-shaft draft for game bags

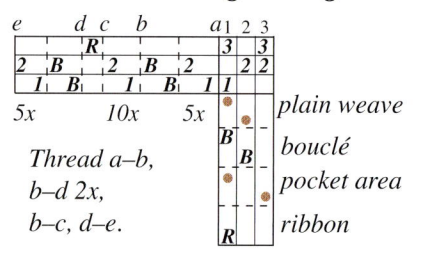

Thread a–b, b–d 2x, b–c, d–e.

B = bouclé
R = ribbon
• = navy

Butt the sides and handsew the side seams with a figure-eight stitch. Tie the ribbon-weft ends on each side, trim neatly, and touch the ends with a drop of glue or Fraycheck.

Thread a 25" length of ribbon in a tapestry needle and beginning at one side seam, make a very long running stitch all around the bag opening through the warp ends in the space left in the top border, and pull the ends even. Thread a bead on these ends and tie an overhand knot to secure the bead. Thread another 25" length of ribbon and beginning from the other side seam, stitch through the same spaces as the first ribbon, thread ends through a bead, and knot. Trim the ribbon ends and touch with a drop of glue or Fraycheck to keep the ribbon ends from raveling. Pulling the two ribbons closes the bag. To make the bag easy to open, loosely stitch a bead on each side of the bag (so they dangle ¼"–½" from the bag) fairly close to the ribbon. Pull on these beads to open the bag. To retain the crispness of freshly woven fabric, do not wash the bags. Fill with treasure! ✄

Double weave provides the pockets that enclose the sequins in these fanciful game bags. Eight shafts are required to form the pockets. On four shafts, you can still achieve the pockets by handsewing the sequins.

sequins and silk: camisole and skirt

Sigrid Piroch

A double weave without doubling the usual number of threads per inch? Yes! This version of 'pocket weave' is a double weave that is sett the same as for a single-layer fabric. The bottom layer weaves plain weave while the upper layer forms the lacy units that create the pockets.

Glittering sequins can be placed in the pockets before they are woven shut. In the fabric for the camisole, the pockets are offset and the design lines run vertically; in the camisole, they are horizontal. Because the original silk yarn used in this project is no longer available, 20/2 silk is recommended as a substitute. It is more softly spun, so a lining may be needed to give the garments more stability.

THE CAMISOLE

- Equipment. 10-shaft loom, 16" weaving width; 15-dent reed; 1 shuttle; an inkle loom and a small flat shuttle for trim and straps (if desired).
- Materials: Warp and weft: 20/2 spun silk (5000 yds/lb), white, 1055 yds; metallic yarn (the metallic used for this fabric is no longer available; substitute Patons Brilliant metallic knitting yarn, 1520 yds/lb or other metallic 1500–2000 yds/lb, white, 145 yds; 3/8" gold sequins (the kind with facets glitter the most) about 550 (1/sq in).
- Wind a warp of 422 ends white silk (S) and 58 ends gold metallic (M) 2½ yds long, 480 ends total: 8S [2S, 2M, 14S, 2M, 12S] 14x, 2S, 2M 20S.
- Sley 2/dent in a 15-dent reed (30 epi); each pair of metallic ends should be in the same dent.
- Following *1*, thread A 2x, B–E 14x, B–C 1x, F 2x.
- Weave 2" plain weave; weave pattern for 50"; end with 2" plain weave. Fill all pockets with sequins.
- Weave two inkle bands in warp-faced plain weave: 16 ends white silk, [4 ends gold metallic, 8 ends silk] 3x for a narrow band (⅞"), 5x for a wide band (1⅜"); end with 16 ends silk. Weave the wide band for 30", the narrow band for 42" with white silk.
- Finish by serging raw edges. Wash in very warm water without rubbing or squeezing. When almost dry, iron on low heat with a press cloth. Finished fabric is 15¼" x 45". Shrinkage for bands is about 4" per woven yard. Cut the narrow band in half for two straps; leave the wide band in one piece.
- Cut and sew following Simplicity pattern #5352 or similar, placing pattern pieces so the warp is horizontal. (Allow 10% shrinkage to plan fabric for a different pattern.) Leave enough side seam allowance for flat felled seams to turn toward the back. Across the top of front piece, sew the wide band over ⅛" of one selvedge (your worst one!) and treat as one piece of fabric for pattern; plan the other selvedge for the lower edge of front and back. After sewing side seams, try on camisole to check length and placement of straps.

THE SKIRT

- Equipment. 6-shaft loom, 24" weaving width; 15-dent reed; 1 shuttle.
- Materials: Warp and weft: 20/2 spun silk (5000 yds/lb), red, 4420 yds; metallic yarn (the metallic used for the skirt fabric is also no longer available; substitute Patons Brilliant metallic knitting yarn, 1520 yds/lb or other metallic yarn at 1500–2000 yds/lb), red, 520 yds; ⅜" gold sequins, about 1800; 2 red buttons; 2 round red Velcro tabs.
- Wind a warp of 626 ends red silk (S) and 86 ends red metallic (M) 4 yds long, 712 ends total: 12S [2S, 2M, 12S] 43x, 12S.
- Sley 2/dent in a 15-dent reed, 30 epi, centered for 23¾". Each pair of metallic ends should be sleyed in the same dent.
- Following *2*, thread A 3x, B–C 43x, A 3x.
- Weave 2" plain weave, weave pattern for 110", and end with 2" plain weave. Begin and end pattern section with six pattern rows in which sequins fill all the pockets for the skirt's borders. For the rest of the yardage, fill the pockets alternately.
- Finish fabric as for camisole.
- Cut, assemble, and sew for a 'one size fits all' skirt (up to 45" hips, waist adjusts from very small to 32"): Fold fabric length in half for front and back panels. Calculate finished length and trim top leaving 2" for turning at waist. Hem each plain-weave end. Sew panels together at sides overlapping 12 edge threads, leaving open 7" at bottom for side pleats and 7½" at top for waist overlap (5½" after waist is sewn down). Add a narrow 1" dart at each hip in front tapering down for 3½" and two ½" by 2½" darts on each side of back (or adjust to fit). Turn under and sew down 2" at waist. Try on skirt and overlap front over back waistband, mark, and sew a button and buttonhole at corners. (A Velcro tab will anchor corner of back waistband under front waistband.) Dry clean when necessary as sequins are not washfast. ✂

1. 10-shaft draft for camisole

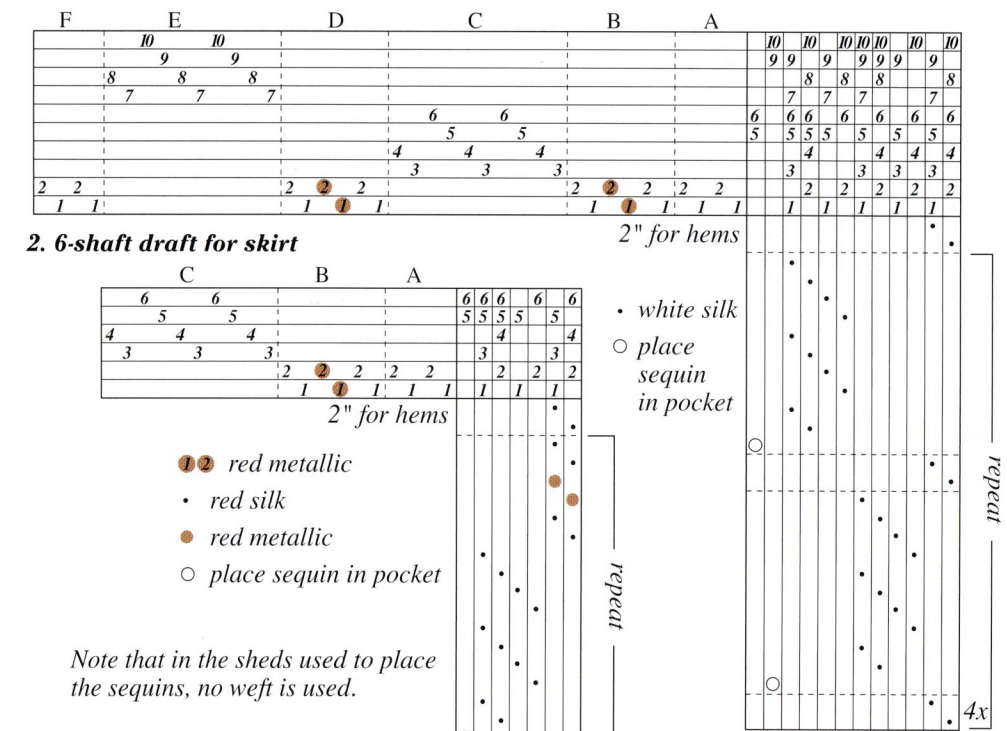

2. 6-shaft draft for skirt

- white silk
- ○ place sequin in pocket
- ●② red metallic
- · red silk
- ● red metallic
- ○ place sequin in pocket

Note that in the sheds used to place the sequins, no weft is used.

Double-woven layers allow the possibility of weaving pockets. For this camisole and skirt, hundreds of tiny pockets enclose sequins in silk. Placing the sequins is not quick, but the results are stunning!

baffle weave: mixing layers on the loom

Alice Schlein

An interesting item in a mail-order catalog caught my eye—a lofty multi-layered down comforter in which staggered baffles prevented 'cold spots' from forming along the stitching lines.

To visualize the cold spots, imagine a comforter in which two cloth layers are joined by parallel stitching lines. The channels between stitching lines are filled with down, but thin places devoid of down occur at the stitching points. If, however, three layers of cloth are used, and the bottom and middle layers are joined by parallel stitching lines and the middle and top layers are joined by offset parallel stitching lines, when down is inserted in all the channels the cold spots of the lower channels do not coincide with the cold spots of the middle and upper channels; see *2*, p. 83.

WOVEN BAFFLES

Staggered baffles can be produced on the loom with triple weave. The layers can be interchanged instead of stitched, as shown in *3*. If different colors or color orders are threaded in each layer, a variety of color effects can be produced.

Six shafts are required for three layers of plain weave: layer A = shafts 1 and 4; layer B = 2 and 5; layer C = 3 and 6. There are six possible ways to weave these three layers, all of them producing an upper and lower stuffing position: ACB (layer A on the top, C in the middle, and B on the bottom), ABC, BAC, BCA, CBA, or CAB. Notice in *3* that when layer A is on top, B and C can change position midway in the channel (the warp is horizontal in *3*; the stuffing is in the weft direction). No 'cold spot' occurs in our woven 'comforter' because the stuffing beneath layer A is continuous across the two lower channels. Similarly, when layer B is on top, A and C can change position midway; when C is on top, B and A can change position.

Materials and setts

Setts for three layers are three times that of one layer, so choose smooth fibers. Polyester quilt batting works well for stuffing; note that the first and last channels require less stuffing than the rest; see the left and right channels in *3*.

Uses for baffle weave

Because of its superior insulating qualities, baffle weave is suitable for hot pads and table mats, bed coverings, floor mats and small rugs, and winter vests. With three distinct layers, opportunities for color-play in warp and weft are seemingly endless.

BAFFLE BAG

This bag begins and ends with a 1" section of two layers woven as a tube (ends on shafts 1-2 weave as one end in the top layer with shaft 5, 3-4 in the bottom layer with 6). The 1" woven tubes at the beginning and end of the bag enable the raw ends of the warp to be tucked inside the tubes and handstitched shut after the fabric is cut from the loom. Add a sturdy inkle or cardwoven band for side panels and handle all in one, a bit of handstitching at the side edges, and —voilà!—a bag to baffle your weaving friends.

- Equipment. 6-shaft loom (10 treadles), 7" weaving width; 15-dent reed; 1 shuttle.
- Materials. Warp: 5/2 pearl cotton (2100 yds/lb), black and white. Weft: 5/2 pearl cotton, white. Total amounts: about ½ lb each color to allow for bag, take-up, some sampling, loom waste, and enough extra for band. Small amount of polyester quilt batting cut into strips: 2 strips 6" x ⅜" (skinny strips) and 37 strips 6" x ¾" (fat strips); piece of black grosgrain ribbon 1½" x ½ yd.
- Wind a warp of 540 ends (225 total black, 315 total white) 2 yds long, repeating the following 12-end color order (use a warping paddle to wind all 12 ends together if available): BBBWBWBWWWWW (this produces BWBW stripes in layer A, BBWW stripes in layer B, and BWWW stripes in layer C).
- Spread warp to 6.4" in raddle so that first thread on right is black; beam.
- Thread according to the draft in *1*.
- Sley 3/dent in a 15-dent reed, 45 epi.
- Weave a few rows with scrap yarn for header (treadles 7, 8, 9; repeat). Weave tube for hem with white for 1" (see treadling for tube in *1*). Weave CBA 3x, then depress treadles 8 and 9 and insert a skinny stuffing strip. (In each 3-layer section, the first letter indicates the layer weaving on top, the second letter the middle layer, and the third letter the bottom layer.) Weave section CAB 3x, depress treadle 9 and insert a fat strip. Then weave all six sections of the treadling sequence ACB through CAB 6x (insert fat strips for all stuffing picks; for the last CAB, insert a skinny strip). Weave second tubular hem for 1". End with a few inches of waste yarn using treadles 7, 8, 9 as needed to seal fabric.
- Cut the fabric from the loom, carefully cut away waste sections, and tuck raw ends to inside of tubes for ½". Carefully handstitch the ends to

1. Draft for baffle bag

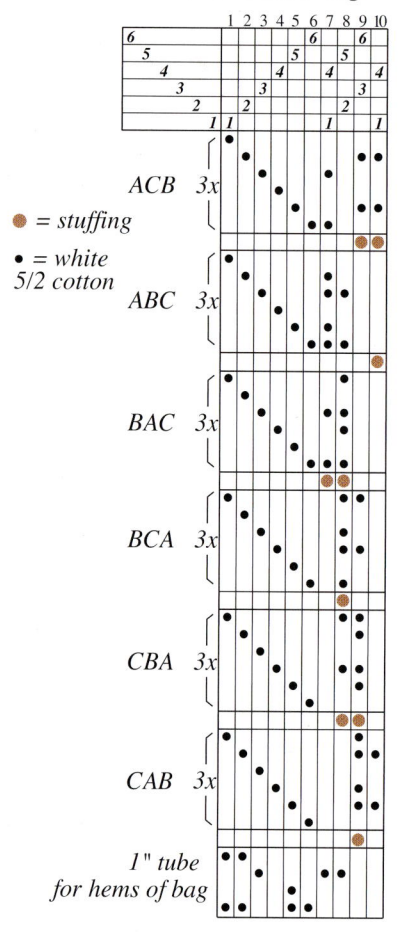

ACB 3x

● = stuffing
• = white 5/2 cotton

ABC 3x

BAC 3x

BCA 3x

CBA 3x

CAB 3x

1" tube for hems of bag

Treadles 7 and 10 are the same so that treadling can be accomplished with two feet, the right foot occasionally depressing two treadles at once.

close them using small overcast stitches.
- Weave an inkle or cardwoven band with remaining black and white pearl cotton 1⅜" wide x 1 yd long.
- Fold bag into an envelope shape, fit band to sides for handle and gussets (with raw ends of band tucked inside bag). Invisibly handstitch selvedges of band to selvedges of bag, leaving flap hanging free. Turn bag inside out and handstitch grosgrain ribbon to sides and bottom of bag, covering raw ends of band and tucking under raw ends of ribbon. Turn bag right side out. Finished size is 6" x 5" x 1¾" plus handle.

Experiment with other color orders for interesting color-and-weave effects, or thread each layer in a different color—and try something bigger—like a handwoven comforter! ✂

2. Down comforter

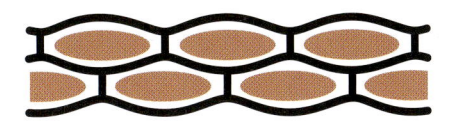

Cross section shows staggered baffles.

3. Baffle weave

Cross section of woven baffle cloth: cloth is cut in the warp direction to show exchange of layers and stuffing weft.

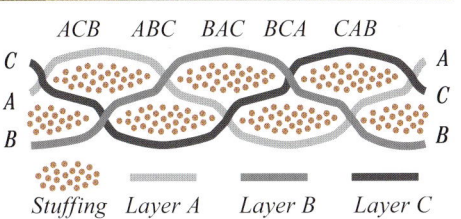

ACB   ABC   BAC   BCA   CAB

Stuffing   Layer A   Layer B   Layer C

Weave three layers of cloth stitched together to form channels for stuffing. Stitching points can be offset so that all areas of the cloth are stuffed. When you get the idea, try a colorful handwoven comforter!

'double, double toil and trouble' runner

Barbara Walker

A longtime wish list led to the draft and the overall design for this double-weave runner. An emerald green supplementary warp floats on the surface to highlight the smooth texture and clear colors of two double-weave blocks while it also mimics their checkerboard design.

Both sides of the runner look the same. When the supplementary warp is not floating on the surface it hides between the layers. You may have to add a 12-shaft loom to the top of your weaving wish list to make this runner!

Design elements can meander in the mind for day, a week, a month, and even longer before they coalesce into an idea that is ready for the loom. This runner began with a design wish list that developed over time: two alternating blocks of solid colors patterned by a 2-block supplementary warp that mimics the checkerboard design of the solid-color blocks but only appears in one of them. It takes double weave, a lot of drafting, and a 12-shaft loom to make these wishes come true!

THE STRUCTURE

Eight shafts are required for two independent blocks of double weave: Block A = 1-2-3-4; Block B = 5-6-7-8. For solid-color blocks, two colors alternate in both warp and weft, one color for each layer. For this runner, dark ends (blue) are threaded on odd shafts, light ends (green) on even shafts.

Only two shafts are needed to weave two blocks with a supplementary warp that patterns a single-layer cloth, but for the pattern floats to appear in one double-weave block at a different time from its appearance in the other, the supplementary warp for each double-weave block requires a separate pair of shafts (9-10 for one and 11-12 for the other).

The drafting challenge for this runner is in determining how to manipulate the supplementary warp to produce pattern when it is desired to show on the surface and yet hide between the layers of double weave when it is not desired to show.

In this runner, the dark block is unpatterned on both surfaces, while the light block shows supplementary-warp pattern on both surfaces. Six treadling sequences are required:

1. Draft for runner

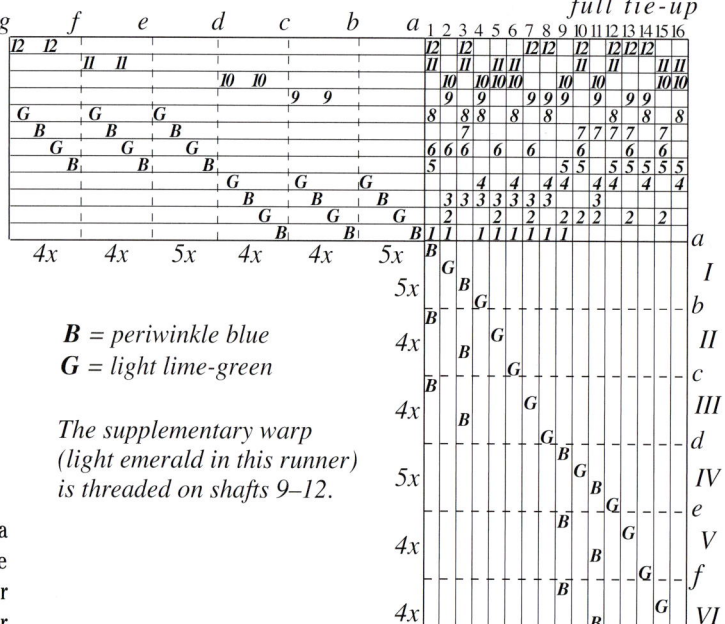

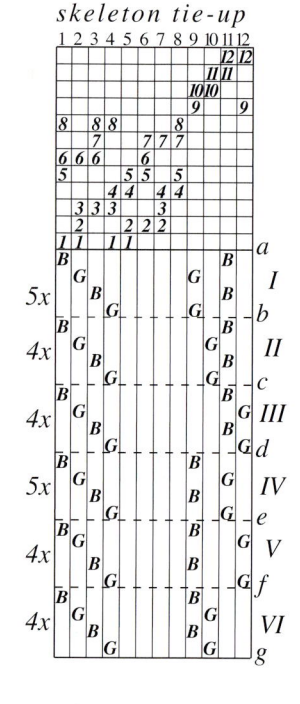

B = periwinkle blue
G = light lime-green

The supplementary warp (light emerald in this runner) is threaded on shafts 9–12.

I. A dark, B light, no supplementary-warp patterning appears
II. A dark, B light, supplementary-warp shaft 11 on top, 9 on bottom
III. A dark, B light, 12 on top, 10 on bottom
IV. B dark, A light, no supplementary-warp patterning appears
V. B dark, A light, 9 on top, 11 on bottom
VI. B dark, A light, 10 on top, 12 on bottom.

The shafts carrying the supplementary warp must be raised for bottom-layer sheds and lowered for top-layer sheds when the floats are hiding between the layers.

- Equipment. 12-shaft loom with 2 warp beams if available, 15" weaving width; 10-dent reed; 2 shuttles.
- Materials. Double-weave warp and weft: 20/2 pearl cotton (8400 yds/lb, Halcyon), periwinkle blue, 2¼ oz; light lime green, 2¼ oz. Pattern warp: 20/2 pearl cotton, light emerald, 1 oz. For different colors from the ones used in this runner, choose two contrasting colors (i.e., dark vs light, warm vs cool) for the double-weave blocks and a third color (a darker or lighter hue in one of the double-weave colors—or a completely contrasting hue) for the supplementary warp.
- Wind a double-weave warp of 600 ends alternating 1 blue/1 green (hold one end blue, one end green together as you wind, keeping them separate with a finger to prevent twisting) 2½ yds long. Wind a separate supplementary-pattern warp of 200 emerald ends, 2½ yds long.
- Spread both warps in a raddle centered for 10"; beam the two warps separately under firm tension. (If you do not have two warp beams, beam the double-weave warp and suspend the supplementary warp in four or more chains from the back beam and weight the chains after both warps are threaded and tied onto the front apron rod.)
- Thread following the draft in *1*: ABABA. Block A: a–b 1x, b–d 2x, b–c 1x, a–b 1x. Block B: d–e 1x, e–g 2x, e–f 1x, d–e 1x.
- Sley 6/dent in a 10-dent reed where ground warp is threaded, 9/dent where ground and pattern warps are threaded, 60 epi ground warp (30 epi/layer), 30 epi pattern warp; center for 10".
- Weave following the treadling in *1* a–b 1x, b–d 2x, b–c 1x, a–b 1x; d–e 1x, e–g 2x, e–f 1x, d–e 1x for desired length (10x for app 40"); end with a–b 1x, b–d 2x, b–c 1x, a–b 1x.
- Finish by removing the runner from the loom; prepare a twisted fringe. Handwash in warm water, Ivory liquid. Lay flat to dry. Press.

'Double, double' (a little) 'toil and' (a little) 'trouble . . .' I wonder if Shakespeare was a weaver in his spare time! ✂

This runner combines two structural elements: double weave and supplementary-warp patterning. Use the 12-shaft draft for a runner in three colors (or more!) that coordinate with your household decor.

network drafting: double weave

Alice Schlein

1. 'Piedmont' pattern line: two repeats

2. Developing a double-weave threading draft

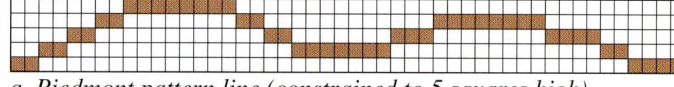

a. Piedmont pattern line (constrained to 5 squares high)

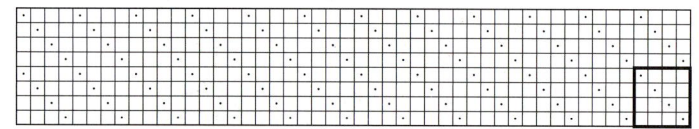

b. Network for 8-shaft threading; dark box = initial

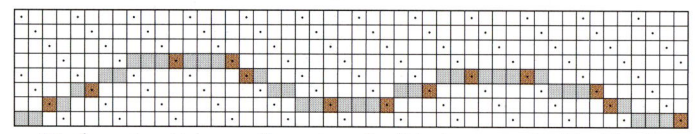

c. Piedmont pattern on the network; 'hits' are marked in black

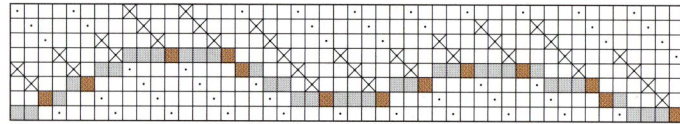

d. Network squares above gray squares in each column are marked 'x'; these and the hits become the threading

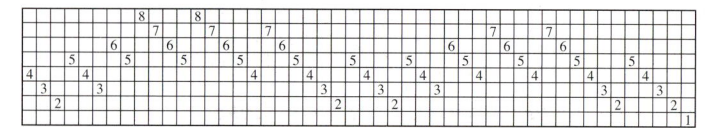

e. Piedmont threading draft; odd ends light, even ends dark

If you are new to network drafting, spend some time reading about network-drafting principles and techniques (see the Bibliography below). You'll appreciate the way networking can transcend the limitations usually imposed by the limited number of shafts on the loom, and you'll love its capacity to override the familiar 'blocky' look of block weaves. In this article we'll apply our networking skills to double weave to find new design opportunities as well as new challenges.

We'll even use an 8-shaft loom for our examples just to prove that network drafting is not the sole property of weavers with sixteen shafts or more! Not just any 8-shaft loom will do, however. A conventional treadle loom does not have enough treadles to manage the many combinations of shafts that must be raised to produce the complex designs. It is necessary to use either a table loom, on which any combination of shafts can be raised with hand levers, or a dobby loom. If you recently purchased an 8-shaft dobby loom and you are wondering what to do with it, networking is for you!

THE THREADING DRAFT

First let's construct a double-weave threading draft. We begin with a pattern line using the same method as with twills. The pattern line used for these double-weave examples is called 'Piedmont,' as it suggests the rolling Appalachian foothills surrounding my South Carolina home. For an 8-shaft loom the pattern line is drawn on five rows as prescribed by basic network-drafting principles. The draft in *1* shows a 'profile drawdown' using the Piedmont pattern line as both the profile threading and the profile treadling.

Next, the pattern line is plotted on a threading grid made up of multiple 'initials.' The 4-shaft initial for double weave is the same as the one used for drafting twills (1-2-3-4), except that the warp ends are alternately light and dark in double weave. The initial is repeated to fill a grid as long as the pattern line and eight rows high (to correspond with the number of shafts on the loom). The Piedmont threading repeat is 48 columns (warp ends) long. Follow the steps in *2* to see how the actual threading draft is derived.

TERMS TO KNOW

initial: a threading group (much like a threading unit but more freely formed) that is used to build a threading grid (network) of more than one initial.
network: a base grid containing initials repeated horizontally and vertically on which the actual threading is plotted.
pattern line: a continuous line drawn on a threading grid that becomes the basis for a pattern drawdown.

BIBLIOGRAPHY

Schlein, Alice. *Network Drafting: An Introduction.* Greenville, South Carolina: Bridgewater Press, 1994.

___. "Network Drafting: More for Less," pp. 62–65; "Network Drafting: Part II," pp. 66–70; "The Pattern Line: Turtles, Snails, and Fleas," pp. 74–77. *Best of Weaver's: Twill Thrills*, Madelyn van der Hoogt, ed. Sioux Falls, South Dakota: XRX, Inc., 2004.

double weave double *weave* double weave double *weave* **double** weave double *weave* double **weave** double weave double *weave* dou
weave double *weave* double *weave* double **weave** double *weave* double *weave* double **weave** double *weave* double **weave** double
weave double *weave* double *weave* dou **double** *weave* double *weave* double *weave* double **weave** double *weave* double **weave** dou

Alice Schlein Alice Schlein Alice Schlein Alice Schlein Alice Schlein Alice Schlein Alice Schle

16-shaft fabric woven from the 'Marrow Bones' pattern line

Alice Schlein's pullover is developed from her 'Cello' pattern line. Network-drafting techniques make possible the rounded and indistinct edges that produce softer, more subtle design shapes.

DOUBLE WEAVE 87

3. Double-weave templates

warp: light ends on odd shafts, dark ends on even shafts
weft: light ends on odd picks, dark ends on even picks

TEMPLATE	APPEARANCE OF CLOTH	
	FACE	REVERSE
1.	dark	light
2.	light	dark
3.	halftone I (dark warp, light weft)	halftone II (light warp, dark weft)
4.	halftone II (light warp, dark weft)	halftone I (dark warp, light weft)
5.	vertical stripe	horizontal stripe
6.	horizontal stripe	vertical stripe

a. Fabric woven in the six possible double-weave effects

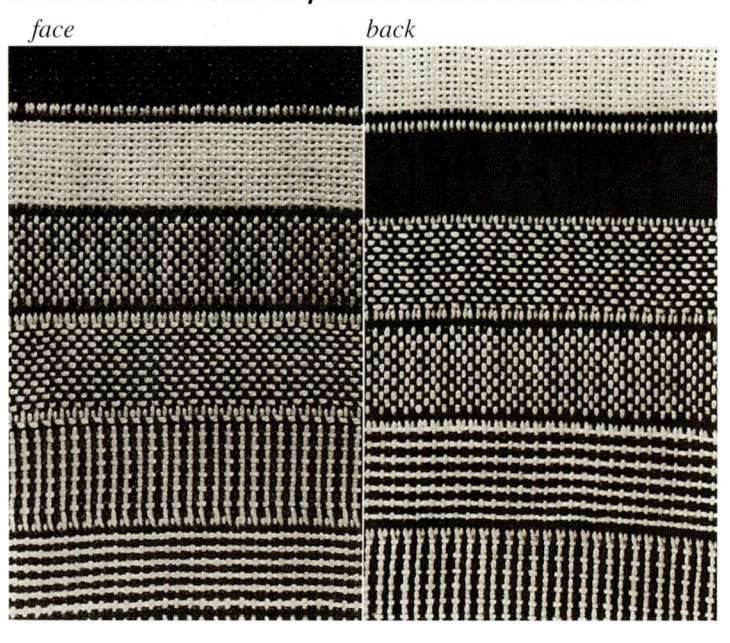

DOUBLE WEAVE LIFTING PLAN MODULES

In order to weave networked threading drafts, row-by-row lifting plans like those used for pegging dobby bars must be developed. The lifting sequences for double weave can be constructed by a 'cut-and-paste' method described in the resources given in the Bibliography.

There are six possible double-weave effects (these occur on one side of the cloth with the reverse on the other side): dark, light, two types of halftones, vertical stripes, and horizontal stripes; see **Photo a**. The dobby lifting plan in *3* (extended to sixteen shafts) shows how each set of four shafts is lifted to create the six effects.

The entire cloth woven with these modules will look the same no matter what pattern line is used or how many shafts are available. Designs that combine the effects within a cloth happen only when more than one effect is used in the lifting plan.

Study the face and reverse of each effect in **Photo a**. Note as well the subtle difference between halftones I and II. It may seem redundant to have more than one halftone effect. But when one is working with many dark and light colors in the warp and weft, instead of a single dark and a single light as in this example, it is useful to have both these options in one's arsenal.

CUT-AND-PASTE LIFTING PLANS

Any 4-pick module in *3* can be repeated as many times as desired to create a peg-plan template of the desired length. If you are using fewer than 16 shafts, trim off the appropriate columns on the right sides of the modules. Templates for all dark and all light effects have been constructed for eight shafts and 48 picks in *4*. Templates for each of the other effects can be constructed in the same way.

The six basic peg-plan templates for these different effects are all interchangeable. Portions of any of them can be pasted onto any of the others as long as the pick numbers are the same (multiples of four) and the shaft columns are kept in line. Remember that light-colored warp ends are on odd-numbered shafts and dark-colored warp ends on even shafts for these fabrics, and that odd-numbered weft picks are light, and even-numbered picks dark (reversing these orders will reverse the effects). If this light-dark convention is observed throughout, then portions of the templates can be interchanged and always give the desired face effect in the desired area.

SOME 8-SHAFT EXAMPLES

The steps for two peg-plan developments for weaving the Piedmont threading from *2* are shown in *5* and *6*. The same development techniques are used for drafts on more shafts. In *5*, the Piedmont pattern line is flipped end to end and rotated 90 degrees counterclockwise. It is then cut out and used as a pattern to trace onto a dark dobby template. The dark template is cut out on the traced lines and then pasted onto a light template (rows and columns are lined up carefully), and the resulting collage is the dobby peg plan (or table loom shaft-lifting plan) for the fabric in **Photo b**.

4. Dark and light templates for eight shafts expanded to 48 picks

5. Developing a peg plan by 'cut-and-paste' method

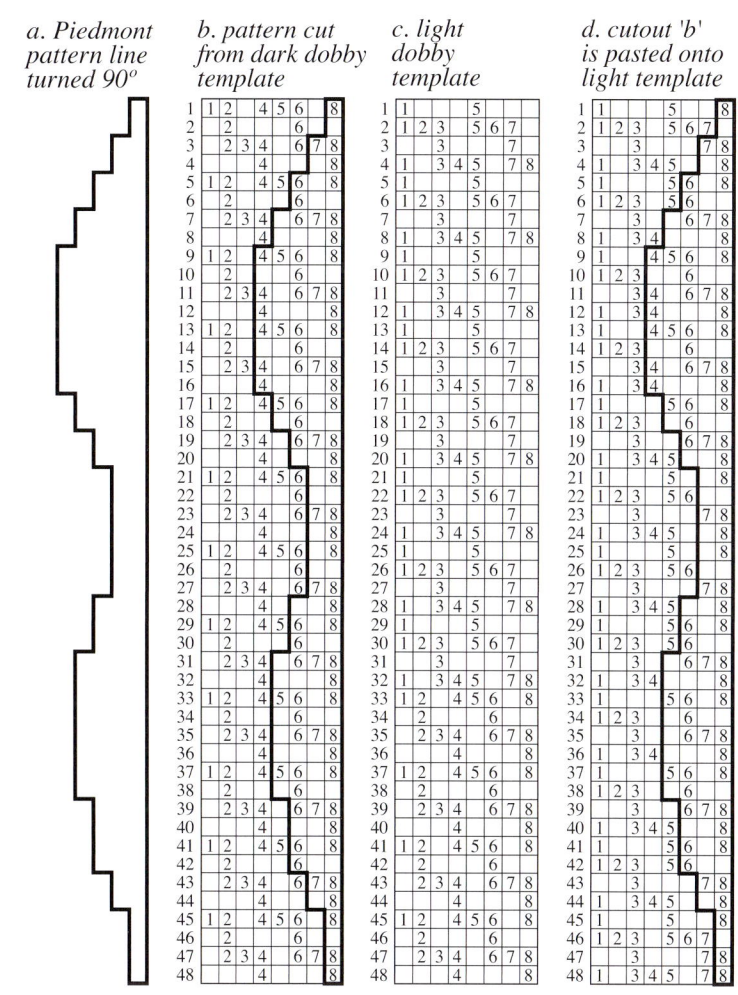

a. Piedmont pattern line turned 90°

b. pattern cut from dark dobby template

c. light dobby template

d. cutout 'b' is pasted onto light template

b. 8-shaft networked double weave using the Piedmont pattern line

Note: The double-weave drawdown disadvantage

An aggravating fact of life with networked double weave (or any form of double weave) is that drawdowns don't give a good idea of the appearance of the cloth (unless you have a very sophisticated computer drawdown program that can show each layer separately). A profile drawdown using the pattern line is better than nothing (the Piedmont line is used for the drawdown in *1*, p. 86), but when you are constructing peg plans, you really have to weave the cloth in order to see its actual appearance. As an example, compare the drawdown in *1* with the woven fabric in *Photo b* (at left)!

DOUBLE WEAVE
89

6. The ribbon style of peg-plan development

Piedmont pattern line expanded to a 4-square ribbon | *ribbon traced onto dark peg plan* | *light peg plan* | *dark cut out and pasted onto light*

7. The Cello pattern line

The Cello pattern line is 13 squares high for a 16-shaft double-weave threading repeat of 88 ends. The pattern line is used as a template for cutting and pasting a dark peg plan onto a light peg plan. (Each square is actually 8 squares wide by 8 squares high. The drawing has been simplified for clarity.) If you have a 16-shaft dobby loom, you'll find it fun to draw interesting shapes (from nature, architecture, interior design, printed fabrics—they can come from almost anywhere!). Translate the line into a double-weave threading and then use cut-and-paste to create a peg plan.

c. Fabric woven from Cello pattern line

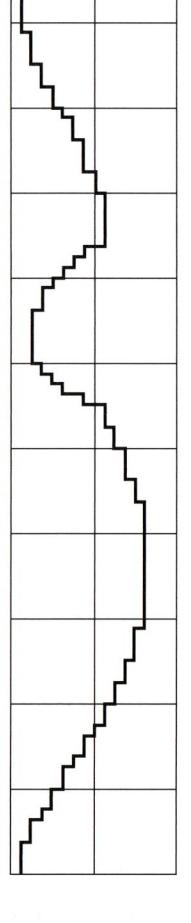

d. Fabric woven from Piedmont pattern line

Another approach is shown in **6**. The Piedmont pattern line is expanded to a 'ribbon' four squares wide (wider ribbons can be used if more shafts are available) and then traced onto the dark template. The dark ribbon is cut out and pasted onto the light template, which results in the peg plan that produces the fabric in *Photo d*.

The dark and light templates are chosen for these examples, but any two of the templates in **3** can be used: light and halftone, dark and horizontal stripes, halftone and vertical stripes, etc. Each one will produce a different effect—all a far cry from the usual 8-shaft block double weave checkerboard look.

SOME 16-SHAFT EXAMPLES

At a string quartet recital one evening, I sketched the 'Cello' pattern line as a starting point for designing the fabric for a pullover (p. 87); see **7** and *Photo c* (above right). The pattern line is used to derive a 16-shaft double-weave threading that repeats on 88 ends. The same pattern line is used to cut a section from a dark template to paste onto a light template for an 88-row dobby peg plan.

It is possible to combine *more* than two templates in one cloth. The peg plan for the 16-shaft 'Marrow Bones' fabric (p. 87), uses dark 'bones' and striped 'marrow' pasted onto a light background. The beginning of this threading draft is shown in **8**. The development of the first 32 rows of the peg plan is detailed in **9** and **10**. More than two templates should not be combined to create 8-shaft drafts, however, since they usually become too muddy. Multiple-weave combinations work best using sixteen or more shafts.

UNIQUE EFFECTS OF NETWORKED DOUBLE WEAVE

The boundary areas where one double-weave effect bleeds into another sometimes appear to contain mistakes, or overlong floats. On inspection of the fabric, however, one can see that adequate interlacement has taken place (dark warp threads always weave plain weave with dark weft threads, light warp threads with light weft threads). A 'color-and-weave' phenomenon gives the appearance of long floats. I have come to like this effect; it suggests the streakiness of ikat weaving. Some people actually assume that my double weaves are ikat until they see the structure up close.

If you are a weaver who likes sharp demarcations between parts of a pattern, you may feel uncomfortable with networked double weave. But if you are willing to put aside preconceived notions of how a weave should look, you may decide that networking is a useful addition to your repertoire. ✂

8. First 56 ends of the Marrow Bones threading draft
Reading from right to left, odd-numbered ends are light, even-numbered ends are dark. The fifth end on shaft 1 is not a mistake.

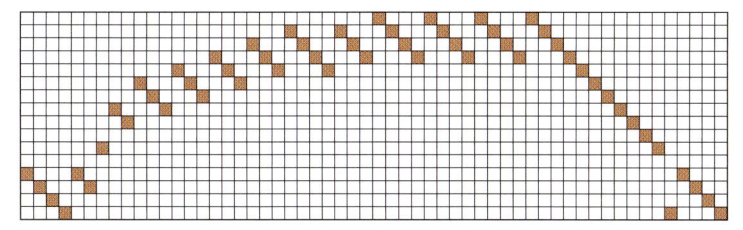

9. Development of first 32 bars of Marrow Bones peg plan
To design a peg plan with three effects (dark face, light face, and vertical stripes), cut out a template along ribbon lines to form sections A, B, and C.

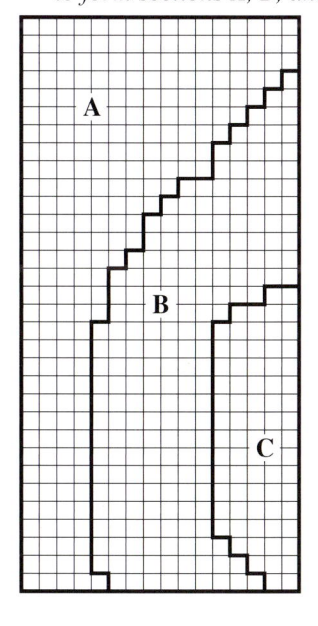

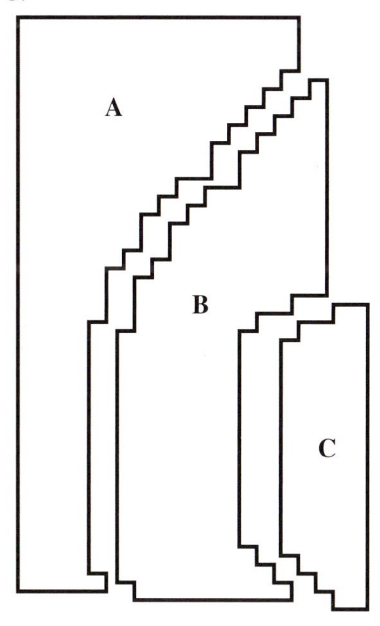

10. Marrow Bones templates applied
Trace A onto the dark peg plan; trace B onto the light peg plan; trace C onto the peg plan for vertical stripes. Then cut and paste them together.

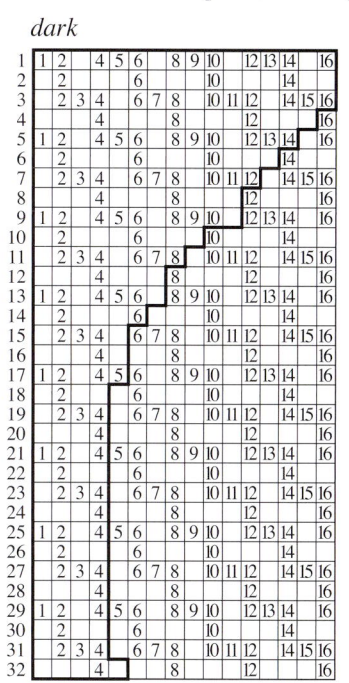

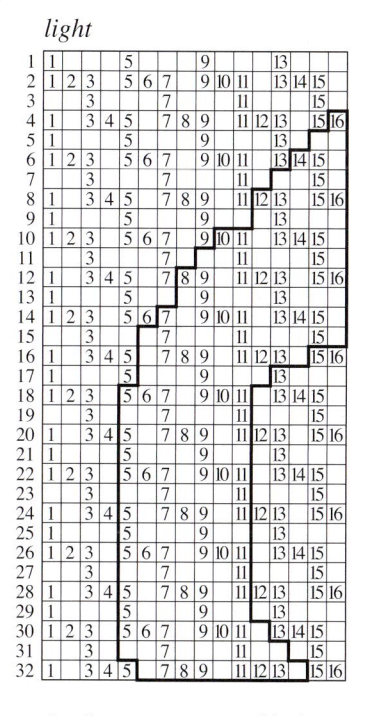

dark

light

vertical stripes

the three parts assembled

DOUBLE WEAVE
91

double weave a la carte

Alice Schlein

Weave drawstring bags on four or sixteen shafts—aside from the side seams and the top hem, the construction of each bag takes place on the loom. You can also use double weave for other items with loom-produced casings, borders, and hems. How about reversible striped placemats with integrated borders? Or polka-dotted scarves with striped borders? Or blankets with wavy stripes and reversible hems? Or a loom-shaped striped pullover with drawstring elastics at the waist and wrist?

Weave the drawstring bag with horizontal stripes on four shafts (vary the size and number of stripes for different designs) or weave it and the polka-dotted, waved, and vertical-striped bags on 16 shafts. The 4-shaft draft is shown in *1a* and the 16-shaft networked threading in *1b* and *2b*, p. 94. White and black alternate in warp and weft in both drafts.

The fabric for each bag is woven in the following order: top hem, drawstring casing, body, drawstring casing, top hem. Off the loom, the fabric is folded; the fold becomes the bottom of the bag, the raw edges of the tops are turned inside and hemmed, and the side seams are butted and sewn.

The weaving order is as follows: first weave a few rows of single-layer plain-weave heading in scrap yarn using one shuttle; these sections also separate each bag. Then with two shuttles interlocking at the selvedges and using the white weft with the white warp in the top layer and the black weft with the black warp in the bottom layer, weave a tubular section to form the top hem of one half of the bag (raw edges are turned to the inside later). Switch layers (bring black layer to top) for four picks; switch layers again. Then with two shuttles not interlocking at selvedges, weave a section of two separate layers to act as the casing for later insertion of the drawstring. Exchange layers two more times to seal casing.

Next weave the body of the bag double the desired bag length in the selected pattern—dots, waves, horizontal or vertical stripes, etc. Interlock shuttles at the selvedges for this section. Exchange layers again; weave drawstring casing as before; exchange layers; weave top hem of other half of the bag. With scrap yarn and one shuttle, weave a few rows of plain weave as before to act as a separator. You are now ready to weave the next bag . . . and the next bag . . . and the next. . . !

1. Drafts for drawstring bags

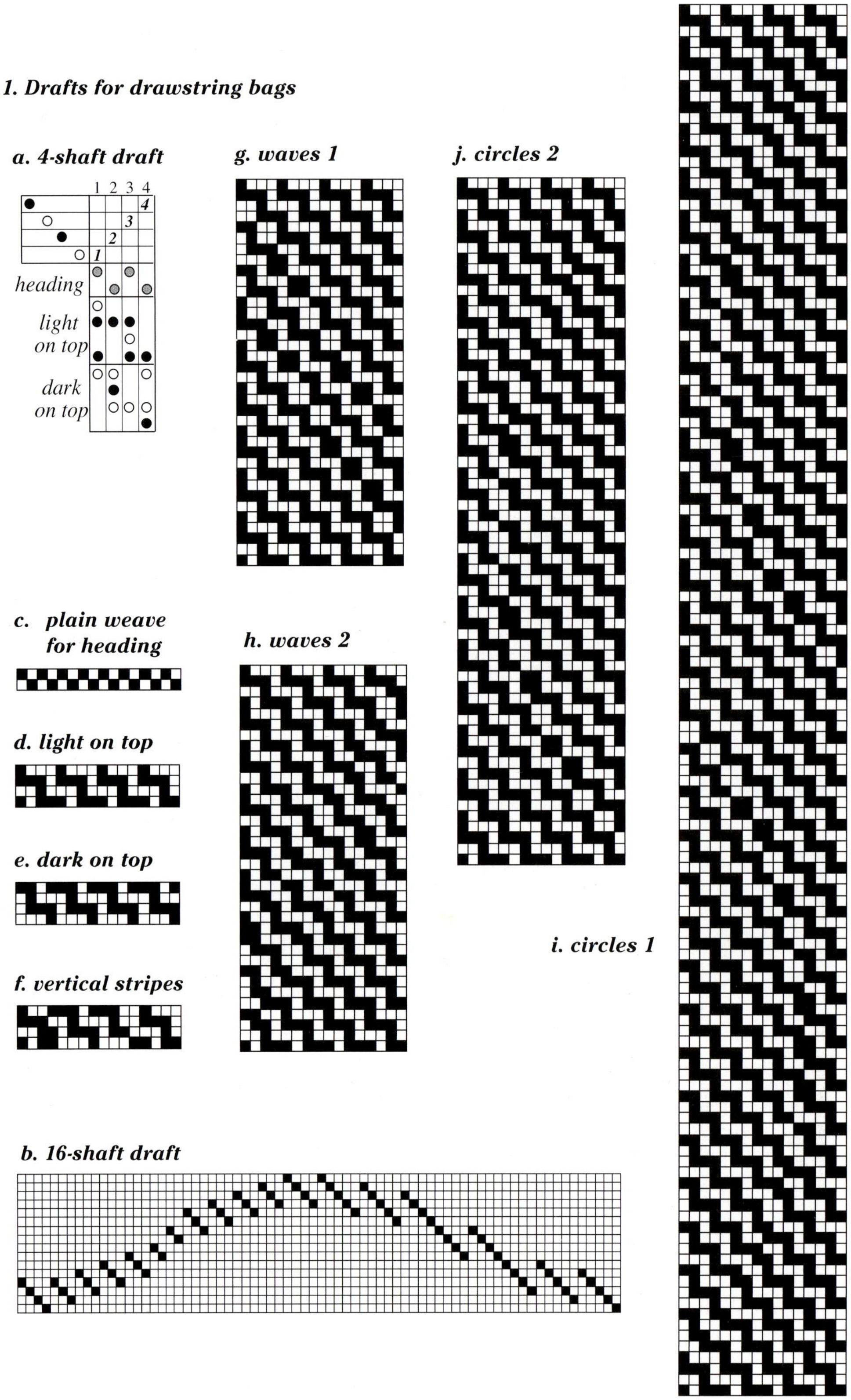

a. 4-shaft draft

c. plain weave for heading

d. light on top

e. dark on top

f. vertical stripes

b. 16-shaft draft

g. waves 1

h. waves 2

i. circles 1

j. circles 2

Use double weave and exchange layers to form on-loom casings for drawstring bags. Weave the striped bag at the left on only four shafts or weave all of the bags—and design more!—on sixteen shafts.

Weave four reversible drawstring bags on one three-yard warp. On four shafts, weave four bags with horizontal stripes; the stripes can be varied in size and number to make each bag unique. On 16 shafts, weave circles, waves, or stripes, or use cut-and-paste peg plans to create additional designs.

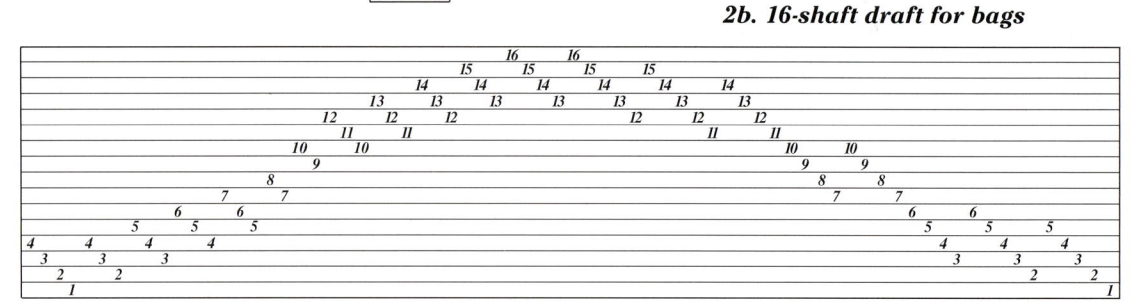

2a. 4-shaft draft for bags

2b. 16-shaft draft for bags

DRAWSTRING BAGS

If your loom has eight or 12 shafts, you can thread a 2-block or 3-block double-weave design from any source. The limitation is that you'll need one set of four treadles for all light on top and one set of four treadles for all dark on top to produce the hems and casings; the remaining treadles can be used for the body of the bag. An 8-shaft dobby or table loom can produce all the required sheds; or on a treadle loom you can retie after the casings to weave the body (the ties that will have to be changed on each set of four treadles are not very many). If your 16-shaft loom is a treadle loom, you'll need eight treadles for the hems and casings—use the remaining treadles for the design or retie.

- Equipment. 4-shaft loom or 16-shaft dobby loom, 12-dent reed, 2 shuttles.
- Materials. Warp and weft: 10/2 pearl cotton (4200 yds/lb), black and natural, 8 oz ea; sewing thread, black and natural; scrap yarn for spacers between bags.
- Wind a warp of 216 ends alternating one end each of natural and black, 3 yds long. Spread warp to 6" in raddle; beam.
- Thread according to 4-shaft or 16-shaft draft; begin with natural on shaft 1 (natural ends are threaded on all odd shafts, black threads on all even shafts).
- Sley 3/dent in 12-dent reed, 36 epi; center for 6" weaving width.
- Weave a few inches with scrap yarn using the plain-weave treadling sequence in *1a*, p. 92, or the peg plan in *1c* to even out the warp. (Also use this sequence with scrap yarn to separate the bags.) Weave the bags with two shuttles, alternating one pick natural and one pick black throughout. Interlock wefts at selvedges; except do not interlock shuttles when you are weaving casings.

a. Top row: bag with wavy stripes. Middle row (left to right): bag with horizontal stripes, bag with vertical stripes, polka dot bag.

- Finish by cutting the bag fabric from the loom. Cut away scrap sections. Tuck raw edges of tubular hems to inside and stitch closed invisibly by hand with matching thread. Fold bags in half and invisibly overcast side edges together by hand, butting selvedge to selvedge, leaving casings and hems unjoined.
- With four strands of black yarn 48" long, make a twisted cord (the four strands become eight strands when doubled over). Make two of these for each bag. With large-eyed needle or bodkin, thread first cord through one casing from left to right then through the other casing from right to left. Knot ends together. Thread second cord through same casings while entering and emerging from other side of bag; knot ends. When cord is correctly inserted, pulling on the knots draws the bag shut. The bag can be reversed and used inside out for a completely different look.

Bag with horizontal stripes

- For hem (interlock weft at selvedges): weave with the threading sequence for light on top in *1a* or use peg plan *1d* 9x. For casing (do not interlock wefts at selvedges): weave with the treadling sequence for dark on top in *1a* or use peg plan *1e* 1x; light on top (*1d*) 3x; dark on top (*1e*) 1x. For body of bag (interlock weft at selvedges): *weave light on top (*1d*) 8x; weave dark on top (*1e*) 3x*. Repeat from * to * 8x. Weave light on top (*1d*) 8x. Weave casing and hem as above. For a number of bags with different-looking designs, vary the number of picks in the strip sections.

Polka dot bag

Weave hem and casing as for bag with horizontal stripes. Weave body of bag (interlock wefts at selvedges): *1d*, 2x; *weave with peg plan *1i* (circles 1) 1x; *1j* (circles 2) 1x*. Repeat from * to * 1x; weave with *1d*, 2x. Again, weave casing and hem as for bag with horizontal stripes.

Wavy bag

Weave hem and casing as above. Weave body of bag with peg plan *1g* (waves 1) 6x; weave with peg plan *1d* (light on top) 5x; weave with peg plan *1h* (waves 2) 6x. Weave casing and hem.

Bag with vertical stripes

Weave hem and casing as above. Weave with peg plan *1f* 88x; weave casing and hem. ✄

raising eyelashes

Alice Schlein

Double weave is full of fun and surprises for the adventuresome weaver. From experiments with forming tubes, making slits, and stuffing pockets come the seeds of new ideas for using layers in weaving. One day as I was weaving double-weave samples on a 4-shaft straight draw (1-2-3-4), I had the following conversation with my Weaving Muse:

WEAVING MUSE On a 4-shaft straight draw you can weave single-layer plain weave, single-layer basket weave, two-layer plain weave…

ALICE … and lots of other structures, like twill!

WEAVING MUSE Right. And you can weave any of them in the same cloth!

ALICE Like horizontal bands of single-layer cloth and double-layer cloth…

WEAVING MUSE Exactly! Now what would happen if you had more shafts?

ALICE Well, on eight shafts I can arrange the single and double areas in blocks. I need four shafts for each block in order to control them independently.

WEAVING MUSE Correct! Now what if…

ALICE What if I had 16 shafts? I could use network drafting to design single-layer and double-layer areas in curved or other non-blocky arrangements.

WEAVING MUSE Work on it! I'll be back!

Derive the threading

A networked threading draft is derived by preparing a network using an 'initial' as the building block. A pattern line is drawn and then placed on the network. Wherever a pattern-line square covers a filled-in network square a 'hit' is marked. In columns with no hits, the nearest filled-in network square above the pattern line is marked. These marks and the hits become the new threading. (See "Network Drafting: Double Weave," pp. 86–91, and the resources given in the Bibliography, p. 86.)

To design the 16-shaft threading draft in *1*, p. 96, that eventually produces the eyelash fabric, I first expanded the 4-shaft initial in Step *a*, p. 96, to a 16-shaft threading network in Step *b*. I then designed a simple zigzag pattern line (Step *c*), and plotted the pattern line on the network (Step *d*). The hits and other legal positions were then marked (Step *e*) to become the final threading.

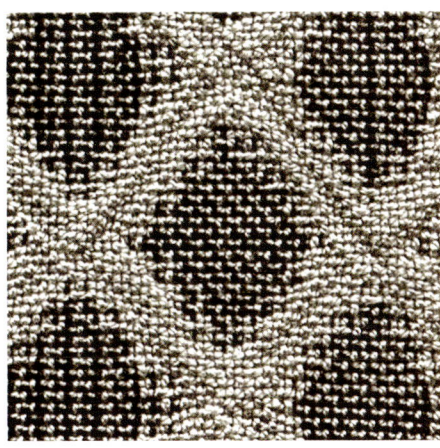

a. Eyelash fabric, front side, uncut

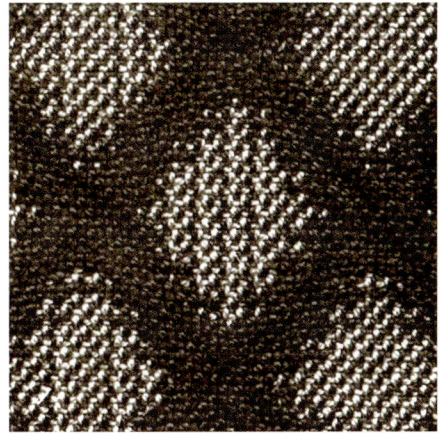

b. Eyelash fabric, reverse, uncut

c. Eyelash fabric, front side, double-weave areas slashed and brushed, machine washed and dried.

d. Eyelash fabric, reverse, double-weave areas slashed and brushed, machine washed and dried.

e. Eyelash fabric, reverse, before cutting. The dashed lines indicate the cutting points.

f. After brushing and washing, the cut warp and weft threads form the long, lush 'eyelash' pile.

1. 16-shaft networked threading draft derived following Steps a–e.

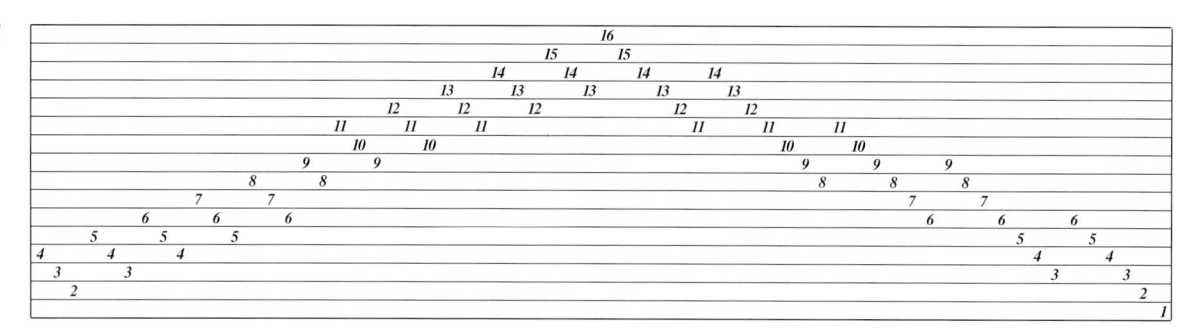

DERIVE THE PEG PLAN

I experimented with peg-plan templates for cutting and pasting, intending to weave a single layer of plain weave *and* two layers of plain weave on this threading. Sample weaving led me to a glaring problem: at the necessary setts for double cloth, the plain-weave areas are too dense and will not beat down to the same level as the double cloth. What next? My Weaving Muse came back just in time.

WEAVING MUSE Why not use basket weave instead of plain weave for the single-cloth areas? It'll beat down closer.

ALICE Good idea! And let's assign a separate color for each layer of the double cloth, for fun.

WEAVING MUSE Just remember to keep a strictly regular color alternation in warp and weft, so you don't get confused. I recommend light threads on odd shafts and dark threads on even shafts, and in the weft, use light for odd picks, light and dark for even picks.

ALICE Gotcha!

THE FINAL PEG PLAN: BASKET WEAVE AND DOUBLE WEAVE

The weaving progressed more smoothly this time. Basket and double weave combine well in the same cloth. The development of the peg plan from the basket-weave and double-weave templates appears in *2*. The shapes in *2a* produce rounded diamonds in the cloth. These shapes are applied to the basket-weave peg plan (*2b*), cut out (*2c*), and then pasted onto the double-weave peg plan (*2d*) to produce the final peg plan (*2e*) which is rewritten in *3*.

A regular color alternation is maintained both in the warp and in the weft: odds light, evens dark.

THE FINAL CUT

When the fabric is removed from the loom, the face shows a latticework of light-colored double cloth

Steps for deriving a networked threading

a. Select an initial. The 4-thread initial shown at **a** is very versatile since threadings based on it can produce plain weave, basket weave, twills, double weave, etc.
b. Make a network: a grid built of repeated initials with as many rows as shafts available and as many columns as ends desired in the repeat.
c. Draw a pattern line that is as many rows high as the bottom row of the top initial (13th row in a 16-row grid) and as wide as the number of ends in the desired repeat.
d. Plot the pattern line on the network. Wherever the pattern line falls on a shaded square, mark a 'hit.'
e. In the columns between 'hits,' blacken shaded squares in next available position above the pattern line. The hits and these squares form the new threading diagram. The final threading appears above.

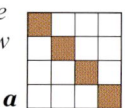

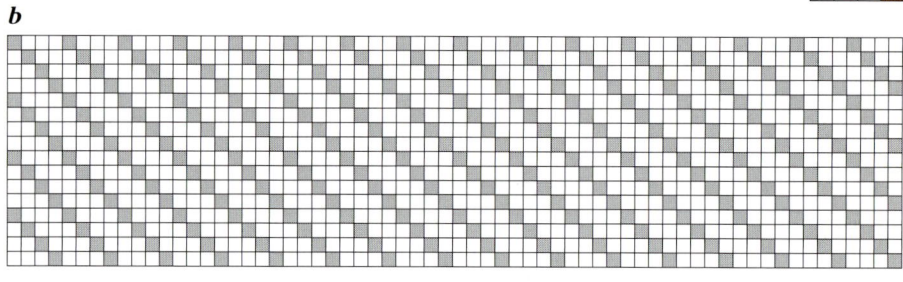

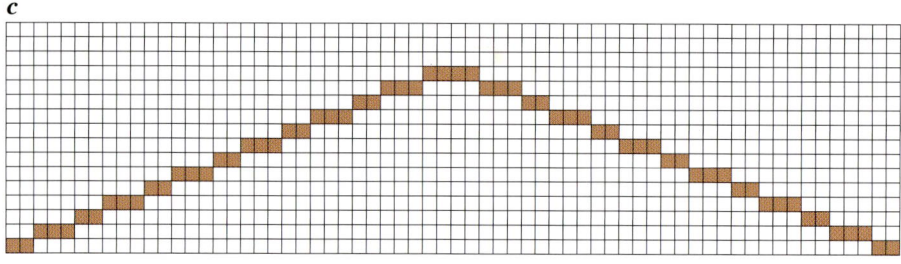

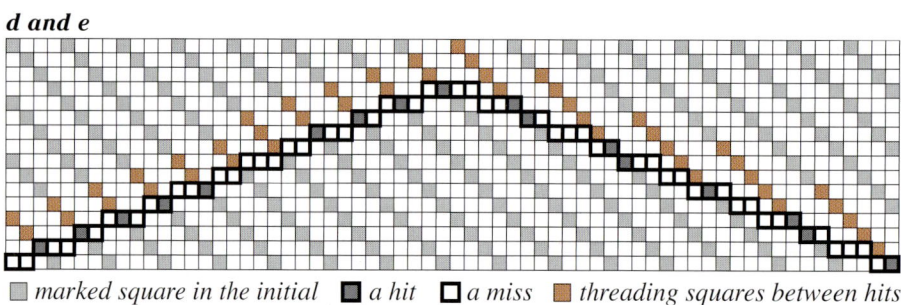

a

b

c

d and e

■ *marked square in the initial*   ■ *a hit*   □ *a miss*   ■ *threading squares between hits*

96

2. Develop a cut-and-paste peg plan for double weave and basket weave

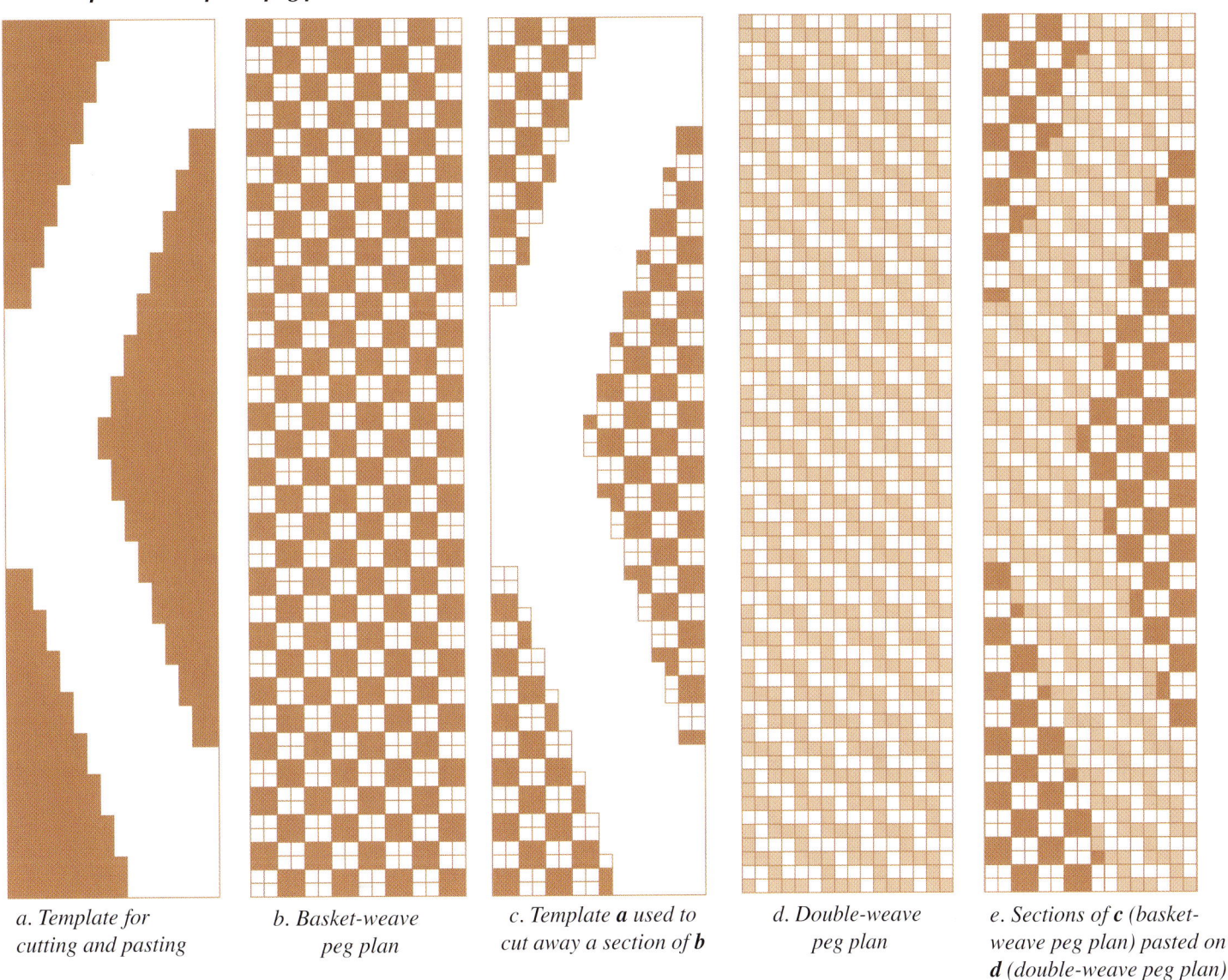

a. Template for cutting and pasting

b. Basket-weave peg plan

*c. Template **a** used to cut away a section of **b***

d. Double-weave peg plan

*e. Sections of **c** (basket-weave peg plan) pasted on **d** (double-weave peg plan)*

framing diamonds of speckled basket weave (**Photo a**, p. 95). On the back, the basket-weave diamonds are framed by a dark-colored double-weave lattice (**Photo b**). Either side can be considered the right side. I thought it was pretty hot stuff, but as usual my Weaving Muse couldn't leave well enough alone.

WEAVING MUSE *(taking a pair of sharp scissors from her pocket)* I wonder what would happen if we just …

ALICE (Gasp!) You aren't going to *cut* it?

WEAVING MUSE Trust me! If we slash the double cloth in one layer only, the fabric will still be held together by the other layer and the basket weave combined (**Photo e**). Just give it a good shake and a washing, and, voilà! Eyelashes! (**Photos c, d, and f**). Slashing the dark-colored layer of the double cloth produces dark eyelashes on light cloth. What would happen if you slashed the light layer instead?

ALICE Light eyelashes on light cloth! Now, one more question…what causes those irregular stripey effects in the basket-weave areas?

WEAVING MUSE Since your warp ends are grouped in the reed dents, the colors lie first one way and then another in the basket-weave cloth, forming random stripes. I think it adds extra zing.

ALICE I love it! I can try it in wool…and play with more colors…and maybe make a shirt with some areas cut and some left uncut…and…

WEAVING MUSE Just remember not to use yarns that are too slippery or setts too open…you don't want the eyelashes to fall out! And a final bit of advice: keep your scissors sharp! ✂

eyelash vest

Alice Schlein

Enjoy this double-and-basket-weave fabric developed through network drafting. Weave enough for two vests: use one side as the right side for one vest (burgundy eyelashes) and the other side as the right side for the second vest (gold eyelashes). The magic happens in the washing machine! As you weave, listen to the ideas your Weaving Muse suggests to you and dream about weaving other eyelash fabrics.

- Equipment. 16-shaft loom with dobby head (mechanical or computerized), 16" weaving width; 10-dent reed; 2 shuttles; sewing machine; steam iron; washing machine; sharp scissors; stiff-bristled hairbrush.
- Materials. Warp and weft: 5/2 pearl cotton (2100 yds/lb, item #83, Halcyon), 12 oz each of colors #110 (gold) and #120 (burgundy); your favorite simple lined-to-the-edge vest pattern with no front darts (Four Corners pattern #5000, medium, is used for this vest); 1½ yds cotton broadcloth to use for both the vest back and lining in a color to match; matching sewing thread.
- Wind a warp of 480 ends (240 ends burgundy, 240 ends gold) 3½ yds long, holding 1 end gold and 1 end burgundy together as you wind but keeping them separated with a finger to prevent twisting. Spread the warp in a raddle at a density of 30 epi, centered for 16" weaving width.
- Beam the warp.
- Thread the heddles according to the draft in *1* (p. 96), gold on odd shafts and burgundy on even. There will be 7½ threading repeats.
- Sley 3/dent in a 10/dent reed for 30 epi; center for 16" weaving width.
- Tie the warp onto the cloth beam apron rod and weave a heading in scrap yarn to spread the warp using about 20 picks of the peg plan in *3*.
- Weave the cloth at 24 ppi following the peg plan in *3*. Alternate weft colors, gold on odd picks and burgundy on even picks. Weave at least 60" to allow take-up and shrinkage of 15% and a little leeway in placing pattern pieces on the cloth.
- Finish by cutting the fabric from the loom. Secure the cut ends by serging or machine zigzagging. Machine wash fabric in hot soapy water; machine dry for maximum preshrinkage. Steam press while still slightly damp.
- Select which side you consider the right side. The Four Corners pattern provides only ¼" seam allowance, so special care must be taken in cutting out vest fronts: Trace pattern outlines on the cloth with marker pen, *cut outside all the lines by at least ½"*, and then serge so that the serger knife cuts exactly on the lines. If no serger is available, machine straightstitch just inside the lines, and then cut on the lines.
- Cut vest back and lining from the broadcloth and assemble vest according to pattern instructions. Press on both sides.
- After the vest is completely sewn, take well-sharpened scissors and ease the point of one blade gently under the center of a double-weave area on the right side of the fabric and snip. Poke the blade farther into the snipped hole and begin to cut carefully down the centers of all the diagonal lattice lines as in *Photo e*, p. 95, making sure to cut through the top layer only. This is easier than it sounds. Be patient; it will take an hour or two.
- Working outdoors, brush the cloth vigorously with a stiff-bristled brush to fluff up the eyelashes and liberate loose bits of yarn (there will be lots of these). Shake the vest well. Machine wash a second time and machine dry along with a few Turkish towels. Check and clean the dryer lint trap frequently. When the vest is dry, a going-over with sticky tape or a commercial lint brush will take care of any remaining lint clinging to the lining. Steam press edges of lining on wrong side if necessary, taking care not to flatten the eyelashes on the right side.

3. Peg plan

1	1 2	5 6	9	13
2	1 2	5 6	9 10 11	13 14 15
3	3 4	7 8	11	15
4	3 4	7 8 9	11 12	15 16
5	1 2	5 6	9	13
6	1 2	5 6	9 10 11	13 14 15
7	3 4	7	11	15
8	3 4	7 8 9	11 12	15 16
9	1 2	5 6	9	13
10	1 2	5 6 7	9 10 11	13 14
11	3 4	7	11	15 16
12	3 4	7 8 9	11 12	15 16
13	1 2	5	9	13 14
14	1 2	5 6 7	9 10 11	13 14
15	3 4	7	11	15 16
16	3 4 5	7 8 9	11 12	15 16
17	1 2	5	9	13
18	1 2	5 6 7	9 10 11	13 14
19	3	7	11 12	15 16
20	3 4 5	7 8 9	11 12	15 16
21	1 2	5	9	13
22	1 2 3	5 6 7	9 10	13 14
23	3	7	11 12	15 16
24	3 4 5	7 8 9	11 12	15 16
25	1	5	9 10	13 14
26	1 2 3	5 6 7	9 10	13 14
27	3	7	11 12	15 16
28	1 3 4 5	7 8	11 12	15 16
29	1	5	9 10	13 14
30	1 2 3	5 6 7	9 10	13 14
31	3	7 8	11 12	15 16
32	1 3 4 5	7 8	11 12	15 16
33	1	5	9 10	13 14
34	1 2 3	5 6 7	9 10	13 14
35	3	7	11 12	15 16
36	1 3 4 5	7 8 9	11 12	15 16
37	1	5	9 10	13 14
38	1 2 3	5 6 7	9 10	13 14
39	3	7	11 12	15 16
40	1 3 4 5	7 8 9	11 12	15 16
41	1 2	5	9	13 14
42	1 2 3	5 6 7	9 10 11	13 14
43	3	7	11 12	15 16
44	3 4	7 8 9	11 12	15 16
45	1 2	5	9	13 14
46	1 2	5 6 7	9 10 11	13 14
47	3 4	7	11	15 16
48	3 4	7 8 9	11 12	15 16
49	1 2	5	9	13 14
50	1 2	5 6 7	9 10 11	13 14
51	3 4	7	11	15 16
52	3 4	7 8 9	11 12	15 16
53	1 2	5 6	9	13
54	1 2	5 6 7	9 10 11	13 14 15
55	3 4	7	11	15
56	3 4	7 8 9	11 12	15 16
57	1 2	5 6	9	13
58	1 2	5 6	9 10 11	13 14 15
59	3 4	7 8	11	15
60	3 4	7 8 9	11 12	15 16
61	1 2	5 6	9	13
62	1 2	5 6	9 10 11	13 14 15
63	3 4	7 8	11	15
64	3 4	7 8	11 12 13	15 16

Weave 'eyelash' fabric and produce patterned pile the easy way: without velvet rods or boutonné pick-up sticks. Use network drafting and double weave for eyelashes that are long and lush!

unconventional double-weave shawl

Miriam Taylor

1. 8-shaft, 2-block double weave

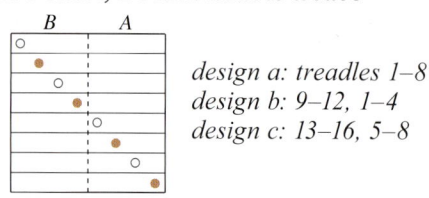

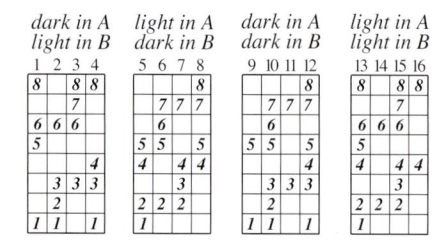

design a: treadles 1–8
design b: 9–12, 1–4
design c: 13–16, 5–8

Arrangements of two blocks

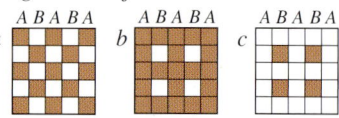

2. 8-shaft, 3-block double weave: blocks are dark or mixed

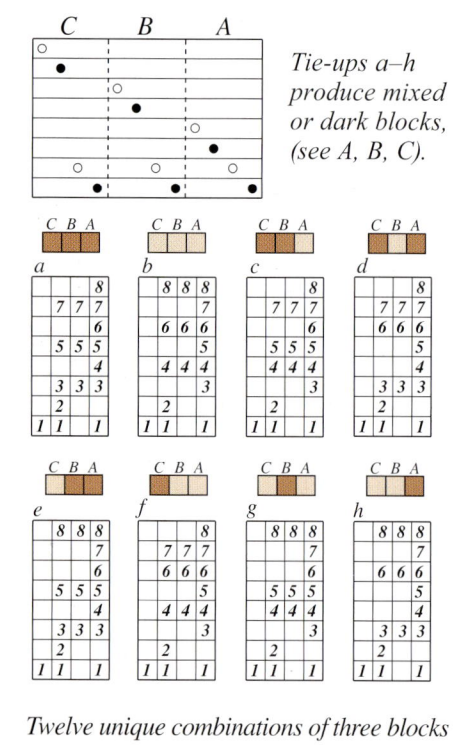

Tie-ups a–h produce mixed or dark blocks, (see A, B, C).

Twelve unique combinations of three blocks

A double weaver's wish: three blocks of double weave on an 8-shaft, 8-treadle loom—but no skeleton tie-up, please! And, I'd like some of the lower layer to be visible while I'm looking at the upper layer. . . .

Impossible? Not really! The good news is that the second of these two features is easily achieved if the two layers of the double-woven fabric are partially offset. Then, the upper layer does not completely cover the lower layer, similar to two sheets of paper lying on top of each other with their edges unaligned.

The first feature is less easily achieved, and then only by a slight compromise—we can relinquish the demand for a solid-colored pattern block without losing the overall effect. (How else to do the impossible!)

CONVENTIONAL DOUBLE WEAVE

Consider 2-block double weave on eight shafts with an 8-treadle tie-up. Let the threading be 1-2-3-4 for Block A and 5-6-7-8 for Block B, and let the warp threads on shafts 1, 3, 5, and 7 be dark and the warp threads on shafts 2, 4, 6, and 8 be light (see the threading in *1*). Depending on the tie-up, one can weave: (*1a*) a checkerboard pattern of dark and light rectangles on both layers, (*1b*) light rectangles on a dark background in one layer and dark rectangles on a light background in the other layer, or (*1c*) the reverse of *1b*.

The change in appearance of a block from light to dark or dark to light is due to the interchange of light and dark warp and weft threads from one layer to the other. In order to appear totally dark all warp threads and all weft threads constituting one layer of a block have to be dark, and in order to appear totally light all warp and all weft threads constituting one layer of a block have to be light.

Eight shafts and eight treadles are required to achieve *either* appearance *1a* or appearance *1b*. If both appearances are to be combined in the same fabric, 12 treadles are needed (see the tie-ups in *1*). All possible combinations of light and dark in both blocks require sixteen treadles.

AN UNCONVENTIONAL DOUBLE-WEAVE VARIATION

Now let's consider a double-weave fabric in which

---

3. Warp positions in conventional and unconventional double weave

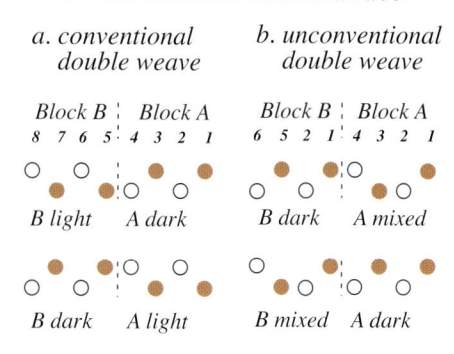

a. conventional double weave

b. unconventional double weave

Block B   Block A
8 7 6 5   4 3 2 1

Block B   Block A
6 5 2 1   4 3 2 1

B light   A dark

B dark   A mixed

B dark   A light

B mixed   A dark

---

partially light rectangles appear on a dark surface on one layer while partially dark rectangles appear on a light surface on the other layer. Since the appearance of a block changes from totally dark to only partially light, not all warp threads nor all weft threads constituting one layer of the block have to be interchanged with all warp and all weft threads constituting the other layer. Some warp threads can continuously weave in the upper layer and some warp threads can continuously weave in the lower layer. The same holds true for the weft threads.

Warp threads that always weave in the same layer, either upper or lower, can be threaded on the same shafts even though they are in different blocks—each block therefore no longer requires four shafts. If in each block one warp thread always weaves in the upper layer and one warp thread always weaves in the lower layer, these threads can be threaded on two shafts, say 1 and 2, no matter what block they are in. On the other hand, in each block the two warp threads that do interchange from layer to layer must be threaded on distinct shafts. In this case, it is possible to weave a 3-block fabric on eight shafts. Let the new threading be 1-2-3-4 for Block A; 1-2-5-6 for Block B, and 1-2-7-8 for Block C. Compare the threading drafts in *1* and *2*, and the warp positions in the two double weaves in *3*.

As in the conventional threading, warp threads on shafts 1, 3, 5, 7 are dark, warp threads on shafts 2, 4, 6, 8 are light. For ease of reference we shall call the partially light and partially dark appearances of a block 'mixed.' In the upper layer the possible appearances of the blocks are: (*2a*) all blocks are dark; (*2b*) all blocks are mixed (i.e., one thread light, one thread dark); (*2c*) Block A mixed, Block B dark, Block C dark; (*2d*) A dark, B mixed, C dark; (*2e*) A dark, B dark, C mixed; (*2f*) A mixed, B mixed, C dark;

100

Here is a lovely variation of double weave that allows three blocks on eight shafts with an easy treadling rotation (no skeleton tie-ups!) to produce a shawl with offset edges that add interest and contrast.

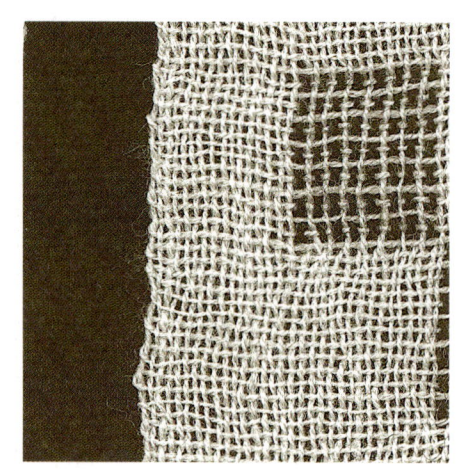

The edges of the shawl's two layers are offset so that both layers show.

This unusual draft in 3-block double weave on eight shafts can provide just enough extra structural stability to be ideal for shawls and stoles. The slightly striped texture of the 'partial warp interchange' in the pattern blocks forms a visual contrast to the solid color of the dark plain-weave background layer. Weave two soft shawls to see how it works, and then design your own unconventional double weave!

4. Draft for shawl

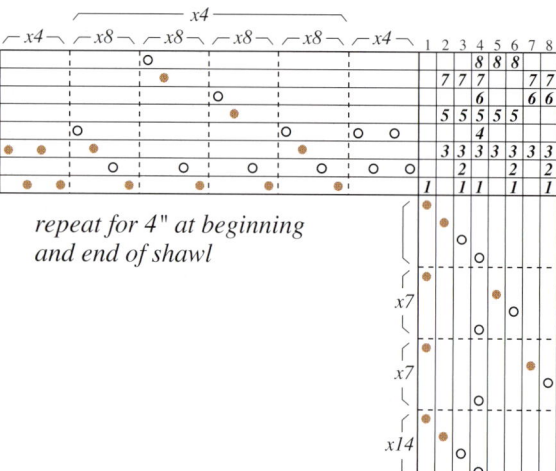

repeat for 4" at beginning and end of shawl

(*2g*) A mixed, B dark, C mixed; (*2h*) A dark, B mixed, C mixed (see the shaded squares in *2a–h*).

In the lower layer the blocks appear light where they are dark in the upper layer and mixed where they are mixed in the upper layer.

The complete tie-ups for these effects (if no weft interchange takes place and each weft thread weaves either in the upper layer only or in the lower layer only) are shown in *2a–h*. Note that warp threads on shaft 1 always weave in the upper layer and warp threads on shaft 2 always weave in the lower layer.

Two of the four treadles are tied in exactly the same way in each tie-up. These are the two treadles that control the weaving of the warp ends on shafts 1 and 2. With eight treadles, any three of these appearances can be combined in the same fabric (see the tie-up in *4*).

The number of possible combinations of the three appearances is 56, but fortunately or unfortunately, depending on one's point of view, only 12 are distinct (these are shown in *2a–h*)—the others are repeats or rearrangements. Of the 12, none have the same appearance on the lower layer as one of the others on the upper layer, since on the upper layer there are dark and mixed blocks and on the lower layer there are light and mixed blocks.

Try using other variations based on weft interchange only or partial warp and weft interchange, or vary the pattern-weft color for color mix in the pattern blocks. The draft for this shawl is only one of many possibilities to consider!

SHAWL IN UNCONVENTIONAL DOUBLE WEAVE

Amounts given are enough are for two shawls, each approximately 15" wide and 80" long.

❑ Equipment. 8-shaft loom, 20" weaving width; 12-dent reed (or 3.5 ends per cm reed); 2 shuttles.

❑ Materials. Warp and weft: 17.5/2 worsted wool or equivalent (4900 yds/lb, J. & H. Clasgens Co., from Glimåkra Looms 'n Yarns) in dark navy and white, 10 oz of each color (for yarn of a similar weight, substitute JaggerSpun 20/2 wool at 5600 yds/lb, 18/2 merino wool at 5040 yds/lb, or 18/2 wool/silk at 5040 yds/lb).

❑ Wind a 2-color warp 5½ yds long for two shawls. Since the two layers do not overlap completely (the edges are purposely offset), wind 16 ends white; 256 pairs of one navy, one white; then 16 ends navy for a total of 544 ends.

❑ Beam the warp, centering for 16½".

❑ Thread following the draft in *4*. Note that since the warp consists of an irregular arrangement of the two colors it is preferable to thread the loom first and sley the reed next (i.e., warp the loom from back to front). The navy-colored warp ends are threaded on the odd-numbered shafts and the white warp ends on the even-numbered shafts.

❑ Sley the sections of the warp which consist of one color differently from the section which combines navy and white ends; i.e., the section of 16 white ends and the section of 16 navy ends are sleyed 18 epi, 1-2 in a 12-dent reed; the section of mixed white and navy ends is sleyed 36 epi, 3 ends per dent. (If you are using a metric reed, sley the monochrome sections 2 ends per dent in a 3.5-dents-per-cm reed, and the navy and white section 4 ends per dent.)

❑ Weave following the treadling draft in *4* taking care not to wind the two weft yarns around each other at the edges of the weaving to ensure that the two layers remain unattached at the selvedges. For speed of weaving, weave two picks of navy followed by two picks of white. Start the shuttle with the navy weft from the right and the shuttle with the white weft from the left. Experiment to determine how hard to beat in order to square the design. The weave is intended to be slightly warp-faced (fewer picks per inch than ends per inch). Leave an unwoven section of 12" between the first and second shawl for fringe.

❑ To finish, remove the fabric from the loom. Cut the two shawls apart in the center of the unwoven (fringe) section. To secure the fringe, for each shawl make overhand knots 3" apart and tie them snug against the fell using four threads as one and making separate knots in each layer. Trim the fringe evenly.

❑ Wash the shawls by hand in warm water and a mild soap; rinse well. Dry flat, and when still slightly damp, press with steam iron on the wool setting. Trim the fringe evenly.

❑ Enjoy using one of your unconventional double-weave shawls and give the other as a gift! ✄

playing with double weave

Raymond Nish

1. 6-shaft draft for 4:1 double weave (see Sample 1)

Double weave is very special in that the woven fabric when it is removed from the loom is often a surprise—and almost always a happy surprise. The surprise in this double-woven cloth is double: one layer creates a lovely lattice-like design, and the finishing produces a drapable, beautifully bumpy fabric. The secret is in the ratio of threads in one cloth to threads in the other: there are four dark threads for every single light thread, and the light threads are much thicker.

I've been playing with double weave for most of my weaving life. These fabrics were inspired by an investigation of an unrelated weave in which a difference in the shrinkage of different fibers caused a dramatic effect. I began to wonder what would happen in double weave if the two fabric layers were constructed of fibers that were likely to shrink differently.

DIFFERENTIAL SHRINKAGE

The fine warp and weft yarn in these fabrics is 20/2 pearl cotton and the heavy warp and weft in all but Sample 3 a soft, unmercerized 6/2 cotton. Washing causes the unmercerized cotton to shrink, puffing the fine gray fabric so that it looks almost quilted. (Note that the difference in shrinkage between these two fibers is not great. Wool used in place of unmercerized cotton would produce much heavier, more crinkled fabric.)

In all the fabrics in this article, eight 20/2 threads (at 32 epi), are threaded between every two 6/2 threads (at 8 epi), a ratio of 4:1. The heavy threads, when appearing on the surface of the cloth, appear as a lacy lattice on a dark gray background of plain weave. The one exception is Sample 3, in which cotton chenille is substituted for the 6/2 cotton. After finishing, the chenille creates a matte, almost pile-like texture, and the interlacement itself is barely visible. Instructions given here are for enough fabric to make a jacket.

- Equipment. 4-shaft, 6-shaft, 8-shaft, or 16-shaft loom for selected fabric, 32" weaving width; 12-dent reed; 2 shuttles.
- Materials. Fine warp and weft: 20/2 pearl cotton (8400 yds/lb), gray, 1½ lbs. Heavy warp and weft: 6/2 unmercerized cotton (2520 yds/lb, Webs), 1¼ lbs, natural (or substitute cotton chenille, 1400 yds/lb, 2 lbs); selected jacket pattern, lining, and notions required by pattern.
- Wind a warp of 960 ends 20/2 pearl cotton and a separate warp of 240 ends 6/2 unmercerized cotton 6 yds long each. (For the 4-shaft draft, you may want to add to warp width; see note with the draft in **4**.)
- Sley 20/2 pearl cotton 4/dent for 2 dents, skip 1 dent, sley 2/skip 1, etc., 32 epi. Sley 2 ends 6/2 unmercerized cotton in every skipped dent, 8 epi; center for 30".
- Thread following selected draft.
- Weave fabric following treadling order in selected draft.
- Finish by removing from loom, serge or machine zigzag ends; sew ends together. Hand wash in very warm water; spin out in machine; hand rinse in very warm water; spin. Hang over cylinder to dry (I use a rolled screen covered in muslin). Steam press.
- Cut, assemble, and sew jacket according to pattern directions.

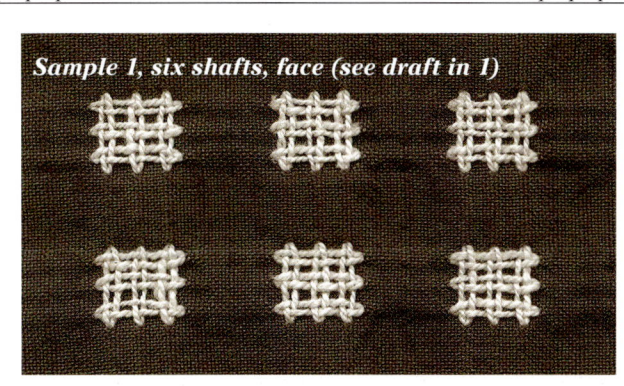

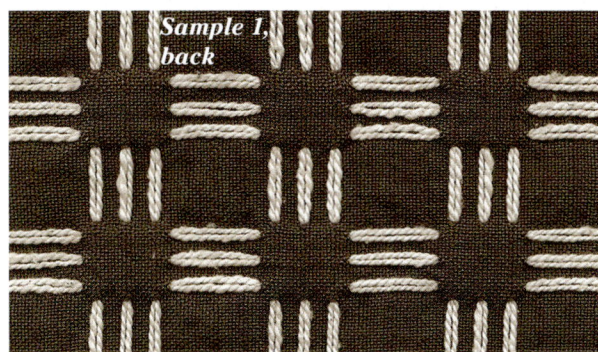

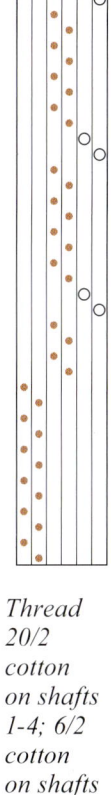

Sample 1, six shafts, face (see draft in 1)

Sample 1, back

Sample 2 face; see draft in 3, p. 104.

Sample 3 face; see draft in 3

Thread 20/2 cotton on shafts 1-4; 6/2 cotton on shafts 5-6.

2. Draft for jacket fabric

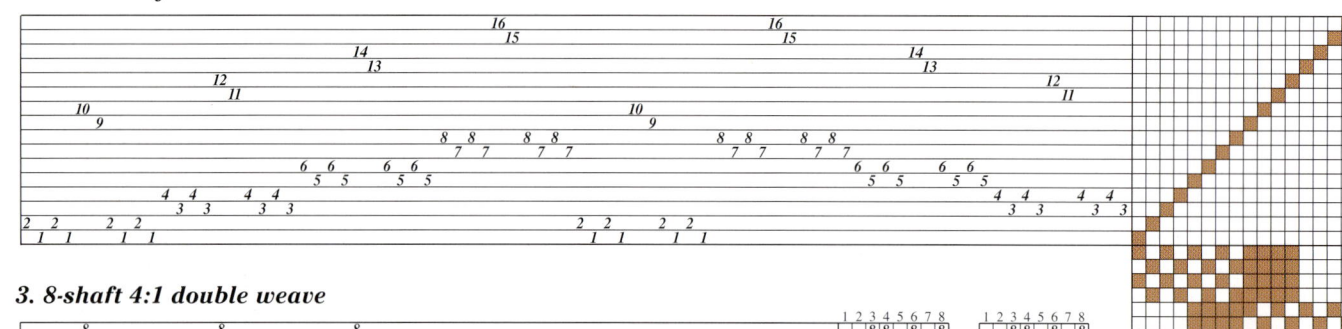

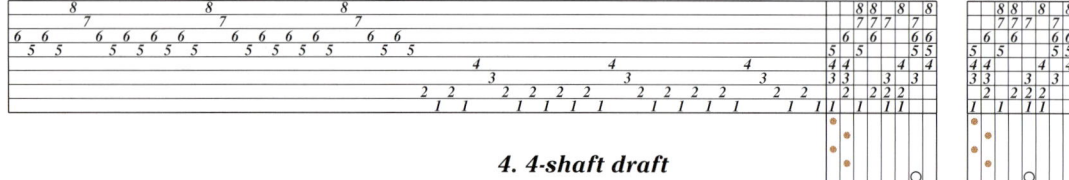

3. 8-shaft 4:1 double weave

4. 4-shaft draft

Fabric from the 16-shaft draft in 2

Fabric from the 8-shaft draft in 3, treadling b

The 4-shaft draft (fabric not shown) produces horizontal stripes of gray on top alternating with horizontal stripes of lattice on top. For clothing, turn stripes so that they are vertical. Increase width on loom (from 30") to add to length of garment if desired.

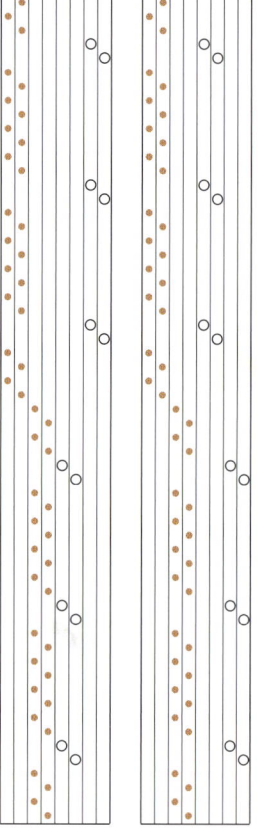

Thread 20/2 pearl cotton on shafts 1, 2 and 5, 6. Thread 6/2 unmercerized cotton (or chenille) on shafts 3, 4 and 7, 8.

Thread 20/2 pearl cotton on shafts 1–8; 6/2 unmercerized cotton on shafts 9–16.

Weave this 4:1 double-weave fabric on sixteen shafts or choose another version on fewer and watch the layers take on dimension during finishing. The finished fabric is soft and supple and never wrinkles!

yarns and suppliers lists

YARNS Yarns are listed with the yards per pound and a range of appropriate setts: wide (as for laces), medium (as for plain weaves), close (as for twills).

20/2 cotton (pearl and unmercerized), 8,400 yds/lb; 30, 36, 48	20/2 wool, 5,600 yds/lb; 20, 24, 30
12/2 cotton (pearl and unmercerized), 5,040 yds/lb; 20, 24, 30	18/2 wool, 5,040 yds/lb; 20, 24, 30
10/2 cotton (pearl and unmercerized) 4,200 yds/lb; 20, 24, 28	17.5 worsted wool, 4,900 yds/lb; 16, 18, 20
8/2 cotton (pearl and unmercerized) 3,360 yds/lb; 16, 20, 24	10/2 wool, 2,800 yds/lb; 12, 16, 20
6/2 unmercerized cotton, 2,520 yds/lb, 14, 18, 24	12/3 wool, 2,100 yds/lb; 12, 15, 20
5/2 pearl cotton, 2,000 yds/lb; 12, 15, 18	2-ply wool, 1,800 yds/lb, Harrisville Shetland; 12, 15, 20
3/2 pearl cotton, 1,260 yds/lb; 10, 12, 15	2-ply wool, 1,620 yds/lb, Munkagarn; 12, 14, 18
cotton chenille, 900 yds/lb; 8, 10, 12	2-ply wool, 1,000 yds/lb; 8, 10, 12
20/2 spun silk, 5,000 yds/lb; 20, 24, 30	2-ply wool, 900 yds/lb, Harrisville Highland; 8, 10, 12
rayon chenille, 1,450 yds/lb; 12, 15, 18	Astra Glow Metallic 3,000 yds/lb

SUPPLIERS

Cotton Clouds
5176 S. 14th Ave., Safford, AZ 85546-9252.
800-322-7888, www.cottonclouds.com.

Earth Guild
33 Haywood St., Asheville NC 28801.
Orders: 800-327-8448, info: 828-255-7818,
www.earthguild.com.

Halcyon Yarn
12 School St., Bath, ME 04530.
800-341-0282, www.halcyonyarn.com.

Harrisville Designs
Center Village, Harrisville, NH 03450.
Orders: 800-338-9415, info: 603-827-3333,
www.harrisville.com.

JaggerSpun
Water St., Springvale, ME 04083.
207-324-4455, 800-225-8023.

Lunatic Fringe
15009 Cromartie Rd., Tallahassee, FL 32309.
800-483-8749, lunatic@talstar.com.

The Mannings
1132 Green Ridge Rd., P.O. Box 687,
East Berlin, PA 17316.
Orders: 800-233-7166, info: 717-624-2223,
www.the-mannings.com.

Nordic Studio
5803 Second St., Katy, TX 77493.
Orders: 888-562-7012, info: 281-467-1575.
www.nordicstudio.com.

PRO Chemical & Dye
P.O. Box 14, Somerset, MA 02726.
Orders: 800-228-9393, info: 508-676-3838.

The Silk Tree
12359-270 A St., Maple Ridge, BC Canada
V2W 1C2. 877-891-2880, www.silkyarn.com.

Treenway Silks
501 Musgrave Rd., Salt Spring Island, BC Canada
V8K 1V5. Orders: 888-383-7455,
info: 250-653-2345, www.treenwaysilks.com.

UKI Supreme Corporation
PO Box 848, Hickory, NC 28603.
888-604-6975.

Webs
PO Box 147, Service Center Rd.,
Northampton, MA 01061-0147.
Orders: 800-367-9327, info: 413-584-2225,
webs@yarn.com, www.yarn.com.

Yarn Barn
930 Massachusetts, Lawrence, KS 66044.
800-468-0035, info@yarnbarn-ks.com,
www.yarnbarn-ks.com.

---

other publications from XRX

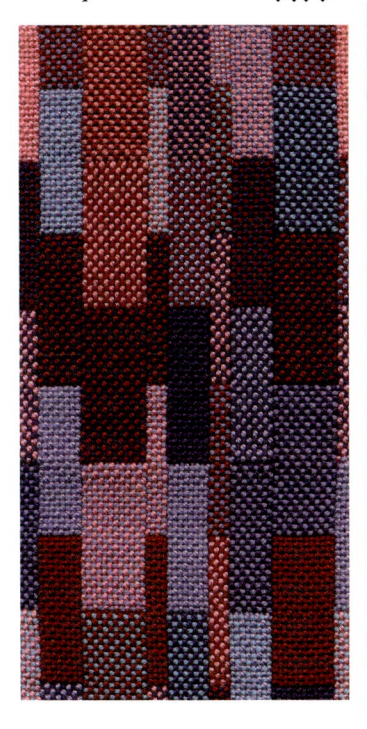

Best of Weaver's to come:

Overshot

Summer and Winter and Beyond

Rugs and Weft-faced Weaves

Double Weave Part II
(Finnweave, Piqué, Llampas, Pick-up)

and more!

For more information:
www.knittinguniverse.com
1-800-232-5648

The Knitter's Handbook

Two sweaters for my father
   by Perri Klass

Module Magic

Maggie's Ireland

Jean Frost Jackets

The Knitting Experience:
   The Knit Stitch
   The Purl Stitch
   Color

A Knitter's Dozen
   Angels
   Bags
   Ponchos & Wraps
   Scarves
   Hats
   Kids

The Best of Lopi

Handpaint Country

A Gathering of Lace

Sculptured Knits

Sally Melville Styles

Magnificent Mittens

Ethnic Socks and Stockings

The Great American Afghan
The Great North American Afghan
The Great American Kid's Afghan
The Great American Aran Afghan

Socks Socks Socks

Kids Kids Kids

The Best of Knitter's
   Arans & Celtics
   Shawls and Scarves

The Best of Weaver's
   Huck Lace
   Thick 'n Thin
   Fabrics That Go Bump
   Twill Thrills

Knitter's Magazine

XRX BOOKS

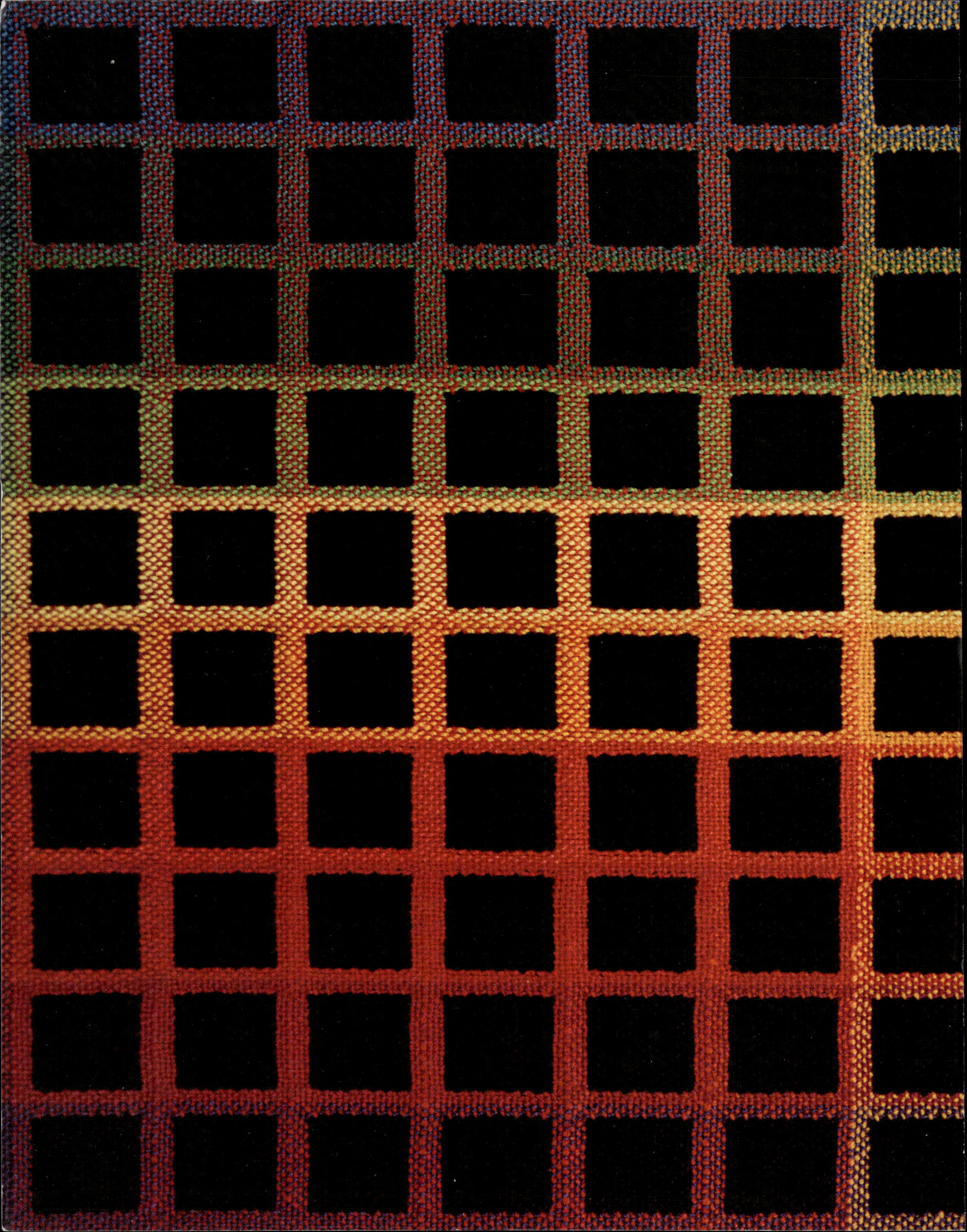